FAITH-HEALING
CHRISTIAN SCIENCE AND
KINDRED PHENOMENA

FAITH-HEALING

CHRISTIAN SCIENCE AND

KINDRED PHENOMENA

BY

J. M. BUCKLEY, LL. D.

NEW YORK
THE CENTURY CO.
1892

THE DE VINNE PRESS.

PROEM

The link connecting the subjects treated in this volume is their dependence upon mental states. Should it be thought that Astrology, Divination, Apparitions, and Witchcraft are based upon objective facts, it is believed that the method of their explanation will show that they are properly classified. The author has adopted certain principles as working laws: namely, that before endeavoring to explain how phenomena exist, it is necessary to determine precisely what exists; and that so long as it is possible to find a rational explanation of what unquestionably is, there is no reason to suspect, and it is superstition to assume, the operation of supernatural causes.

CONTENTS

I

FAITH-HEALING

II

ASTROLOGY, DIVINATION, AND COINCIDENCES

III

DREAMS, NIGHTMARE, AND SOMNAMBULISM

IV

PRESENTIMENTS, VISIONS, AND APPARITIONS

V

WITCHCRAFT

VI

"CHRISTIAN SCIENCE" AND "MIND CURE"

FAITH–HEALING

IN 1849 I first saw performances in "animal magnetism." A "professor," of fluency, fine appearance, and marked self-possession, lectured with illustrations; feeble men after being "magnetized"
became strong, and persons ordinarily reticent spoke
eloquently on subjects suggested by the audience.
Great excitement arose, and the attention of medical
men was attracted to the curative powers of "magnetism." A dentist, who was also a physician, acquired the art, and a paralytic when under "the
influence" moved an arm long useless. Persons
whose teeth were extracted felt no pain during the
operation.

Some years afterward, at boarding-school, a young
man who was very devout occupied a room with
me. A revival in town extended to the school, and
the young man was brought from a meeting in a
"trance" and placed upon the bed. He was unconscious for some hours; his limbs were rigid, and it
was possible to lift him by the head and feet without
his body yielding in the least degree; nor could the
strongest man bend his arms. At length he opened
his eyes, uttered pious ejaculations, and relapsed; this
recurred at irregular intervals. By one o'clock in the
morning he had resumed his natural state. Feeling

that he had been the subject of an unusual manifestation of the favor of God, he was very happy for some days. Similar seizures occurred to him during his stay at the institution, whenever religious meetings were unusually fervent.

In 1856, while in college, I first saw the phenomena of spiritualism as displayed by a "trance medium" and "inspirational speaker." Soon afterward I visited the Perfectionist community established by John H. Noyes, where the cure of disease without medicine and the possibility of escaping death were expounded.

In 1857 I found certain "Millerites" or "Adventists" in the interior of Connecticut who claimed power to heal by prayer and without medicine, and—if they could attain sufficient faith—to raise the dead. This they attempted in the case of a young woman who had died of fever, and continued in prayer for her until decomposition compelled the civil authorities to interfere. This case has been paralleled several times recently. Trances were also common among the Millerites at their camp-meetings, as they had been among the early Methodists, Congregationalists in the time of Jonathan Edwards, and certain Presbyterians and Baptists in the early part of this century in the West and South.

In 1859 the famous Dr. Newton arrived in Boston on one of his periodical visits, causing an extraordinary sensation. The lame who visited him leaped for joy, and left their crutches when they departed; in some instances blindness was cured; several chronic cases were relieved, and astonishing results reported confounding ordinary practitioners, and puzzling one or two medical men of national reputation. I made Dr. Newton's acquaintance, and conversed with him at length and with entire freedom. His disciples became numerous; and "healing mediums" and physicians who cure by "laying on of hands" still exist, increasing rather than diminishing in number.

The circumstance of meeting a person who had been in the habit of going into trances in religious meetings, was an easy subject for "mesmerizers," had been cured by a "healer," and finally became a spiritualist and "trance medium," suggested the question whether there might not be a natural susceptibility acted upon by a general law. Nothing which could shed light upon this problem has been knowingly neglected by the writer during the past thirty years.

Two root questions arise concerning the phenomena; they are the inquiries which lie at the foundation of all knowledge : What are the facts, and how may they be explained ?

THE FACTS

THE career of Prince Hohenlohe, Roman Catholic Bishop of Sardica, is as well authenticated as any fact in history. Dr. Tuke, in his thoroughly scientific work on the "Influence of the Mind upon the Body," admits his cures as facts. The Prince, who was born in 1794, in Waldenburg, was of high position and broad education, having studied at several universities. When twenty-six years of age, he met a peasant who had performed several astonishing cures, "and from him caught the enthusiasm which he subsequently manifested in healing the sick." I quote two cases on the authority of Professor Onymus of the University of Würtzburg. "Captain Ruthlein, an old gentleman of Thundorf, 70 years of age, who had long been pronounced incurable of paralysis which kept his hand clinched, and who had not left his room for many years, was perfectly cured.

Eight days after his cure he paid me a visit, rejoicing
in the happiness of being able to walk freely. . . . A
student of Burglauer, near Murmerstadt, had lost for
two years the use of his legs; and though he was
only partially relieved by the first and second prayer
of the Prince, at the third he found himself perfectly
well."

Father Mathew was very successful in relieving
the sick; after his death multitudes visited his tomb,
and of these many were helped and left their crutches
there.

In all parts of Roman Catholic countries, and in the
Greek churches of Russia, great stacks of crutches,
canes, and splints may be seen, which have been left
by those who, as Dr. Tuke says, "there is no reason to
doubt, have been cured and relieved of contracted
joints by the prayers offered at some shrine, or by
the supposed efficacy of their relics." Similar results
have been seen in Montreal, Canada, within a few
years, at solemnities connected with the deaths of
certain bishops, one of whom had performed many
cures through a long career.

It cannot be denied that many cures occurred at
Knock Chapel in Ireland; and also at Lourdes in
France, whose fame "is entirely associated with the
grotto of Massavielle, where the Virgin Mary is believed, in the Catholic world, to have revealed herself
repeatedly to a peasant girl in 1858." This place is
resorted to by multitudes of pilgrims from all parts
of the world, whose gifts have rendered possible the
building of a large church above the grotto, "conse-
crated in 1876 in the presence of thirty-five cardinals
and other high ecclesiastical dignitaries." The gifts
have been made by devotees, many of whom claim to
have been cured of ailments that defied medical treatment; besides, a large trade is carried on in the water,

which is distributed to all parts of the world. I stood by the fountain for hours observing the pilgrims drinking and filling their bottles. A flask which was filled for me has stood on my mantel for several years, and I am bound to say that no serious illness has occurred in the family during that time. Many recoveries follow its use.

Nor is there any reason to doubt that Joseph Gassner, a Catholic priest in Swabia, effected many cures.

Turning from the Roman Catholic and Greek churches to Protestantism, five or six names are conspicuous in connection with the production of cures without the use of medicine, and in answer to prayer.

Dorothea Trudel, a woman living at Manheim, long had an establishment there. Marvelous tales have been told of the cures, some of which have been thoroughly authenticated.

Another name widely known is that of the late Rev. W. E. Boardman, with whom I was acquainted for many years. He had an establishment in the north of London which is designated "Bethshan," and has created quite a sensation. There hundreds of remarkable cures are claimed of cancer, paralysis, advanced consumption, chronic rheumatism, and lameness; and the usual trophies in the shape of canes, crutches, etc., are left behind. They will not allow the place to be called a *hospital*, but the "Nursery of Faith." Their usual mode is to anoint the sufferer with oil and then pray; though considerable variety in method is practised apparently to stimulate faith. They profess to effect many cures by correspondence, and assert that the healing virtues claimed for French and Irish relics by Roman Catholics are not to be compared with those exercised in answer to their prayers.

Dr. Charles Cullis, of Boston, recently deceased, was long noted in connection with healing diseases by faith and prayer, and among his followers has given Old Orchard, Maine, a reputation as great as the grotto at Lourdes has among Catholics.

The Rev. Mr. Simpson, formerly a Presbyterian minister, and now an Independent in the city of New York, has also become prominent, and there can be no doubt of the improvement in health of many of the persons for whom he has prayed. His devotees have enabled him to open a house here to which various persons, among them some ministers, resort when ill.

Mrs. Mix, a colored woman living in the State of Connecticut, had great fame; having been the instrument of the cure of persons who have devoted themselves to faith-healing, attending conventions, writing books, etc. Her death was bewailed by many respectable persons, without distinction of creed, sex, age, or color, who believed that they had been cured through her prayers.

One of the elements of the notoriety of George O. Barnes, the "Mountain Evangelist," of Kentucky, was his oft-announced power to heal.

Having admitted in general that real cures of real diseases are often made, it is necessary to consider more closely the subject of testimony.

TESTIMONY TO PARTICULARS

ALL honest and rational persons are competent to testify whether they feel sick, and whether they seem better, or believe themselves to have entirely recovered after being prayed for and anointed by Boardman, Simpson, or Cullis; but their testimony as to what disease they had, or whether they are entirely cured, is a different matter, and to have value must be scrutinized in every case by competent judges.

In general, diseases are internal or external. It is clear that no individual can know positively the nature of any *internal* disease that he has. The diagnosis of the most skilful physicians may be in error. Post-mortems in celebrated cases have often shown that there had been an entire misunderstanding of the malady. Hysteria can simulate every known complaint: paralysis, heart-disease, and the worst forms of fever and ague. Hypochondria, to which intelligent and highly educated persons of sedentary habits brooding over their sensations are liable, especially if they are accustomed to read medical works and accounts of diseases and of their treatment, will do the same. Dyspepsia has various forms, and indigestion can produce symptoms of organic heart-disease, while diseases of the liver have often been mistaken by eminent physicians for pulmonary consumption. Especially in women do the troubles to which they are most subject give rise to hysteria, in which condition they may firmly believe that they are afflicted with disease of the spine, of the heart, or indeed of all the organs. I heard an intelligent woman "testify" that she had "heart-disease, irritation of the spinal cord, and Bright's disease of the kidneys, and had suffered from them all for *ten years*." She certainly had some symptoms of all of them. Within eight years a "regular" physician died, the cause, as he supposed on the authority of several examinations, being consumption. A post-mortem showed his lungs sound, and his death to have been caused by diseases the result of the enormous quantities of food and stimulants he had taken to "fight off consumption." The object of these observations is simply to show that testimony that a person has been cured reflects no light upon the problem as to what he or she was cured of, if it was claimed to be an *internal* disease. The solemn assertion of a responsible person that he was cured of heart-disease, can prove only that the symptoms of what he thought was heart-disease have disappeared.

Also, in any state not accompanied with acute pain, testimony to an immediate cure is of no value unless the disease be of an external character and actually disappears before the eye of the witness. All other cures must have the test of time; hence testimony given on the spot, at the grave of Father Mathew, or at Lourdes, or at the camp-meeting at Old Orchard, or in the Tabernacle of Mr. Simpson, can prove merely that then and there the witness was not conscious of pain or weakness, or of the symptoms of the disease which he believed he had.

The foregoing observations relate to internal diseases, but it is by no means easy to determine what an *external* disease is. Tumors are often mistaken for cancers, and cancers are of different species — some incurable by any means known to the medical profession, others curable. It is by these differences that quack cancer-doctors thrive. When the patient has anything resembling cancer, they promptly apply some salve, and if the patient recovers he signs a certificate saying that he was cured of a cancer of a most terrible character which would have been fatal in three months or six weeks; or when the *quack himself writes the certificate for the patient to sign*, which is generally the case, the time in which the cancer would have proved fatal may be reduced to a few days. There is also a difference in tumors: some under no circumstances cause death; others are liable to become as fatal as a malignant pustule.

In supposed injuries to the joints, the exact cause of the swelling is not always easily determined; and internal abscesses have sometimes been months in reaching a condition which would enable the most skilful physicians and surgeons to locate them, or decide positively their cause. The converse of this is true, that swellings have been supposed to be caused by abscesses, incisions made, and a totally different and comparatively harmless condition found. Hence it is by no means certain that an external disease is properly named. The patient and his attending physicians may be in serious error as to the exact character of what at a first glance it might be supposed easy to identify.

I have already spoken of the power of hysteria to simulate the symptoms of any internal disease. It may be new to some that it can produce very remarkable external developments. On the authority of Dr. Marvin R. Vincent, of this city, I give the following. Says Dr. Vincent: "I was told of a case at St. Luke's Hospital in this city: a woman with a swelling which was pronounced by the physicians to be an ovarian tumor, but which disappeared on the administration of ether, and was discovered to be merely the result of hysteria."

Consumption is a subject of painful interest to almost every family in the country. The peculiarity of this disease is that it advances and retreats. In the more common form there comes a time when what is commonly called softening of the tubercles takes place. The patient is then very ill; hectic fever with the succeeding chill occurs every day, and sometimes several times a day; night-sweats, profuse expectoration, and other evidences and causes of debility complicate the situation, and the end is thought to be not far off. To the surprise of the friends, in a few days he greatly improves. Night-sweats cease, the fever greatly diminishes or disappears, the cough lessens; he rejoices, perhaps resumes his business and re-

ceives congratulations. Whatever he had been taking now has the credit,—whether what his physician
prescribed or hypophosphites, cod-liver oil, balsams,
pectorals, expectorants, "compound oxygen," benzoic;
when the fact is that the tubercles have softened.
As foreign bodies they produced fever and other
symptoms; they have been eliminated by coughing
and other natural processes. Meanwhile others are
forming which give no uneasiness except a slight
increase of shortness of breath. When the second
softening period comes the patient sinks lower than
before; new remedies, of course, are tried, radical
change of diet is made, but if death does not end
the scene similar apparent recovery takes place. At
either of these stages a visit to a grotto, the operations of "faith-healers," or a magnetic belt or pad,
might seem to produce a great effect; but decline
would occur at the periods of softening, and the
patient afterward improve or sink beyond the possibility of recovery, if none of these things had been
done.

A fact concerning consumption is known to medical
men and stated in works on hygiene, but often dis-
believed. That fact is that pulmonary consumption,
genuine and unmistakable, often terminates spontaneously in recovery, and frequently yields to hygienic
methods. It is the opinion of one of the most celebrated physicians of Europe that for every two cases
of death from consumption there is one case that
is either indefinitely prolonged, the patient living to
be old, or entirely recovering and dying of old age,
or of some entirely different disease. It may be asked
how such a fact as this can be established. By two
modes — one probable, the other conclusive. The
probable is where the patient had all the external
symptoms of the disease, and examination of the

lungs by competent specialists gave results which agreed with each other and with the external symptoms, and the patient, by changing from a sedentary to an outdoor and active life, entirely recovers and lives for many years without return of the symptoms. Possibility of error in the diagnosis remains, but where all these conditions exist it is reduced to a minimum. Such cases are numerous. Conclusive demonstration is found in post-mortem examinations. The late Prof. Austin Flint of New York, author of the "Practice of Medicine," was also the author of a "Clinical Report on Consumption," and describes sixty-two cases in which an arrest of the disease took place; in seven cases it occurred without any special medical or hygienic treatment, and in four of the seven he declares that recovery was complete.

Prof. J. Hughes Bennett, of the Royal Infirmary at Edinburgh, in a lecture says: "Up to a recent period the general opinion has been that consumption almost always marches on to a fatal termination, and that the cases of those known to be restored were so few as to be merely an exception to the general rule. Morbid anatomy has now, I think, demonstrated that tubercles in an early stage degenerate and become abortive with extreme frequency, in the proportion of one third to one half of all the incurables who die over forty."

Both the Edinburgh "Journal of Medical Science" and the London "Lancet" indorse this conclusion. It is equivalent to saying that from one third to one half of all the incurables of Scotland who die over forty have had incipient consumption and got well of it. To meet those who would say that practically consumption does not mean the existence of a few isolated tubercles, but an advanced stage in which the lungs are in a state of ulceration, and the powers are so lowered that perfect recovery seldom or never takes place, Dr. Bennett proceeds to say that "Laennec, Andral, Cruveilhier, Kingston, Pressat, Boudet, and many others have published cases where all the functional symptoms of the disease, even in its most advanced state, were present, and yet the individual lived many years and ultimately died of some other disorder, and on dissection cicatrices and concretions have been found in the lungs." In that lecture Prof. Bennett exhibited the lungs of a man who died suddenly of congestion of the brain, aged fifty years. At twenty-two he had been given up to die of pulmonary consumption, recovered, lived nearly thirty years, and his lungs exhibited most indubitable marks of the progress and termination of the disease. It is easy to see that in such cases of recovery there came a time when the last tubercles softened; at such a time, any powerful mental stimulus, or pleasing change in circumstances, or physical stimulant compelling exercise in the open air, might be the element which would decide the question whether the system would rally or the process of innutrition and decay go on.

The heating of the minds of witnesses by a succession of testimonies must not be forgotten.

In one of the meetings conducted by the Rev. A. B. Simpson, I heard witnesses testify to the healing power of God, and one witness, who seemed to be a pillar and was specially called upon by Mr. Simpson, testified, stating that no one had greater reason to praise God than he, "for during the past year I have *several* times been *miraculously* and *instantaneously* raised from the *jaws of death.*"

In Adelaide, Australia, at a meeting held in the Workmen's Hall, which was crowded, a Mrs. Morgan testified that for twenty years she had suffered from heart-disease, but the moment "Mr. Wood laid his curative hands upon me, I felt a quiet within and was conscious I was cured." The Rev. W. B. Shorthouse tendered some wonderful testimony; he described his own career of weakness which interfered with his ministerial duties, but now he was completely restored to health. Only two weeks previous, he said, some of his congregation told him that he looked like death. As he grew warm in his testimony, he described several marvelous cases, *one of a man brought in dead* who walked away without assistance. He had seen hundreds "touch the border of Mr. Wood's garment," and finally concluded by saying he was himself "a *living example of miracles greater than those performed by the disciples of Christ.*"

After seeing this in "Galignani's Messenger" in Paris, I ascertained from high authority in Australia that these narratives were greatly exaggerated, and that many relapses had occurred.

If such dangers exist in connection with the testimony of witnesses in religious meetings to *physical facts*, it may be thought that accounts of cases carefully written by honest men might be taken without so many grains of allowance. Having inquired into several of the most conspicuous with whose subjects I am acquainted, I have found that the condition of the patient *prior to the alleged cure* has been magnified in the description. This has not always been so, but in most of the celebrated cases which I have personally investigated.

Many important facts have been omitted, sometimes because the witness did not regard them as of consequence; in other cases, it must be confessed, because the luster of the cure would be dimmed by their recital. A female evangelist, whose astonishing cure has been told to thousands, never mentions a surgical operation from which her friends know that she de-

2

rived great benefit; and when asked why she did not tell of that, she replied, in substance, that she did not wish to divert attention from the great work that God had really wrought in her. Often the account of the *cure* has been exaggerated: relapses have not been published, peculiar sensations still felt, and resisted, have been omitted from the description, and the mode of the cure has been restricted to one act or a single moment of time, when in response to questions it appeared that it was weeks or months before the person could properly be said to be well. In all such cases it is obvious that the written testimony is of little value; indeed, it is seldom that a published account in books supporting marvels of this kind shows any signs of being written by a person who took the pains, if he possessed the capacity, to investigate the facts accurately. Frequent quotation of such accounts adds nothing to their credibility or value.

But after all deductions have been made, that most extraordinary recoveries have been produced, some of them instantaneously, from disease in some cases generally considered to be incurable by ordinary treatment, in others known to be curable in the ordinary process of medicine and in surgery only by slow degrees, must be admitted.

The object of these remarks is not to discredit all testimony, but to show the conditions upon which its value depends.

EXPLANATION OF THE FACTS

HAVE these facts a common cause? To solve the problem requires us to ascertain whether the effects are the same, and the limitations of the cause or causes are the same? Do recoveries under the prayers and anointings of Dr. Cullis surpass in the nature of disease, rapidity of cure, and proportion of recoveries to the whole number of persons prayed for, those attested in connection with Mrs. Mix or those of the Rev. A. B. Simpson? Is there any reason to believe that Dr. Newton was less successful in the number, character, or permanence of the cures attributed to his touch and voice than those of the persons before named? Again, is there any testimony that they have achieved greater success than "Bethshan" in London? Further, can these be proved to have done any more than Prince Hohenlohe, or the priest Gassner, or the water of Lourdes? The subjects of these cures will, of course, chant the praises of the respective schools; but does the impartial student of the testimony see any reason to distinguish between them as to the number or character of the effects? They all sometimes cure paralysis, convulsions, cancers, tumors, spinal diseases, those peculiar to women, and relieve or cure chronic cases frequently, especially rheumatism, sciatica, neuralgia, and similar maladies. They succeed in some forms of acute disease. "Schools" in religion and medicine are prone to magnify their own achievements and depreciate those of others. Nor does this always spring from dishonesty; since faith often prevents that scrutiny which would reveal reasons for discounting testimony or appearances, while suspicion would lead to a treatment of the reports of others the opposite of that accorded to their own. I have seen subjects of spiritualist healers, mesmeric and magnetic healers, Roman Catholic and Russo-Greek miracles, and of the most conspicuous "faith-healers" and "mind-curers" in this country, and find no reason to believe that one has been more or less successful than others.

A very important question is whether their *limita-*

tions are the same. The limitations must have respect
to what and how they heal, and the permanence of the
cure. It will be noted that none of them can raise
the dead, or if any profess ability to do so, or by
prayer to restore to life, the rest will unite to deny
the claim of the others, and so fully support our view.
Nor can they give sight to one born blind, nor healing
to one born deaf, where the cause of deafness is the
absence of any of the organs necessary to hearing.
Instances have been published where children who
had lost their hearing by scarlet fever or other disease, have been made to hear by the manipulations of
spiritualists or by the prayers of Catholics or Protestants; but whether true or not, no case which can
be shown to be one of congenital deafness or blindness can be attested where sight or hearing has been
made possible by any other than surgical treatment.
Further, none of them can restore a limb that has
been cut off, or an eye that has been lost.

In mental derangement it is to be admitted that all
have been successful in some cases of a functional
character, and in some of protracted melancholia; but
no authentic account has been adduced of the cure of
dementia or idiocy.

Another common limitation is the existence of
many cases of the same disease in which cures are
effected, which they cannot relieve in the least. Piti-
ful instances could be detailed of persons who have
traveled long distances, or have believed in the water,
or the power of the dead body of an ecclesiastic, or of
prayers at his tomb, or of the mystic touch of Newton, or of Dr. Cullis, or of a coterie who have made
their headquarters at a famous resort on the coast
of the Atlantic, and have died bitterly disappointed.
Many have died while firmly believing that God would
heal them, and that they were not about to die. Neither

Catholic, Spiritualist, nor Protestant has any prëemi-
nence with regard to this limitation.

A remarkable attempt to Christianize the interior
of Africa is now proceeding under the auspices of
William Taylor, a missionary bishop. One of the
company which he took out was an obstinate believer
in the power of faith to draw from God such help as
to enable him to dispense with medicine. This young
man fanatically refused to take any medicine, and
died a martyr to superstition which he mistook for
faith. The last entry in his diary was: "I have n't
the fever, but a weak feeling; but I take the promise
'He giveth power to the faint,' and I do receive the
fact." The testimony of his medical adviser to his
last conversation is: " Charlie, your temperature is
105, and pulse 130; normal is 98; the dividing line
between life and death is 103. You are now dying.
It is only a question of time; and if you do not take
something to break up this fever, it will surely kill
you." The reply of the misguided youth was, "Well,
then, I 'll die; for I won't take any medicine." Bishop
Taylor himself does not hold the view which, con-
sistently carried out, practically caused the suicide
of this young man. Almost all in the party had
the African fever, and by the aid of medical skill
recovered.

The limitations common to all are further illustrated
by the following case, an account of which I received
in writing from the eminent physician who had it in
charge until the fatal termination. A minister of the
gospel and his wife, widely known both in Europe
and America, had a daughter-in-law to whom they
were greatly attached. Her health began to fail, and
all that medical treatment could do was done without
avail. The diagnosis was one of ovarian tumor, and
little hope was offered either to the invalid or to her

friends. Finally she was made a subject of prayer by the minister and his wife, who earnestly besought God to heal her. They believed that they received an evidence in answer to their prayers that she would be cured; but being about to make a long evangelizing tour throughout the world, they prayed that if she was to get well, they might receive a certain sign which they suggested in prayer; and the event was in harmony with the suggestion. Thoroughly persuaded, they made a farewell visit and had a season of prayer in which both they and she received "the assurance" that the disease was checked and that she would finally recover. Previous to their embarking on the voyage, at a meeting which was attended by thousands, her case was spoken of and prayers were offered for her recovery; and this happened on several occasions during the long tour following. But the disease progressed and ended in death, according to the prognosis given by the physician, who is himself a Christian. These facts show the deceptive character of the assurances which many claim to receive on matters of fact of this kind.

Another element of limitation has respect to relapses. In many cases those who suppose that they have been cured relapse and die of the malady of which they testified they had been cured. This is true of the results of medical practice, and is a consequence of the law of human mortality and general limitations of human knowledge; but it is specially true of quack medicines involving anodynes, alcohol, or other stimulants which disguise symptoms, develop latent energy, or divert attention.

Lord Gardenstone, himself a valetudinarian, spent a great deal of time "inquiring for those persons who had actually attested marvelous cures, and found that more than two thirds of the number died very shortly after they had been cured." That the proportion of relapses among persons who have attested cures under the Spiritualists, Magnetizers, Roman Catholics, and Protestants is as great as this, I do not affirm; but I have no doubt that it is greater than among those who have supposed themselves to be cured either by hygienic means without medicine, or under the best attainable medical treatment, which always attends to hygiene in proportion to the intellectual and moral elevation of the physician above the sphere of quackery.

Some years since a member of the Christian church in the city of Boston solemnly testified that he had been entirely cured of pulmonary consumption through the anointing and prayer of Dr. Cullis. In less than six months afterward he died of consumption. "Zion's Herald," a paper published in the same city, in an editorial upon the results of a faith-healing convention at Old Orchard, says: "We are not surprised to learn that some who esteemed themselves healed are suffering again from their old infirmities, in some instances more severely than before." Such relapses are exceedingly numerous, but they are not published; the jubilant testimonies are telegraphed throughout the land and dilated upon in books; the subsequent relapses are not spoken of in religious meetings nor published anywhere, but a little pains enabled me in a single year to collect a large number.

If we are not able to conclude a common cause from these concurrences in effects, limitations, and relapses, neither the deductive nor the inductive process is of value, and all modes of acquiring knowledge or tracing causes would seem to be useless.

But what is that common cause? Can these effects be proved to be natural by constructing a formula by

which they can be produced? If there be phenomena
in which the results cannot be traced to their sources,
can they be shown to be similar to other effects whose
causes can be thus traced?

In investigating phenomena, some of which it is
claimed are connected with religion and others with
occult forces, it is necessary to proceed *without regard
to the question of religion*, in determining whether the
facts can be accounted for upon natural principles,
and paralleled by the application thereof.

In searching for analogies I avail myself of authentic cases found in John Hunter, in Dr. Tuke's
work previously referred to, in the "Mental Physiology" of Dr. Carpenter, and in the psychological
researches of Sir Benjamin Brodie and Sir Henry
Holland; selecting, however, only such facts as have
been paralleled under my own observation.

First. Cases where the effect is unquestionably
produced by a natural mental cause.

(*a*) The charming away of warts is well established.
Dr. Tuke says of them: "They are so apparent that
there cannot be much room for mistake as to whether
they have or have not disappeared, and in some instances within my own knowledge their disappearance was in such close connection with the psychical
treatment adopted, that I could hardly suppose the
cure was only *post hoc*. In one case, a relative of mine
had a troublesome wart on the hand, for which I made
use of the usual local remedies, but without effect.
After they were discontinued, it remained *in statu quo*
for some time, when a gentleman 'charmed' it away
in a few days." He then tells of a case the particulars of which he received of a surgeon. His daughter
had about a dozen warts on her hands, and they had
been there eighteen months; her father had applied
caustic and other remedies without success. A gen-

tlemen called, noticed her warts, and asked how many she had. She said she did not know, but thought about a dozen. "Count them, will you?" said he, and solemnly took down her counting, remarking, "You will not be troubled with your warts after next Sunday." Dr. Tuke adds, "It is a fact that by the day named the warts had disappeared and did not return." Francis Bacon had a similar experience, including the removal of a wart which had been with him from childhood, on which he says: "At the rest I did little marvel, because they came in a short time, and might go away in a short time again; but the going away of that which had stayed so long doth yet stick with me."

(b) Blood-diseases, such as scurvy, have been cured in the same way. At the siege of Breda in 1625, scurvy prevailed to such an extent that the Prince of Orange was about to capitulate. The following experiment was resorted to: "Three small phials of medicine were given to each physician, not enough for recovery of two patients. It was publicly given out that three or four drops were sufficient to impart a healing virtue to a gallon of liquor." Dr. Frederic Van der Mye, who was present and one of the physicians, says: "The effect of the delusion was really astonishing; for many quickly and perfectly recovered. Such as had not moved their limbs for a month before were seen walking the streets, sound, upright, and in perfect health." Dr. Van der Mye says that before this happy experiment was tried they were in a condition of absolute despair, and the scurvy and the despair had produced "fluxes, dropsies, and every species of distress, attended with a great mortality."

(c) Van Swieten and Smollett speak of consumptive patients recovering health from falling into cold water. Dr. Tuke says that Dr. Rush refers to these cases, and "inclines to think that fright and the consequent exertion produced a beneficial result."

(*d*) Abernethy gives a case of a woman who was permanently cured of dropsy by being frightened by a bull, relief coming through the kidneys.

(*e*) Of the famous metallic tractors of Dr. Perkins, which produced most extraordinary results, attracting the attention of the medical world, the effects of the use of the tractors being attributed to galvanism, and of the production of the same effects by two wooden tractors of nearly the same shape, and painted so as to resemble them in color, it is hardly necessary to say anything. But wooden and metallic were equally efficient, and cured cases of chronic rheumatism in the ankle, knee, wrist, and hip, where the joints were swollen and the patient had been ill for a long time; and even a case of lockjaw of three or four days' standing was cured in fifty minutes, when the physicians had lost all hope.

(*f*) I have frequently tested this principle. The application of a silver dollar wrapped in silk to ulcerated teeth, where the patient had been suffering for many hours, and in some instances for days, relieved the pain, the patient supposing that it was an infallible remedy. After I had explained that the effect was wholly mental, the magic power of the remedy was gone.

(*g*) In 1867 a well-known public singer was taken dangerously ill on the evening of his concert, having great nausea and intense headache; two applications of the silver dollar to his forehead entirely relieved him, and he performed a full program with his usual energy. Anything else would have been as effectual as the dollar, which was used merely because it was at hand.

(*h*) The following case is taken from a pamphlet published by me in 1875, entitled "Supposed Miracles."

In company with the Rev. J. B. Faulks I called at a place near Englewood, N. J., to procure a boat. There was a delay of half an hour, and the day being chilly, we repaired to a house near by and there saw a most pitiable spectacle. The mother of the family was suffering from inflammatory rheumatism in its worst form. She was terribly swollen, could not move, nor bear to be touched. I said to Mr. Faulks, "You shall now have an illustration of the truth of the theory you have so often heard me advance." He mildly demurred, and intimated that he did not wish to be mixed up in anything of the kind. But, after making various remarks solely to inspire confidence and expectation, I called for a pair of knitting-needles. After some delay, improved to increase confidence and surround the proceedings with mystery, operations were begun. One of the hands of the patient was so swollen that the fingers were very nearly as large as the wrist of an ordinary child three years of age. In fact, almost all the space naturally between the fingers was occupied, and the fist was clinched. It was plain that to open them voluntarily was impossible, and to move them intensely painful. The daughter informed us that the hand had not been opened for several weeks. When all was ready I held the needle about two inches from the end of the woman's fingers, just above the clinched hand, and said, "Now, Madam, do not think of your fingers, and above all do not try to move them, but fix your eyes on the ends of these needles." She did so, and to her own wonder and that of her daughter the fingers straightened out and became flexible without the least pain. I then moved the needles about, over the hand, and she declared that all pain left her hand except in one spot about half an inch in diameter.

(*i*) The efficacy of the touch of the king to cure scrofula is authenticated beyond question. Charles II. touched nearly 100,000 persons; James in one of his journeys touched 800 persons in Chester Cathedral. Macaulay's History shows how, when William III. refused to exercise this power, it brought upon him "an avalanche of the tears and cries of parents of the children who were suffering from scrofula. Bigots lifted up their hands and eyes in horror at his impiety." His opponents insinuated that he dared not try a power which belonged only to legitimate sovereigns; but this sarcasm was without basis, as an old author says: "The curing of the king's evil by the touch of the king does much puzzle our philosophers, *for whether our kings were of the house of York or Lancaster*, it did cure for the most part." This reminds the student of ecclesiastical history of the consternation of the Jesuits when the extraordinary "miracle" was wrought upon the niece of the famous Blaise Pascal.

(*j*) The daughter of an eminent clergyman in this city had been sick for a long time, entirely unable to move and suffering intense pain. One of the most famous surgeons of New York declared, after careful examination, that she had diseases of the breast-bone and ribs which would require incisions of so severe a character as to be horrible to contemplate. Three times the surgeon came with his instruments to perform the operation, but the parents could not bring themselves to consent to it, and it was postponed. At last the late Dr. Krackowitzer was called in; he solemnly and very thoroughly examined her from head to foot, taking a long time, and at last suddenly exclaimed, "Get out of bed, put on your clothes, and

go down-stairs to meet your mother in the parlor!"
The young lady automatically arose and obeyed him.
The next day she took a walk with her mother, and
soon entirely recovered. Dr. Krackowitzer stated
that he recognized in her an obstinate case of hysteria, which needed the stimulus of sudden command
from a stronger will than her own. I received this
narrative from the young lady's father; she has
never had a relapse, and is still living in excellent
health. Had she been cured by a faith-healer believed
in by the family, the mistaken diagnosis of the eminent surgeon would have been heralded far and wide,
and the cure considered a miracle.

(k) The cure of obstinate constipation when all
medicine had lost its effect, by a medical man who
required the patient to uncover the abdomen and
direct his thoughts entirely to the sensations experienced in that region, is vouched for by Dr. Carpenter.

(l) The cure of a case of paralysis by Sir Humphrey Davy is a scientific fact of the first importance.
He placed a thermometer under the tongue of the
patient simply to ascertain the temperature; the patient at once claimed to experience relief, so the same
treatment was continued for two weeks, and by that
time the patient was well. In this case the imagination of the patient was not assisted by an application
to the affected part.

In all the foregoing cases the cure or relief was a
natural result of mental or emotional states. As long
ago as the time of John Hunter, it was established
by a variety of experiments and by his own experience that the concentration of attention upon any
part of the human system affects first the sensations,
next produces a change in the circulation, then a
modification of the nutrition, and finally an alteration in structure.

3

Second. Cases in which the operation of occult causes is claimed. These will be treated here *only so far as they reflect light upon "faith-cures."*

(*a*) That trances and healings occurred under the performances of Mesmer is as well established as any fact depending upon testimony. French scientists who investigated the subject divided into two hostile parties upon the explanation, and in some cases as to whether they were genuine or fraudulent; but they agreed as to the genuineness of many of the cures. The Government established a commission of physicians and members of the Academy of Sciences to investigate the phenomena. Benjamin Franklin, who was at that time in Paris in the interest of the United States, and the distinguished J. S. Bailly were of that commission, with Lavoisier, Darcet, and others. They presented an elaborate report, specifically admitting many of the alleged facts, but denying the necessity of assuming "animal magnetism." Forty years afterward,— namely, on October 11, 1825,— the Royal Academy of Medicine in Paris was addressed by a noted physician, Foissac, who called its attention to the importance of a new inquiry. After a long debate the Academy appointed a committee to inquire whether it would or would not become the Academy to investigate "animal magnetism." The report was favorable, and was debated at great length; it was finally decided to investigate, and the Academy, by a majority of ten in a total vote of sixty, appointed a permanent committee on the subject. This committee reaffirmed the facts, and did not divide as in the former instance, two merely declining to sign the report because not present at the experiments. The subject was reopened in 1837, and further reports and discussions of great importance resulted. These are referred to here simply to show the amount of testimony to certain facts of trance conditions, so called, and cures.

The following is given on the authority of Dr. Tuke, who says, "It is afforded by a highly respectable surgeon and attributed by him to mesmerism." It is the case of Edward Wine, aged seventy-five, who had been paralyzed two years in one arm and leg. The left arm was spasmodically fixed to the chest, the fingers drawn toward the palm of the hand and wasted, quite incapable of holding anything; walked with a crutch, drawing the left leg after him. After several mesmerizing operations the surgeon put "a nosegay in his coat and posted him off to church, and he tells me he walked like a gentleman down the aisle, carrying his stick in his lame arm."

The noted Mr. Braid in many authentic instances restored lost sight, greatly improved the condition of the paralyzed, in some instances entirely curing the patient, and had very little difficulty with most cases of rheumatism. Dr. W. B. Carpenter investigated many of these cases.

But what is mesmerism, magnetism, electro-biology, etc.? It is a subjective condition. The notion that a magnetic fluid passes from the body, or that passes are of utility in producing the state except as they act upon the mind of the candidate, was exploded long since; and both in Europe and America the discovery of the real principle was accidental and made by a number of persons. About fifty years ago an itinerant lecturer on these phenomena, who had great success in experiments, used an old-fashioned cylinder electrical machine. The "subjects" took hold of the wire. He gave them a slight electrical shock, and "concentrated his will upon them." Those that were susceptible passed into the trance state. On a certain occasion, when trying the experiment with several gentlemen in a private room, the operator was called out just as the candidates had taken hold of the wire. He remained twenty minutes, not supposing that the experiment was being tried; on his return, to his great surprise, he found three of them as much "magnetized," "mesmerized," electro-biologized," "hypnotized," or "psycodunamized" as any he had ever seen. This showed that the entire effect was caused by their own mental states. Further experiments made it clear that neither the will of the operator, nor any "magnetism" from his body, nor electricity, nor the influence of the candidates upon each other had anything to do with the result. Mesmer himself used magnets until he fell in with the Roman Catholic priest Gassner, before mentioned, when, perceiving that he used none, he renounced magnets, afterward depending solely on manipulation.

Twenty-three years ago I was present at a private meeting of twenty-five ladies and gentlemen, at the residence of Mr. Henry R. Towne, president of the Yale and Towne Manufacturing Company. On two successive evenings these phenomena had been explained. It had been maintained that all the results were subjective, arising from the concentrated attention, expectancy, and reverence of the persons trying the experiment. At the close of the two lectures, after divesting the subject of mystery, and, apparently, rendering it impossible to produce reverence or confidence, I was urged to test the theory by experiment. Accordingly eight gentlemen and ladies were requested to rise, stand without personal contact with one another or myself, close their eyes, and clasp their hands. In a few minutes five passed more or less fully into the trance state, two becoming unconscious of their surroundings and the others exhibiting peculiar phenomena. One thus affected was a

prominent lawyer of the city of New York, another
a recent graduate of the Sheffield Scientific School,
and the third the bookkeeper in a large establishment. *Nothing* was done by the experimenter during
the interval after these persons closed their eyes and
clasped their hands, save to wait in silence and require silence from spectators. Among those who witnessed and critically studied these phenomena with
the writer were Professor Fuertes, Dean of the Department of Civil Engineering in Cornell University,
whose letter, herewith printed,[1] explains itself; Mr.
Henry R. Towne, before mentioned; the Rev. Dr.

[1] DR. J. M. BUCKLEY. DEAR SIR: My recollection of the
"séance" referred to in your letter of the 25th ult. is not as
distinct in some points as in others you do not mention. The
study of psychology is so important that it is necessary to be
exact beyond measure in order not to mislead. An immense
amount of rubbish has been piled upon slender foundations in
the study of psycho-genesis, and no progress can be made so
long as people assent easily to become witnesses with external aid to recollect facts which happened long ago. I am very
positive as to the truth of the following facts: I belonged to a
literary club, composed of the most cultivated people residing
in Stamford in 1864–71. At one of our meetings, I was present
when you performed some experiments upon ten or fifteen of its
members by asking them to stand in a circle, with closed eyes,
and holding their hands before their faces as in the conventional attitude for praying; the gas was partly turned down.
Some of the members of this group laughed, and you perempto-
rily excluded them from the circle, as previously agreed upon. A
short time afterward one of my neighbors began to breathe hard,
and he was followed by several others, who gave indications,
plainly visible, that something unusual was happening to them.

If human testimony is to be depended upon at all, I am sure
that the social position of the persons so affected, their high
culture, refinement, and surroundings, entitled their actions to
be believed, as representing truthfully the conditions causing
their strange behavior, even if the following circumstances did
not reinforce the necessity of believing their candid sincerity in
this question. One of the first "subjects" was a young lady,

A. S. Twombly, pastor of the Winthrop Congregational Church of Charlestown, Mass.; and J. B. Williams, Esquire, of the city of New York.

On the 14th of April, 1868, in the City Hall of Dover,
New Hampshire, in the presence of a thousand persons, the same principles were set forth. At the close
Dr. L. G. Hill, of that city, long President of the State
Medical Society, called for the proof of the theory
that the effects attributed to animal magnetism were
the result of subjective mental condition. The result,
as described in the "Dover Gazette" of Friday, April
17, 1868, by the editor, who refers to himself in the
account, is as follows: "Ten or twelve gentlemen at
his [the lecturer's] request took the platform and were
requested to shut their eyes, close their hands, and
remain quiet. They did so. One complete trance
medium and two partial ones at once developed.

who was made to believe that she was writing a letter to a
friend, and immediately began to simulate the act of writing;
but other subjects proving to be most amusingly affected, she
was, unfortunately, forgotten, and allowed to go on "writing"
for nearly three hours consecutively, earnestly engaged at her
task, oblivious of her surroundings, neither laughing, nor apparently caring for what was going on. The effect of holding
her hand in mid-air for so long a time, and moving her fingers
all the time, is a feat of endurance of which she was not physically able, if conscious. Her arm and shoulder were swollen
and lame for several days after this performance. [Owing to the
crowded condition of the room, I did not observe this till the interview terminated. AUTHOR.] Another subject was a young lady
who had recently lost a friend. The mother of her dead friend
had also recently arrived from Europe and was present in the
room; and after the young lady affected had expressed her
ability to go to heaven and described what she saw there, she
paused a moment, as if surprised and filled with terror; then,
uttering a piercing scream, moved forward as if to embrace the
dead friend, whose name she mentioned, in a manner so tragic
and out of keeping with her usual lovely and bashful demeanor
that the impression produced on the company was quite pro-

Three of the other gentlemen, among whom was the
writer of this article, felt the trance force in a slight
degree. The completely developed medium was in the
most perfect trance; could be convinced of anything
at once; was clairvoyant, ecstatic, mesmeric, somnam-
bulic, and in fact took any form of ideomania at will.
We have been at perhaps over a hundred séances of
mesmeric, biologic, and so-called spiritual subjects or
mediums, but have never seen so perfect a subject so
soon developed and upon so pure a principle." These
cases are adduced to show the effect of the mind upon
the body, and of the mind upon its own faculties.
The young man particularly mentioned by the "Gazette" could have had every tooth extracted, or even
a limb amputated, without consciousness. After he
had resumed his normal state, such was his susceptibility that a word would have sent him back to sleep.

found. This behavior, both brutal and coarse, and cruel to the
mother of the dead young girl, is, I am very sure, incompatible
with any theory of Miss —— being in her usual senses. In fact
she was made ill by this circumstance, and conceived the greatest aversion toward you. Her friend had been buried but a few
days. [These facts were unknown to me, and as soon as possible her attention was diverted from them. As the whole was
imaginary, this was easily done. AUTHOR.]

One of the most amusing incidents was the honest conviction
with which a prominent lawyer believed himself sitting on a
log looking into the muddy bottom of a stream of water. Another, that of a young man whose trembling legs were made to
bend under the enormous weight of an envelope placed over his
head, when told it weighed a ton. The above are a few of the
things I saw about which I am positive my memory of the
events is perfect. Also, that you stated that you would not and
did not exercise any act of volition or influence upon your
"subjects," but merely waited for them to fall into the hypnotic
state giving rise to the phenomena described.

Believe me, sincerely,

E. A. Fuertes.

ITHACA, NEW YORK, January 30, 1886.

If he had been ill of any disease which "faith-healers" or "magnetizers" could relieve, he would have received equal help. While these persons were standing and the susceptible were passing "under the influence," I was *simply waiting*, "only this and nothing more."

(*b*) As for causing the bedridden to rise, and breaking up morbid conditions that had defied medicine while being aggravated by it, these are among the simplest applications of the principle involved. The confidence of those unfamiliar with the subject would be taxed beyond endurance by the narration of illustrative facts to which there is abundant testimony and which can be paralleled easily.

(*c*) Intelligent missionaries and travelers in heathen lands, where they have given any investigation to the subject, unite in testifying that extraordinary cures follow the enchantments and magical rites employed by priests and physicians claiming supernatural powers.

(*d*) The influence of witch-doctors among the negroes of Africa, both to produce disease and cure it, is as well authenticated as any facts concerning the "Dark Continent"; nor is it necessary to go there for illustrations, which can be found in great numbers in the South. Not long since an entire community in the vicinity of Atlanta, Georgia, were greatly excited by the terrible diseases which followed threats made by a doctor of this sort. Voodooism has power to bring on diseases and also to cure; nor need this burden be placed upon the negroes and American Indians exclusively. In various parts of Austria, Germany, and Russia, among the peasantry and ignorant classes, belief in witchcraft, and the coincidences which sustain it, still exists; and on the authority of most distinguished physicians and surgeons in those

countries, I state that the results both in inflicting
and in removing what they never inflicted, which follow the operations of these witch-doctors, are often
astonishing.

(e) There is an old proverb that "when rogues fall
out, honest men get their dues." It is also true that
when quacks fall to discrediting each other, principles may be discovered. In 1865 there came to
Detroit, Michigan, a pupil of Dr. Newton, Bryant by
name, who performed cures as successfully as Newton
himself. In company with Dr. J. P. Scott, a Presbyterian minister there, I visited Dr. Bryant, and
saw him operate upon a score or more of patients
(one of whom had been supposed to be doomed to a
speedy death with ovarian tumor; Dr. Bryant removed the tumor, after which she lived some months
and died of debility). To comprehend his methods
fully I was operated upon for dyspepsia. About
a year later, returning from New Orleans to Mem-
phis, Tennessee, I found on board the steamer Dr.
Newton, who had just come from Havana. He
told me that in one day eight hundred persons had
applied to him in that city. On the same steamer
was Dr. B—— of St. Louis, an aged physician who
had been to Havana with a wealthy patient. I inquired of Dr. B—— and others whether such great
numbers had visited Dr. Newton, and was told that
such was the report, that vast crowds had surrounded
him from the day he arrived till he embarked, and
that marvelous tales were told of the cures he performed. For several hours a day during four days
I conversed with him concerning his career and principles. My conviction is that he believed in himself,
and also that he would use any means to accomplish
his ends. He would glide from fanaticism into hypoc-
risy, then into fanaticism, and from that into common

sense, with the rapidity of thought. He said that he
was influenced by spirits who told him what to say.
He would use the name of Jesus Christ in what would
seem a blasphemous manner; standing before an audience he would say, "I am now about to send forth
shocks of vitality." He would move his arms back-
ward and forward and exclaim, "In the name of Jesus
Christ, I command the diseases in the persons now
present to disappear!" He would go to the paralytic
or lame and exclaim, "In the name of Jesus Christ,
be healed of your infirmity." When I mentioned
having seen "Dr." Bryant, Dr. Newton instantly denounced him as an "unmitigated fraud who had no
genuine healing power." He claimed that he had
cured Bryant of a malignant disease with which he
found him suffering in a hospital; that Bryant had
acted as his amanuensis for some time, and then left
him, and had since been acting in opposition to him.
Knowing that the manipulations by Bryant had been
followed by some wonderful results in Detroit, I said
to Dr. Newton:

"If Bryant be an unmitigated fraud, how do you
account for his cures?"

"Oh!" said the doctor, "they are caused by the
faith of the people and the concentration of their
minds upon his operations, with the expectation of
being cured. Now," said he, "none would go to see
Bryant unless they had some faith that he might cure
them, and when he begins his operations with great
positiveness of manner, and they see the crutches he
has, and hear the people testify that they have been
cured, it produces a tremendous influence upon them;
and then he gets them started in the way of exercising, and they do a good many things they thought
they could not do; their appetites and spirits revive,

and if toning them up can possibly reduce the diseased tendency, many of them will get well."

Said I, "Doctor, pardon me, is not that a correct account of the manner in which you perform your wonderful works?"

"Oh, no," said he; "the difference between a genuine healer and a quack like Bryant is as wide as the poles."

To question him further upon this line would have put an end to the conversation sooner than I desired.

But testing fundamentally the same methods before and since that interview on many occasions, always under the great disadvantage of not being able to profess supernatural aid, either of spirits or of God, and thus being shut up to affecting the mind by the laws of suggestion and association, and by the manner assumed, and finding a result similar in kind, and in some cases equal in extent, to any produced by Newton or others, I know that when he was explaining to me the success of Bryant upon the assumption that he had no healing power, he gave inadvertently the whole explanation of the healing as far as it is independent of mere physical manipulation. Dr. Newton had been to Havana with his daughter, very low with consumption. He was taking her North, doubtful if she would reach home alive. On my saying, "Doctor, why could you not heal her?" he mournfully replied, "It seems as if we cannot always affect our own kindred!"

(f) In working miraculous cures, the Mormons are fully equal to Catholics or Protestants. In Europe one of their chief methods of making converts is praying with the sick, who often recover; and similar success has often aided them in making converts in this country. The Rev. Nathaniel Mead, a highly respected clergyman, to whom Dr. Baird refers in his "History of the Town of Rye," authorized me to publish the following facts, with the sanction of his name.

In the year 1839 a Mormon priest came to the neighborhood where Mr. Mead resided, and obtained access to the room of an intelligent member of a Christian church, who had long been hopelessly ill. He asked permission to pray for her. Catching at anything, she consented. He prayed with great earnestness, and she at once began to improve and recovered with surprising rapidity. Convinced by the supposed miracle that God was with the Mormon priest, she left the Christian church and identified herself with the Mormons to the extent of deserting friends and home.

In the same locality, another member of a Christian church had been severely injured by a bar of iron which fell upon his foot, mangling and crushing it. The same Mormon priest prayed with him, with a similar result; the wound healed very soon, and the man became a convert to Mormonism.

So great was the faith of certain Mormon proselytes in Europe that the priesthood could work miracles, that one who had lost a leg and could not secure another through the prayers of the Mormon missionaries, crossed the Atlantic and made a pilgrimage to Salt Lake City, where he had an interview with Brigham Young. This fox-like prophet and miracle-worker, who could cope in intellectual keenness with Horace Greeley, said to him, "It would be easy for me to give you another leg, but it is my duty to explain to you the consequences. You are now well advanced in life. If I give you another leg, you will indeed have two legs until you die, which will be a great convenience; but in the resurrection, not only will the leg which you lost rise and be

united to your body, but also the one which I now
give you; thus you will be encumbered with three
legs throughout eternity.   It is for you to decide
whether you would prefer the transient inconve-
nience of getting along with one leg till you die, or
the deformity of an extra leg forever." The pilgrim
concluded to remain maimed in this life, that he
might not be deformed in that which is to come.
This may be a myth, but it falls in well with Brigham Young's known character, and is as worthy of
respect as the reasons given by professedly Christian
faith-healers for not working miracles of this kind,
which are that they do not find "any special promise
for such cases," and that "they find no instance where
the apostles gave new limbs."

INDUCTIONS

THE inductions from these cases, and from the fact
that they are constantly paralleled, are:

(1) That subjective mental states, such as concentration of the attention upon a part with or without belief, can produce effects either of the nature of
disease or cure.

(2) Active incredulity in persons not acquainted
with these laws, but willing to be experimented upon,
is often more favorable to sudden effects than mere
stupid, acquiescent credulity.   The first thing the in-
credulous, hard-headed man, who believes that "there
is nothing in it," sees, that he cannot fathom, may
lead him to succumb instantly to the dominant idea.

(3) That concentrated attention, with faith, can
produce powerful effects; may operate efficiently in
acute diseases, with instantaneous rapidity upon nervous diseases, or upon any condition capable of being

4

modified by direct action through the nervous or circulatory system.

(4) That cures can be wrought in diseases of accumulation, such as dropsy and tumors, with surprising rapidity, where the increased action of the various excretory functions can eliminate morbid growths.

(5) That rheumatism, sciatica, gout, neuralgia, contraction of the joints, and certain inflammatory conditions, may suddenly disappear under similar mental states, so as to admit of helpful exercise; which exercise by its effect upon the circulation, and through it upon the nutrition of diseased parts, may produce a permanent cure.

(6) That the "mind-cure," apart from the absurd philosophy of the different sects into which it is already divided, and its repudiation of all medicine, has a basis in the laws of nature. The pretense of mystery, however, is either honest ignorance or consummate quackery.

(7) That all are unable to dispense with surgery, where the case is in the slightest degree complex and mechanical adjustments are necessary; also that they cannot restore a limb, or eye, or finger, or even a tooth. But in certain displacements of internal organs the consequence of nervous debility, which are sometimes aided by surgery, they all sometimes succeed by developing latent energy through mental stimulus.

THE MIRACLES OF CHRIST AND HIS APOSTLES

WE find that in comparison with the Mormons, Spiritualists, Mind-Curers, Roman Catholics, and Magnetizers, the Protestant Faith-Healers can accomplish as much, but no more; that they have the same limitations as to diseases they cannot heal, and injuries they cannot repair; as to particular cases of diseases that they can generally cure, but which occasionally defy them; and as to their liability to relapses. We also find that their phenomena can be paralleled under the operation of laws with which "experts" upon the subject, whether medical or otherwise, are acquainted, but which are not recognized by the general public, including many physicians of various schools, clergymen, lawyers, educators, and literary persons of both sexes who might be expected to understand them.

It is necessary to examine the New Testament, to ascertain whether Christ was subject to the limitations which have marked all these. The record states that *he* healed "*all* manner of disease, and all manner of sickness." It declares that "they brought unto him *all* that were sick, holden of divers diseases and torments, possessed with devils, and those that were lunatic [new version, epileptic] and palsied; and he healed them." He did these things uniformly, and sent word to John, "The *blind* receive their sight and the *lame* walk, the *lepers* are cleansed and the *deaf* hear, and the *dead are raised up*." He restored the withered hand, not by the slow process of a change in the circulation, and gradual change in the nutrition, followed by structural alteration; but it was instantly made "whole like as the other." Not only so, he restored limbs that had been cut off. See New Revision, Matthew xv. 30: "And there came unto him great multitudes having with them the lame, blind, dumb, *maimed*, and many others, and they cast them down at his feet; and he healed them; insomuch that the multitude wondered, when they saw the dumb speaking, the *maimed whole*, and the lame walking, and the blind seeing." The last miracle that Christ wrought before his crucifixion, according to St. Luke, was one that could defy all these "faith-healers" of every species to parallel. See New Revision, Luke xxii. 50: "And a certain one of them smote the servant of the high priest and *struck off his right ear.* But Jesus answered and said, Suffer ye thus far. And he touched his ear and *healed him.*"

Rational men familiar with the laws expounded in this paper could not believe this record if the mighty works told of Christ and the apostles were comprised simply in an account of wonderful tales. They would reason that it is much more probable that those who testified to these things were deceived or exaggerated, or that those who received the original accounts added to them, than that they should have happened. But when those who make the record convey to us ancient prophecies attested and still preserved by the Jews and fulfilled in the character and works of Christ; the account of his rejection and crucifixion by the Jews; the Sermon on the Mount; the parable of the prodigal son; the Golden Rule; the sublime and spiritual doctrines taught by Christ; and the picture of a life and of a death scene that have no parallel in human history or fiction, and declare that he who taught these things did such and such mighty works before us, we saw them and were convinced by the miracles that he did, "that he was a teacher come from God," it is no longer a question simply of believing things not included in the laws of nature. When these doctrines are applied to men's own needs and lives, they prove their divine origin by the radical and permanent changes which they make in character. Then the subjects of these changes accept the truthfulness of the record of miracles in a remote past which they cannot now test upon the authority of the spiritual truths which they are capable of subjecting to the test of practical experience.

Some allege that even the apostles could not restore limbs that had been cut off, or that had been wanting from birth. The record shows that the apostles made no distinction in cases. Ananias prayed for Paul, and "straightway there fell from his eyes as it had been scales." When Tabitha lay dead, Peter, after prayer, "turning to the body said, 'Tabitha, arise,'" and he "presented her alive." The chains fell off Peter in the prison, and "the iron gate opened for him and the angel of its own accord." As Peter had, in the first miracle after Pentecost, given strength to a man who had been *lame from his mother's womb*, so Paul, seeing a man at Lystra, "a cripple from his mother's womb who had never walked," said, "with a loud voice, 'Stand upright on thy feet,' and he leaped up and walked." They cast out devils wherever it was necessary, and when Eutychus fell from the third story, and "was taken up dead," Paul restored him to life again. On the island of Melita, a viper hung upon the hand of Paul, and "when the barbarians saw the beast hanging from his hand, they said one to another, No doubt this man is a murderer, whom, though he hath escaped from the sea, yet justice hath not suffered to live"; but when they remained long in expectation and beheld nothing amiss come to him, they changed their minds and said he was a "god." We are informed that after that the diseases of the entire population of the island were healed.

CLAIMS OF "CHRISTIAN FAITH-HEALERS," TECHNICALLY SO CALLED, EFFECTUALLY DISCREDITED

IN examining the healing works both of Christ and the apostles, it appears that there is not a uniform law that the sick should exercise faith, and that it was not necessary that their friends should exercise it, nor that either they or their friends should do so. Sometimes the sick alone believed; at others, their friends believed and they knew nothing about it; again, both the sick and their friends believed, and on some occasions neither the sick nor the friends. No account of failure on the part of Christ, or of the apostles after his ascension, to cure *any* case can be found. Neither is there a syllable concerning any *relapse* or the danger of such a thing, nor any cautions to the cured, "*not to mind sensations*," or that "*sensations are tests of faith*," nor any other such quackery, in the New Testament.

Claims of Christian faith-healers to supernatural powers are discredited by three facts:

(1) They exhibit no supremacy over pagans, spiritualists, magnetizers, mind-curers, etc.

(2) They cannot parallel the mighty works that Christ produced, nor the works of the apostles.

(3) All that they really accomplish can be paralleled without assuming any supernatural cause, and a formula can be constructed out of the elements of the human mind which will give as high average results as their prayers or anointings.

That formula in its lowest form is "*concentrated attention.*" If to this be added reverence, whether for the true and ever-living God, false gods, spirits, the operator, witches, magnetism, electricity, or simple unnamed *mystery*, the effect is increased greatly. If to that be added confident expectancy of particular results, the effect in causing sickness or relieving it may be appalling. Passes, magnets, anointings with oil, are useful only as they produce concentration of attention, reverence, and confident expectancy. Those whose reputation or personal force of thought, manner, or speech can produce these mental states, may dispense with them all, as Mesmer finally did with the "magnets," and as many faith-healers and the Roman Catholics do with the oil.[1]

THE CHRISTIAN DOCTRINE OF ANSWER TO PRAYER

Is there then no warrant in the New Testament for the ordinary Christian to pray for the sick, and is there no utility in such prayers? "There's a Divinity that shapes our ends, rough hew them how we will." The New Testament affirms that "All things work together for good to them that love God." It teaches that the highest good is the knowledge and love of God, and that the Spirit of God has constant access to the minds of men, and sets forth an all-inclusive doctrine of Providence without whom not even a sparrow falls. It does *not* say that prayer will always secure the recovery of the sick, for it gives the instance of Paul who had a "thorn in the flesh," and who besought the Lord thrice that this thing should depart from him, but received, "My grace is sufficient for thee."

None can demonstrate that God cannot work through second causes, bringing about results which, when they come, appear to be entirely natural, but which would not have come except through special providence, or in answer to prayer. The New Testament declares that he does so interpose "according to his will." It was not his will for Paul, and he did not remove the thorn, but gave spiritual blessings instead. Prayer for the sick is one of the most consoling privileges, and it would be a strange omission

[1] The Roman Catholics use oil in the "sacrament of extreme unction," which is administered in view of death.

if we were not entitled to pray for comfort, for spiritual help, for such graces as will render continued chastening unnecessary, and for recovery, when that which is desired is in harmony with the will of God. Belief that when the prayer is in accordance with the mind of God, "the prayer of faith shall save the sick, and the Lord shall raise him up," is supported by many explicit promises. But as all who die must die from disease, old age, accident, or intentional violence, every person must at some time be in a state when prayer cannot prolong his life.

When we or others are suffering from any malady, the Christian doctrine is that we are to use the best means at command, and to pray, "Father, if it be possible, let this cup pass from me; nevertheless, not my will but thine be done." The prayer may be answered by its effect upon the mind of the patient; by directing the physician, the nurse, or the friends to the use of such means as may hasten recovery; or, by a direct effect produced upon the physical system, behind the visible system of causes and effects, but reaching the patient through them; if the patient recovers, it will seem as though he recovered naturally, though it may be in an unusual manner. The Christian in his personal religious experience may believe that his prayer was the element that induced God to interfere with the course of nature and prolong life. Assuming that there is a God, who made and loves men, none can show his faith irrational or unscriptural; but such testimony can be of no value to demonstrate to others a fact in the plane of science. When the Christian comes to die, he must then rest, even while praying for life, upon the promise, "My grace is sufficient for thee."

Faith-healers represent God as interfering constantly, not by cause and effect in the order of nature, but affecting the result directly. That they do not surpass those who are not Christians, but use either false pretenses or natural laws, and that they are inferior in healing power to Christ and the apostles, condemn their pretensions. Nor does it avail them to say, "Christ would not come down from the cross when taunted by unbelievers." They might perhaps with propriety refuse a test for *the test's sake;* — though Elijah forced one. But a radical difference between their work and what it accomplishes, and those who, they say, have no divine help, should be manifest. Some of them affirm that the Mormons, Newton, and others do their mighty works by the aid of devils. If so, since casting out devils was miracle-working power of low grade, it is wonderful that none of these persons have been able to cast out the devils from any of the large number who are working in this way, and thus demonstrate their superiority as the apostles vindicated their claims against Simon the sorcerer and others.

Faith-cure, technically so called, as now held by many Protestants, is a pitiable superstition, dangerous in its final effects.

It may be asked, What harm can result from allowing persons to believe in "faith-healing"? Very great indeed. Its tendency is to produce an effeminate type of character which shrinks from pain and concentrates attention upon self and its sensations. It sets up false grounds for determining whether a person is or is not in the favor of God. It opens the door to every superstition, such as attaching importance to dreams; signs; opening the Bible at random, expecting the Lord so to influence their thoughts and minds that they can gather his will from the first passage they see; "impressions," "assurances," etc. Practically it gives support to other delusions which claim a supernatural element. It seriously diminishes the influence of Christianity by subjecting it to a test which it cannot endure. It diverts attention from the moral and spiritual transformation which Christianity professes to work, a transformation which wherever made manifests its divinity, so that none who behold it need any other proof that it is of God. It destroys the ascendancy of reason, and thus, like similar delusions, it is self-perpetuating; and its natural and, in some minds, irresistible tendency is to mental derangement.

Little hope exists of freeing those already entangled, but it is highly important to prevent others from falling into so plausible and luxurious a snare, and to show that Christianity is not to be held responsible for aberrations of the imagination which belong exclusively to no race, clime, age, party, or creed.

DEFENSE OF FAITH-HEALERS EXAMINED

PRESENTATION to the public, through "The Century Magazine," of the substance of the foregoing excited much discussion, and led the most conspicuous advocates of "faith-healing" therein exposed to make such defense as they could. But confident assertions of supernatural powers, and vehement denials of the sufficiency of natural causes to account for their results, and quotations of misapplied passages of Scripture, have been the only defensive weapons of the faith-healers. They have, however, been compelled to avow that "they keep no record of failures, as they do not depend upon phenomena or cases, but upon the divine Word."

This admission is fatal. If they cannot do the works, either they have not the faith, or they misunderstand the promises they quote. Christ and the apostles depended upon the phenomena to sustain their claims; and when the apostles failed in a single instance Christ called them a faithless and perverse generation. The failure of these religious thaumaturgists to surpass other manipulators in the same line in the nature and extent of their mighty works has compelled them to say that they do not depend upon phenomena, and make no record of unsuccessful attempts and relapses.

The difficulty is that they apply promises to the ordinary Christian life which relate to the power of working miracles. That they misunderstand and misapply them is clear also from the fact that most spiritually minded Christians in the greatest emergencies have been unable to work miracles. The reformers—Calvin, Knox, Luther, etc.—could not. John Wesley, in his letter to the Bishop of Gloucester, enumerates all the miraculous gifts possessed by the apostles, and expressly denies that he lays claim to any of them. Judson, Carey, Martyn, Duff, Brainerd,[1] and other eminent missionaries trying to preach the Gospel among Pagans, Mohammedans, and Pantheists, most of whose priests are believed by the people to be able to work miracles, were unable to

[1] Brainerd, in his narrative of his work among the American Indians, confesses his great embarrassment as follows:

"When I have instructed them respecting the miracles wrought by Christ in healing the sick, etc., and mentioned them as evidences of his divine mission, and of the truth of his doctrines, they have quickly referred to the wonders of that kind which [a diviner] had performed by his magic charms, whence they had a high opinion of him and of his superstitious notions, which seemed to be a fatal obstruction to some of them in the way of their receiving the Gospel."

Yet, though Brainerd could do none of these mighty works, he was the means of the conversion of that very diviner by the influence of his own life and the spiritual truths which he taught.

prove their commission by any special power over disease, or by other mighty works. In Algiers, after its conquest by the French, the power of juggling priests was so great that it was impossible to preserve order until Robert Houdin, the magician, was sent over, whose power so far surpassed that of the priests that their ascendancy over the people was broken.

The charge that the writer is not a spiritually minded man was to be expected: this is the common cry of the superstitious when their errors are exposed. But the most extraordinary allegation was made by A. B. Simpson, founder of a sect of faith-healers in the city of New York. He states his belief that the cases " of healing and other supernatural phenomena ascribed to Spiritualism cannot be explained away either as tricks of clever performers or the mere effects of will power, but are, in very many instances, directly supernatural and superhuman"; and asserts that: " The cures to which Dr. Buckley refers among heathen nations, the Voodoos of the negroes, and the Indian medicine men, are all of the same character as Spiritualism." On the subject of Roman Catholic miracles he says:

" Where there is a simple and genuine faith in a Romanist,— and we have found it in some,— God will honor it as well as in a Protestant. . . . But when, on the other hand, they are corrupted by the errors of their Church, and exercising faith, not in God, but in the relics of superstition, or the image of the Virgin, we see no difference between the Romanist and the Spiritualist, and we should not wonder at all if the devil should be permitted to work his lying wonders for them, as he does for the superstitious Pagan or the possessed medium."

This means that if the Roman Catholics are devout, it is God who does the mighty works for them; if

superstitious it is the devil. As many of the most remarkable phenomena connected with Roman Catholicism have occurred where the Virgin is most prominent, as at the Grotto of Lourdes, and at Knock
Chapel (a girl having been cured recently by drinking water with which some of the mortar of the
chapel had been mingled), it is pertinent to ask, if
supernatural operations are involved in both, whether
the works of God might not be expected to be superior
to those of the devil?

Mr. Simpson goes so far as to say that what he calls
"divine healing" is "a great practical, Scriptural, and
uniform principle, which does not content itself with
a few incidental cases for psychological diversion or
illustration, but meets the tens of thousands of God's
suffering children with a simple practical remedy
which all may take and claim if they will." Such
propositions as this are as wild as the weather predictions that terrify the ignorant and superstitious,
but are the amusement and scorn of all rational and
educated persons; as the following, from the "Con-
gregationalist" of Boston, shows:

We have taken pains, before publishing it, to confirm, by
correspondence, the singular case of a woman's death in a religious meeting at Peekskill, N. Y. Rev. Mr. Simpson, formerly a Presbyterian preacher, was holding a Holiness Convention, Major Cole, the "Michigan Evangelist," being a helper. In
an "anointing service" an elderly lady, long afflicted with heart-
disease, who had walked a long way after a hard day's work,
presented herself for "divine healing," and was anointed by
Mr. Simpson. A few minutes after she fainted and died, the
finding of the jury of inquest being that her death was from
heart-disease, but hastened by the excitement of the service.
One would suppose that the case would be a warning against
the danger of such experiments, if not a rebuke of the almost
blasphemous assumption of miraculous power.

5

ERROR IN MENTAL PHYSIOLOGY

A RADICAL error in mental physiology which most of these persons hold relates to the will. Referring to the theory which explains the cure of many diseases by bringing the person to exercise special will power, Mr. Simpson says:

> Why is it that our physicians and philanthropists cannot get the sick to rise up and exercise this will power? Oh! that is the trouble to which we have already adverted. The will is as weak as the frame, and the power that is needed to energize both is God: and Faith is just another name for the new divine WILL which God breathes into the paralyzed mind, enabling it to call upon the enfeebled body to claim the same divine power for its healing. We are quite willing to admit the blessed effect of a quickened faith and hope and will upon the body of the sick. This is not all. There must also be a direct physical touch.

A hotel-keeper in New Hampshire, lingering at the point of death, as was supposed, for weeks with typhus, saw the flames burst from his barn. "Great God!" cried he, "there is nobody to let the cattle out!" He sprang from the bed, cared for the cattle, broke out in a profuse perspiration, and recovered. The burning barn gave him no strength, but the excitement developed latent energy and will.

Mrs. H. had long been ill, was emaciated and so weak that she could not raise a glass of water to her lips. One day the house took fire. She sprang from the bed, seized a chest full of odds and ends, and carried it out of doors. This, as a result of an effort of will, she could not have done when in health without help.

A letter recently received from the Rev. J. L. Humphrey, for many years a missionary in India, now of Richfield Springs, N. Y., says:

The following instance came under my observation in India. An officer of the Government was compelled to send native messengers out into a district infected with cholera. As he sent them out they took the disease and died; and it came to such a pass among the Government peons under his charge that a man thought himself doomed when selected for that duty. A German doctor in that region had put forth the theory that inoculation with a preparation of quassia was a specific for cholera — a simon-pure humbug. But this gentleman seized the idea; he cut the skin of the messenger's arm with a lancet so as to draw some blood, and then rubbed in the quassia, telling them what the doctor had said about it. Not a man thus treated died.

The surprising strength and endurance exhibited by lunatics and delirious persons often show that the amount of power which can be commanded by the will under an ordinary stimulant by no means equals the latent strength. Equally true is it that mental and emotional excitement often renders the subject of it unconscious of pain, which otherwise would be unendurable. Even without such excitement, a sudden shock may cause a disease to disappear.

The following was narrated to me by an eminent physician:

I was once called to see a lady, not a regular patient of mine, who had suffered for months with rheumatism. Her situation was desperate, and everything had been done that I could think of except to give her a vapor bath. There was no suitable apparatus, and I was obliged to extemporize it. Finding some old tin pipe, I attached it to the spout of the tea-kettle and then put the other end of the pipe under the bed-clothes, and directed the servant to half fill the kettle, so as to leave room for the vapor to generate and pass through the pipe into the bed. I then sat down to read, and waited for the result. The servant girl, however, desiring to do all she could for her mistress, had filled the kettle to the very lid. Of course there was no room for steam to form, and the hot water — boiling, in fact — ran through the pipe and reached the body of the patient. The instant it struck her she gave a shriek and said, "Doctor, you have scalded me!" and as she said this she leaped out of bed.

"But now," said the physician, "came the wonder. The rheumatism was all gone in that instant, nor did she have any return of it, to my knowledge."

A "MISSING LINK"

IF there were no other, a fatal stumbling-block in the way of the faith-healers is their failure in surgical cases. But they seize everything that could even point at extrahuman interference with the order of nature. The following is taken from the "Provincial Medical Journal" of Leicester and London, June 1, 1886, and is an illustration of the subject:

Another "wonderful cure" at the Bethshan. T. M. N., during a voyage from Liverpool to New York on board the steamship *Helvetia*, sustained a compound fracture of the left humerus at about the line of junction of the middle with the lower third. The injury was treated for a few days by the mercantile surgeon. On his arrival at New York on December 29, 1883 (four days after the accident), he was transferred to a public hospital. He was at once treated, the fracture being fixed in a plaster-of-Paris dressing, and this mode of mechanical fixation was continued for three months, when the surgeon, perceiving no progress toward union, performed the operation of resetting the fractured ends. The arm and forearm were again put in plaster-of-Paris, and retained until his arrival in Liverpool, five months after the date of the injury. On June 10, 1884, he submitted his arm for my inspection, when on removal of the dressing I found there was no attempt at repair, and that the cutaneous wound pertaining to the operation had not healed. The method of treatment I pursued was the following: The forearm was first slung from the neck by its wrist; the ulcer was attended to, and an area inclusive of the fracture partially strangulated by means of india-rubber bands. This was continued for three months, but without appreciable result. I therefore, in addition to this treatment, percussed the site of fracture every three weeks. Four months passed, and yet no change. After seven months the ulceration was healed, and the limb slung as before, partially strangulated and percussed monthly, but, in addition, maintained well fixed by a splint, and carefully readjusted on the occasion when percussion was employed. At length I found evidence that repair was progressing, for at this date, December, 1885, it required some force to spring the connection. I now knew it could only be a question of a few weeks for consolidation to be complete, but thought it wise for some little time to leave the arm protected, lest rough usage should destroy the good attained. However, the patient suddenly disappeared, and on the 13th of April I received the following interesting document:

"No. 2 Woodhouse St., Walton Road,
"Monday, April 12th.

"Dear Sir: I trust after a very careful perusal of the few following words I may retain the same share of your favorable esteem as previously, and that you will not think too hardly of me because, although I have done a deed which you would not sanction, and which was against your injunctions. Still, I must write and let you know all about it, because I know you have been so kind to me from a purely disinterested motive. I dare say you remember me mentioning the 'faith-healing' some time ago, and to which you remarked that 'it would do no harm to try it, but that you thought I should require *mighty* faith.'

"Well, I have tried it, and I am sure that you will be glad to hear that my arm is not only in my sleeve, but in actual use, and has been for the past three weeks. The pain I bore after the last beating was something dreadful, and being in great trouble at my lodgings at the time, I was downhearted. I was thrown out of my lodgings, and being quite destitute, I reasoned in myself, and came to the conclusion that if I really asked God to make it better right away he would, and I was told that if I would do away with all means and leave it to him, it would be all right. So I just took off all your bandages and splint, and put it in my sleeve. I have now the use of my arm, and it is just the same as my right one — just as strong. Several times I called at your house when on my way to the Bethshan, George's street, but Dr. Gormley slammed me out, and therefore I did not like to come again.

"I cannot describe how thankful I am, doctor, for your past kindness and goodness to me, and that is one reason I have not seen you. I know you will be glad to see me with it in my sleeve. Yours very truly,

"Tom M. Nicholson.

"Dr. H. O. Thomas.

"P. S.— Any communication will reach me if addressed to me at the above, *should you desire to write.*"

There is very little to add to this case. . . . It affords, however, a typical instance of the way a Bethshan thrives. The surgeon tells a patient all but recovered to be cautious lest the results of months of care be nullified, and "fools rush in" and tell him "to dispense with means and all will be well." In this particular instance the result was harmless, but it would be interesting to inquire how many poor deluded victims are consigned to irremediable defects by an ignorant and fanatical display which is a satire upon our civilization.

In this country the case that has been most frequently quoted is narrated by the late W. E. Boardman, who had the story from Dr. Cullis and gives it thus:

The children were jumping off from a bench, and my little son fell and *broke both bones of his arm below the elbow.* My brother, who is a professor of surgery in the college at Chicago, was here on a visit. I asked him to set and dress the arm. He did so; put it in splints, bandages, and in a sling. The dear child was very patient, and went about without a murmur all that day. The next morning he came to me and said, "Dear papa, please take off these things." "Oh, no, my son; you will have to wear these five or six weeks before it will be well!" "Why, papa, it is well." "Oh, no, my dear child; that is impossible!" "Why, papa, you believe in prayer, don't you?" "You know I do, my son." "Well, last night when I went to bed, it hurt me very bad, and I asked Jesus to make it well." I did not like to say a word to chill his faith. A happy thought came. I said, "My dear child, your uncle put the things on, and if they are taken off, he must do it." Away he went to his uncle, who told him he would have to go as he was six or seven weeks, and must be very patient; and when the little fellow told him that Jesus had made him well, he said, "Pooh! pooh! nonsense!" and sent him away. The next morning the poor boy came to me and pleaded with so much sincerity and confidence, that I more than half believed, and went to my brother and said, "Had you not better undo his arm and let him see for himself? Then he will be satisfied. If you do not, I fear, though he is very obedient, he may be tempted to undo it himself, and then it may be worse for him." My brother yielded, took off the bandages and the splints, and exclaimed, "It is well, absolutely well!" and hastened to the door to keep from fainting.

Afterward the Rev. Mr. Gordon introduced the above alleged occurrence into his " Mystery of Healing."

This case was thoroughly investigated by Dr. James Henry Lloyd, of the University of Pennsylvania, and in the "Medical Record" for March 27, 1886, Dr. Lloyd published a letter from the *very child*, who has become a physician.

DEAR SIR: The case you cite, when robbed of all its sensational surroundings, is as follows: The child was a spoiled youngster who would have his own way; and when he had a *green stick* fracture of the forearm, and, after having had it bandaged for several days, concluded he would much prefer going without a splint, to please the spoiled child the splint was removed, and the arm carefully adjusted in a sling. As a matter of course, the bone soon united, as is customary in children, and being only partially broken, of course all the sooner. This is the miracle.

Some nurse or crank or religious enthusiast, ignorant of matters physiological and histological, evidently started the story, and unfortunately my name — for I am the party — is being circulated in circles of faith-curites, and is given the sort of notoriety I do not crave. . . .

Very respectfully yours,

CARL H. REED.

EVILS OF THIS SUPERSTITION

MANY well-attested cases of irreparable damage to religion, individuals, and to the peace of churches and families have been placed in my hands or ascertained by investigation. From them I select the following:

A lady, a member of the Christian church, aged about fifty-five years, had been ailing for two or three years. She fell and bruised her side, and was confined to her bed for some weeks. She was better for a month perhaps, and then the disease developed into internal abscess of the stomach, and she slowly declined until her death, which occurred about five months afterward. She and her family became very anxious for her recovery, and, being very devout, their minds turned to faith-cures and faith-healers. A month before her death she was in correspondence with one of these persons. This lady appointed an hour in which to pray, and directed that friends in the place where she resided should meet and pray at that time. Her pastor went and prayed. At the close of this interview the patient told him she had received just then a great blessing, so that now she felt reconciled to die, and subsequently said nothing about healing, but much about the heavenly rest which she expected soon to enter. For a long time her nourishment had been, and then was, taken entirely in the form of injections of beef tea. On a certain day a layman who had been healed, and was himself a healer and a prime mover in faith-healing conventions, visited her about noon and stayed until near evening. He told the lady and her children that the Lord had sent him there that she might be instantly healed, read and expounded the book of James, brought out his phial of oil, anointed her forehead, knelt by her bedside, holding her hand in his, and prayed very earnestly for her immediate cure, claiming present conscious testimony by the Holy Spirit that the cure was wrought. On rising from his knees, still holding her hand, he lifted the lady in bed to a sitting posture, and pronounced her cured in the name of the Holy Trinity. A member of the family protested that it was hazardous for her to sit up in that way, as she had not been able to sit up for many weeks. Finally the patient laid down exhausted, and the visitor left, assuring the family that "in four days mother would be up and about." Shortly after this (perhaps an hour) intense pain in the stomach began and kept increasing until the agony became unendurable, so that groans and screams of distress were wrung from her. This continued for twelve hours, when exhaustion and stupor ensued, which lasted until her death, the next day. An autopsy was held by physicians who had been in attendance, and they reported a lesion of the stomach, caused, in their opinion, by the exertion of the patient in arising and sitting up in bed. When our informant met the visiting brother who had had a revelation of the Spirit that the patient was to recover, he inquired after the case, and on being told that our informant was about to go to the funeral, he expressed great surprise and said, "It sometimes happens that way."

Can anything more blasphemous be imagined than the presumptuous claim of a revelation through the

Holy Spirit of a matter of fact, and the pronouncing the dying cured in the name of the Holy Trinity?

Families have been broken up by the doctrine taught in some leading "Faith-Homes" that friends who do not believe this truth are to be separated from because of the weakening effect of their disbelief upon faith. A heartrending letter has reached me from a gentleman whose mother and sister are now residing in a faith-institution of New York, refusing all intercourse with their friends, and neglecting obvious duties of life.

Certain advocates of faith-healing and faith-homes have influenced women to leave their husbands and parents and reside in the homes, and have persuaded them to give thousands of dollars for their purposes, on the ground that "the Lord had need of the money."

This system is connected with every other superstition. The Bible is used as a book of magic. Many open it at random, expecting to be guided by the first passage they see, as Peter was told to open the mouth of the first fish that came up and he would find in it a piece of money. A missionary of high standing with whom I am acquainted was cured of this form of superstition by consulting the Bible on an important matter of Christian duty, and the passage that met his gaze was, "Hell from beneath is moved to meet thee at thy coming." Paganism can produce nothing more superstitious, though many Christians, instead of "searching the Scriptures," still use the Bible as though it were a divining-rod.

It feeds upon impressions, makes great use of dreams and signs, and puts forth statements untrue and pernicious in their influence. A young lady long ill was visited by a minister who prayed with her, in great joy arose from his knees, and said, "Jennie, you are sure to recover. Dismiss all fear.

The Lord has revealed it to me." Soon after, physicians in consultation decided that she had cancer of
the stomach, of which she subsequently died. He
who had received the impression that she would
recover, when met by the pastor of the family, said,
"Jennie will certainly get well. The Lord will raise
her up. He has revealed it to me." Said the minister, "She has not the nervous disease she had some
years ago. The physicians have decided that she has
cancer of the stomach." "Oh, well," was the reply,
"if that is the case, she is sure to die."

A family living in the city of St. Louis had a daughter who was very ill. They were well acquainted with
one of the prominent advocates of faith-healing in
the East, who made her case a subject of prayer, and
whose wife wrote her a letter declaring that she would
certainly be cured, and the Lord had revealed it. The
letter arrived in St. Louis one day after her death.

These are cases taken not from the operations of
recognized fanatics, but from those of leading lights
in this *ignis fatuus* movement.

It is a means of obtaining money under false pretenses. Some who promulgate these views are honest, but underneath their proceedings runs a subtle
sophistry. They establish institutions which they
call faith-homes, declaring that they are supported
entirely by faith, and that they use no means to make
their work known or to persuade persons to contribute. Meanwhile they advertise their work and institutions in every possible way, publishing reports in
which, though in many instances wanting in business
accuracy, they exhibit the most cunning wisdom of
the children of this world in the conspicuous publication of letters such as the following:

DEAR BROTHER: The Lord told me to send you fifty dollars
for your glorious work. I did so, and have been a great deal

happier than I ever was before; and from unexpected quarters *more than three times the amount has come in.*

In one of the papers devoted to this subject this letter recently appeared:

DEAR BROTHER: Please announce through the "Crown of Glory" that I will sail for the western coast of Africa to preach a full salvation in the name of the Lord Jesus Christ, and to heal whomsoever the Lord will by faith, as soon as the Lord sends the balance of the money to pay my fare. I have renounced all rum, wine, cider, tobacco, beer, ale, and medicines — only Jesus! Only Jesus my Savior! I will sail October 10, if the Lord sends the balance of the money to Brother Heller, 48 Orchard st., Newark, N. J.   Yours, in Christ,
                                                S. B. MYLER.

A prominent English advocate of this method of raising money, who has done an extraordinary and useful work, on one of his missionary tours in this country explained his curious system with so much eloquence that the founders of certain faith-homes in the United States called upon the editors of various religious papers and endeavored to induce them to set forth that there are institutions in this country conducted on the same principle, naïvely observing that they did not wish his presence and eloquence to divert to England money that should be expended here. Yet they "do not use means"! But as in the case of the supposed faith-healings, for every successful instance there are a large number of unrecorded grievous failures; and many subjects of delusion who have established faith-homes to which the public has not responded have suffered the agonies of death. Some have starved, some have been relieved by benevolent Christian friends, and others have been taken to asylums for the insane. Similar wrecks are to be found all through the land, dazzled and deceived by the careers of the few who have succeeded in getting their enterprises under way and enjoy a monopoly of their limited method of obtaining revenue. Some who succeed are doubtless as sincere men and women as ever lived. Others oscillate between knavery and unbridled fanaticism.

The horrible mixture of superstition and blasphemy to which these views frequently lead is not known to all. I quote from a paper published in Newark, N. J., in the interest of faith-healing:

DEATH.—Three of the richest men in Ocean Park, N. J., have died. Faith-healing has been taught in the place, but was rejected by them, so death came.

CHARLESTON, S. C.—A few years ago the Holy Ghost sent me to preach in that city. But they rejected the Gospel and me. A wicked man shot at me and tried to kill me, but God saved me so that I was not harmed. . . . But I had to leave Charleston and do as the great Head of the Church said: . . . "when ye depart out of that house or city, shake off the dust from your feet." Earthquake, September 1, 1886; one-half the city in ruins. It has a population of about fifty thousand people. Ye wicked cities in the world, take warning! God lives!

SUPPOSED DIFFICULTIES

IT has been suggested that if faith-healing can be demonstrated to be subjective, what is called conversion can be accounted for similarly. If by conversion is meant the cataleptic condition which occurred among Congregationalists in the time of Jonathan Edwards, certain Presbyterians and Baptists in the early part of this century in the South and West, and the early Methodists, and is still common among colored people, Second Adventists, and the Salvation Army, and not wholly unknown among others, I admit that such phenomena are of natural origin.

But if conversion is understood to mean a recognition of sinfulness, genuine repentance, and complete trust in the promises of God, accompanied by a controlling determination to live hereafter in obedience to the law of God, this is radically different. Such an experience may be sufficiently intense to produce tears of sorrow or joy, trances, or even lunacy. But neither the lunacy, the trances, nor the tears are essential parts of the conversion. They are results of emotional excitement, differing in individuals according to temperament and education. If these results are believed to have a divine origin—especially when the susceptible are exposed to the contagion of immense crowds swayed by a common impulse and acted upon by oratory—hundreds may succumb to the epidemic who do not experience any moral change, while others who are thus excited may at the same time be genuinely reformed.

The inquiry has been made why these principles do not apply to the miracles of Christ; why I do not sift the evidence in the same way, and explain the facts on the same grounds. What, then, does the New Testament say, and is it rational to believe it?

The first question relates to the issue with the faith-healers. If they performed such works as are recorded of Jesus Christ, a writer professing to believe in his divinity would be compelled to admit their claims to supernatural assistance. But the point made against them is that they do *not* perform works similar to his.

The credibility of the record concerning Christ's works is a question which cannot be raised by Christians, whether they hold the superstitions of the faith-healers or not.

It is conceded that probably no such sifting of the evidence was attempted as can be made of what takes place in this scientific age, that there was a predisposition to accept miracles, and that the ascendancy of

6

religious teachers was maintained largely by the belief of the people in their power to work miracles. To affirm, however, as some do, that there was no investigation, is an exaggeration. The Jews, who did not believe Christ, had every motive to examine the evidence as thoroughly as possible. Still, we possess only the testimony of those who thought they saw. If they beheld and understood, their testimony is conclusive; but standing alone it would be insufficient.

Yet it is rational to accept the record, although we have not the opportunity of seeing the miracles or testing the evidence by scientific methods. A miracle of wisdom may be as convincing as one of physical force. The resurrection from the dead declared of Jesus Christ could not be more contrary to the laws of nature than the conception of such a life and character as his if he never existed. His discourses are as far above human wisdom as his recorded works transcend human power.

The prophecies which the Jews then held and still preserve, taken in connection with their character and history as a nation, afford a powerful presumption of the truth of the narrative. In the ordinary course of human events the death of Christ, after he had made such claims, would have destroyed the confidence of his apostles and scattered them; but their lives were transformed after his death. This is inexplicable unless he appeared again and sustained them by miraculous gifts.

Of the effect of a belief in the teachings of Christ I have had much observation. It convinces me of their truth; for what reforms human nature, developing all that is good, sustaining it in the endeavor to suppress what is evil, supporting it in the difficulties of life, and illuminating death with a loftier hope than life had ever allowed, furnishes evidence of its truth, not in the scientific method, but in a manner equally convincing. Because the record of miraculous facts concerning Christ is inseparably connected with these teachings, it is rational to believe it.

Later ages have had no experience of the ways of God in making special revelations to men; but these things were performed for such a purpose. To allege the experience of modern times against the credibility of extraordinary events *then* appears no less unphilosophical than to bring forward that record in favor of miracles *now*.

Faraday, "the father of modern experimental chemistry," began his celebrated lecture on the Education of the Judgment thus:

Before entering upon the subject, I must make one distinction, which, however it may appear to others, is to me of the utmost importance. High as man is placed above the creatures around him, there is a higher and far more exalted position within his view; and the ways are infinite in which he occupies his thoughts about the fears or hopes or expectations of a future life. I believe that the truth of that future cannot be brought to his knowledge by any exertion of his mental powers, however exalted they may be; that it is made known to him by other teaching than his own, and is received through simple belief of the testimony given. Let no one suppose for a moment that the self-education I am about to commend in respect of the things of this life extends to any considerations of the hope set before us, as if man by reasoning could find out God. It would be improper here to enter upon this subject further than to claim an absolute distinction between religious and ordinary belief. I shall be reproached with the weakness of refusing to apply those mental operations which I think good in respect of high things to the very highest. I am content to bear the reproach. Yet, even in earthly matters, I believe that the invisible things of him from the creation of the world are clearly seen, being understood by the things that are made, even his eternal power and Godhead; and I have never seen anything incompatible between those things of man which can

be known by the spirit of man which is within him, and those
higher things concerning his future which he cannot know by
that spirit.

I would not shield myself behind a great name
from the charge of inconsistency, but have brought
forward this passage because it states, what the life
of Faraday illustrated;—the compatibility of intense
devotion to the scientific method in its proper sphere,
with a full recognition of its limitations, of the value
of moral evidence, and of the difference between
grounds of belief in nature and revelation.

ASTROLOGY, DIVINATION,
AND COINCIDENCES

IT is incorrect to suppose that astrology has no votaries at the present time. Zadkiel's Almanac,
which has been published for nearly forty consecutive years, sells more than one hundred and twenty
thousand copies per annum, and it is not a publication which ignorant persons could understand,—nor
does it appear to appeal to that class. The "Satur-
day Review" for July 4, 1863, says: "Without doubt
there are a million of people who have some sort of
confidence in Zadkiel; certainly there is ample en-
couragement to them in the countenance afforded
Zadkiel by the great and wise and learned of the
land." This writer also states that "society believes
in astrology." It is quite possible that this is exaggerated, for "society" affects the study of all strange
or new things. If its interest in a passing novelty
or new aspect of something old should be allowed
any value as indicating what it "believed," it might
be held to accept almost anything.

I should not, however, think it a prudent economy
of effort to treat astrology merely to delay its final
disappearance. It is because the exhibition of its
principles and methods will afford us almost indis-
pensable aid in accounting for and explaining certain
conditions of current thought, that it is worthy of
investigation.

Goethe's autobiography commences with these words:

On the 29th of August, 1749, at midday, as the clock struck 12, I came into the world at Frankfort-on-the-Main. My horoscope was propitious: the Sun stood in the sign of the Virgin, and had culminated for the day; Jupiter and Venus looked on him with a friendly eye and Mercury not adversely, while Saturn and Mars kept themselves indifferent; the Moon alone, just full, exerted the power of her reflection all the more as she had then reached her planetary hour. She opposed herself, therefore, to my birth, which could not be accomplished until this hour was passed. These good aspects, which the astrologers managed subsequently to reckon very auspicious for me, may have been the causes of my preservation; for, through the unskillfulness of the midwife, I came into the world as dead, and only after various efforts was I enabled to see the light.

This mighty intellect, representing, according to Madame de Staël, in himself alone the whole of German literature, whose knowledge, insight, sensibility, and imagination were so extraordinary as to elevate him for all time to the highest rank, appears to have been somewhat under the influence of that belief in astrology which, from earliest ages, had dominated the human mind, and from which, at the date of his birth, even the most enlightened, with comparatively few exceptions, had not been emancipated. For there was scarcely an extraordinary character in antiquity who did not believe in astrology. Hippocrates and Galen,—the first names in medicine,—Pythagoras, Democritus, and Thales gave it credit. Hippocrates said in substance that a physician who was ignorant of astrology deserved to be called a fool rather than a physician; and Galen, that no man should "trust himself to that physician, or rather pretender, who is not skilled in astrology." In China, Persia, Egypt, Greece, and Rome it was universally accepted, while Chaldea was the center of its power.

There are many references to it in the Bible, such as "The stars in their courses fought against Sisera," and "Canst thou bind the sweet influences of Pleiades, or loose the bands of Orion?" The Magi, who came from the East following the star of Christ, were astrologers. From some passages it seems probable that Daniel, who accepted the office of Chief of the Magi, studied the heavens and astrological books. Only when the astrologers contradicted the direct revelation of God's word were they specially condemned. On such occasions the prophets denounced them: though seeming to admit that there might be an influence from the stars, they declared that they could not prevail against the will of God—as when Jeremiah says, " Be not dismayed at the signs of heaven, for the heathen are dismayed at them"; or the similar injunction by Isaiah, "Let now the astrologers, the stargazers, the monthly prognosticators, stand up, and save thee."

The ancient poets—Æschylus, Virgil, Horace, Homer, and many others—rose to the loftiest strains when praising astrology. In more modern times the chief physicians on the continent of Europe were astrologers, some of them most famous. One was Cardan of Milan, who was not only a physician but an algebraist. The "Text-book of Astrology" gives a list of eminent men in England who believed in astrology,—Roger Bacon; Duns Scotus; Baron Napier, the inventor of logarithms; Tycho Brahe; Francis Bacon; [?] Kepler; Flamstead, first Astronomer Royal; Sir Elias Ashmole, founder of the Ashmolean Museum. Chaucer was also a believer, and wrote a treatise on the astrolabe. John Dryden, skilled in the theory, computed the nativities of his children, and foretold certain severe accidents to his son Charles.

Astrology has exerted a powerful influence upon language and literature. Many words most frequently used are derived from astrology or kindred subjects — *augur, augury, auspices,* the common word *talisman;* and especially *influence.* In literature appeals to the heavens are common, as well as references to stars as sources of prosperity.

Trench says we seem to affirm that we believe that

the planet under which a man may happen to be born will affect his temperament, will make him for life of a disposition grave or gay, lively or severe. . . . For we speak of a person as "jovial," or "saturnine," or "mercurial"—jovial as being born under the planet Jupiter or Jove, which was the joyfullest star and of the happiest augury of all; a gloomy, severe person is said to be "saturnine" as born under the planet Saturn, who was considered to make those that owned his influence, and were born when he was in the ascendant, grave and stern as himself; another we call "mercurial," that is, light-hearted, as those born under the planet Mercury were accounted to be. The same faith in the influence of the stars survives, so far at least as words go, in "disaster," "disastrous," "ill-starred," "ascendant," "ascendancy," and, indeed, in the word "influence" itself.[1]

Or, again, do we keep in mind, or are we even aware, that whenever the word "influence" occurs in our English poetry, down to a comparatively modern date, there is always more or less remote allusion to the skyey, planetary influences supposed to be exercised by the heavenly luminaries upon men? How many a passage starts into new life and beauty and fullness of allusion, when this is present with us! Even Milton's

> Store of ladies, whose bright eyes
> Rain *influence,*

as spectators of the tournament, gain something when we regard them—and using this language, he intended we should— as the luminaries of this lower sphere, shedding by their propitious presence strength and valor into the hearts of their knights.[2]

[1] Trench, " On the Study of Words."
[2] Trench, " English Past and Present."

If we turn to Shakspere, we find the belief molding some of his most beautiful expressions:

> Comets, importing change of times and states,
> Brandish your crystal tresses in the sky.

When *Romeo* and *Juliet* are married the prayer is:

> So smile the heavens upon this holy act,
> That after hours with sorrow chide us not.

In one of the most frequently quoted passages of Shakspere the astrological reference is generally omitted:

In my stars I am above thee: . . . some are born great, some achieve greatness, and some have greatness thrust upon them.

From Byron astrologers quote a fine passage, using it as though he were a believer:

> Ye stars! which are the poetry of heaven,
> If in your bright leaves we would read the fate
> Of men and empires — 't is to be forgiven
> That, in our aspirations to be great,
> Our destinies o'erleap their mortal state,
> And claim a kindred with you; for ye are
> A beauty and a mystery, and create
> In us such love and reverence from afar,
> That fortune, fame, power, life, have named themselves
>   a star.

Dante, writing of Mars, says:

> With him shalt thou see
> That immortal who was at his birth impressed
> So strongly with this star, that of his deeds
> The nations shall take note.

And speaks in another place thus:

> Where the planets roll
> To pour their wished influence on the world.

Longfellow, in a passage which has touched many a parent's heart, says:

> O child! O new-born denizen
> Of life's great city! on thy head
> The glory of the morn is shed,
> Like a celestial benison!
> .   .   .   .   .   .
> By what astrology of fear or hope
> Dare I to cast thy horoscope!

WHAT IS ASTROLOGY?

ACCORDING to Zadkiel's "Grammar of Astrology" the science consists of four branches or distinct parts, which are essentially different from each other. These are: *Nativities, Mundane Astrology, Atmospheric Astrology*, and *Horary Astrology*.

Nativities comprise "the art of foreseeing, from the figurings of the heavens at the moment of birth, the future fate and character of individuals."

Mundane Astrology is "the art of foreseeing, by the positions of the heavenly bodies at certain periods, the circumstances of nations, such as wars, pestilences, inundations, earthquakes, etc."

Atmospheric Astrology, Zadkiel defines as "the art of foreseeing, by the positions of the planets at the periods of the sun and moon being in mutual aspect, and some other circumstances, the quality of the weather at any required time or place."

Horary Astrology is "the art of foreseeing, by the positions of the heavens at any period when an individual may be anxious about the matter, the result of any business or circumstance whatever."

Concerning Atmospheric Astrology, which is merely a system of meteorology based on the theory that changes of the weather are produced by the influence of the planets, I shall say nothing. Mundane Astrology is in some respects more complex than either Nativities or Horary Astrology.

The nature of the influence of the heavens upon human destiny has been differently represented by different astrologers, some claiming that the heavens merely exhibit signs of events, so that when these are properly interpreted the future can be foretold, and others holding that they are causes of the events. Most, however, seem to believe that they are both.

Astrological calculations are made by means of the sun, moon, and planets, the signs of the Zodiac, and the various aspects and relations of the planets. To work the problems, a "figure of the heavens" is drawn. This is merely a map to represent the heavens at any particular moment, such as when a child is born, a question asked, etc. It is made by drawing three circles and then drawing lines to represent the horizon, and others at right angles with them to represent the meridian. Thus will be shown the natural divisions formed by the rising and setting of the sun, and by his passing the meridian at noon and midnight. Each of these quarters or quadrants is to be divided again into three equal parts, forming the twelve houses. The accompanying figure, from Lilly's "Introduction to Astrology," exhibits the method.

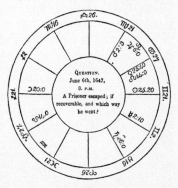

QUESTION.
June 6th, 1647,
8. P.M.
A Prisoner escaped; if recoverable, and which way he went?

In calculating a *nativity*, the horoscope must be cast for the instant the child is born, and the figure show exactly the state of the heavens at that instant as viewed from the place of birth: the signs of the Zodiac and the planets, with their latitudes, declinations, etc., have to be determined, and the figure when completed must exhibit all these. This is difficult, and cannot be done without the knowledge of astronomical tables.

Suppose, then, the figure completed; what is the method of judging? Here we enter the most interesting part of the subject. From the time of Ptolemy down to the present, a system of significations has existed. These significations, which have been more or less changed and modified by the various astrologers who have arisen since his time, are assigned to the signs of the Zodiac, and also to the planets and to their relations to each other and to the Zodiac. *Aries*, one of the four cardinal signs, influences Britain, Germany, Denmark, Lesser Poland, Burgundy, Palestine, Syria, and Judea. Astrologers go so far as to specify towns: Naples, Capua, Florence, Verona, Padua, Brunswick, Marseilles, Cracow, and Utrecht. *Gemini* relates to the northeast coast of Africa, Lower Egypt, Flanders, Lombardy, Sardinia, Brabant, and Belgium. It is of particular interest to us because it rules the west of England and the United States. London, Marseilles, and other cities also come under its sway, and, the "Science of the Stars" modestly says, "perhaps Melbourne."

Astrologers hold that the signs of the Zodiac affect not only nations, but individuals — that Aries, for example, produces a spare and strong body, of stature rather above the average, face long, eyebrows bushy, neck long, etc.; while Taurus gives a middle stature, thick, well-set body, broad forehead, full face and prominent eyes, neck and lips thick, nose and mouth wide. Aries governs the head and face of man; and the diseases it produces (when evil planets are located in it) are smallpox, measles, ringworm, apoplexy, palsy, etc. Gemini governs the arms and shoulders. Its diseases are brain-fever, croup, fractures of the head, arms, etc.

Certain planets are called *malefics*. These are Mars, Saturn, and Uranus. Venus and Jupiter are specified as *benefics*. A planet is spoken of as being *afflicted* whenever the malefics are in certain relations to it, and as being free from affliction when the benefics are in these relations. Of the sun they say that if it is afflicted at birth, the tendency is to destruction of life. In order to have great prosperity, both the sun and the moon must be free from affliction; and if both are afflicted, the person will have a life-long struggle. If the sun is in good aspect with Mars, the child born will be very fortunate in war, surgery, chemistry, etc.; if it is in the zenith and free from affliction, he will have a great public career. If it is rising at the birth, it makes him bold, courageous, and proud. But if it is afflicted by Saturn, he is liable to consumption or paralysis; if by Mars, he will be cruel and bloodthirsty, unless Jupiter happens to assist the sun. If the moon is properly related it has a good, but if otherwise an exceedingly bad, effect. Its diseases are rheumatism, consumption, palsy, lunacy, scrofula, smallpox, and dropsy.

There are certain "eminent" fixed stars, to which great significance is attached. Some of these are Aldebaran, Hercules, and Regulus. Alfred J. Pearce predicts that when "the martial star Aldebaran (*α* Tauri), of the first magnitude, shall arrive at 17 degrees, 54 minutes, Gemini, 700 years hence, there will probably happen a fearful conflagration in, if not the total destruction of, London." This is safer than anything which Professor E. Stone Wiggins has as yet attempted, since the author of the "Science of the

7

Stars" will not be upon the scene at that time to rejoice at the fulfilment of his prophecy or to mourn over the destruction of London.

When the figure is completed, and the positions and aspects of the planets are duly marked, preparation is made to form a judgment.

The exact way of judicature in astrology is, first, by being perfect in the nature of the planets and signs; secondly, by knowing the strength, fortitude, or debility of the significators and well-poise of them (that is, the various rules, directions, aspects, etc., and several mixtures in your judgment); thirdly, by applying the influence of the figure of heaven erected and the planets' aspects to one another at the time of the question or nativity.[1]

To make the proper calculation is a work requiring experience.

The above is the famous figure which William Lilly drew to decide whether Presbytery should stand in England. Zadkiel adduces this figure with the judgment pronounced upon it as a decisive proof of the science, and of its ability to decide the most important questions, but public and private.

EVIDENCE RELIED UPON

To demonstrate the truth of astrology, its votaries appeal to the history of England for the past six

[1] Lilly, "Introduction to Astrology," p. 29.

hundred years. Aries is the principal sign influencing England. Saturn is a malefic planet, and they assign various coincidences of misfortune to England during the times Saturn was in Aries, of which I give a few. In 1290, the desperate war with the Scots was waged by Edward I. and the English army defeated at Roslin, near Edinburgh; in 1378, the rebellion by Wat Tyler; in 1555, Queen Mary's time, 277 persons burned at the stake; in 1643, civil war between Charles I. and Parliament. The whole list is remarkable.

On the other hand, in 896 Jupiter was in Aries, and King Alfred beat the Danes; in 1215 King John signed the Magna Charta; in 1856 peace was signed between the allies, and the Crimean war ended; in 1868 the tide of prosperity set in.

An important incident is related to the United States. Gemini rules the United States and also the west of England. The rebellion of the American colonies coincided with the transit of Uranus through the sign Gemini; and on the very next occasion, as the "Science of the Stars" points out, when the same planet passed through the same sign, 1859 to 1866, the American civil war waged four years. During the same time the west of England suffered fearfully from the cotton famine, nearly a million people being in a state of semi-starvation.

Of the eclipses in their relation to Mundane Astrology the following illustrations may serve: On April 10, 1865, there occurred a partial eclipse of the moon at Washington; Jupiter was in the ascendant in Sagittarius, and about that time General Lee surrendered to General Grant. They make the point also upon the death of President Garfield, that in the mid-heavens of his horoscope the comet B appeared, and that this same comet was seen in the second decanate of Gemini on the 22d of May, and on the 2d of July, 1881, Garfield was shot.

Another class of coincidences is striking. It is claimed by astrology that mental disease is likely to occur when Mars and Saturn — to which modern research has added Uranus — are at birth in conjunction, quadrature, or opposition with Mercury and the moon, but Mercury more particularly. The "Science of the Stars," from which we take some of these coincidences (quoted by it from another work), says: "It is by no means asserted that insanity always or even often occurs with such opposition; what is asserted is, that it rarely occurs without it." This proposition should be scrutinized, for it contains a serious if not fatal weakness.

There are nine great princes notoriously insane or deficient in intellect, upon whose birth Mercury or the moon, or both, will be found to have been afflicted by Mars, Saturn, or Uranus. These are: Paul of Russia, George III. of England, Gustavus IV. of Sweden, Ferdinand II. of Austria, Maria of Portugal, Charlotte, Empress of Mexico, Charles II. of Spain, Murad V. of Turkey, and Constantine of Russia. Six persons of genius, born under the same configuration — Gérard de Nerval; Alfred Rethel, the painter of "Der Tod als Freund"; Agnes Bury, the actress; Julien; Paul Morphy, the chess-player; and Pugin — became insane. Four distinguished men who lost their faculties in old age are also given — Swift, Southey, Moore, and Faraday. The histories of the Bourbon family, as derived from documents now in the British Museum, agree with the state of the heavens at the time of their births, according to the theories of astrology; their misfortunes, insanity, violent deaths, etc., are too well known to need recapitulation. Many coincidences between the aspect of the heavens at her birth and the events of her career are found in the life of Queen Victoria.

Lilly predicted, it is claimed, in 1651 the Great Plague which occurred in London in 1665. The accompanying is a facsimile of the hieroglyphic of the Great Plague.

FAC-SIMILE *of the* HIEROGLYPHIC *of the* GREAT PLAGUE *in* 1665, *published by* W. LILLY, *in the* YEAR 1651.

This hieroglyphic, as explained by Zadkiel,

signifies a great mortality, in which the vast number of deaths should so far exceed the supply of coffins that the dead should be buried in their shrouds, or merely stitched up in sheets, as therein rudely represented.

Lilly also predicted, in the same year, by means of an astrological hieroglyphic, the Great Fire in London, which took place September 3, 1666.

FAC-SIMILE *of the* ASTROLOGICAL HIEROGLYPHIC *of the* GREAT FIRE *in* LONDON, SEPTEMBER 3d, 1666, *published by* W. LILLY, *in the* YEAR 1651.

Zadkiel says that the hieroglyphic forecasting the Great Fire may be understood

by the horoscope being introduced therein, and the twins are intended to represent the sign Gemini, which in astrology is known to rule London, and the twins are, therefore, intended to denote that city. Their falling headlong into the fire signifies the extensive injury to be done to London by that element fifteen years afterward.

The astrologers made a great deal out of these hieroglyphics, Zadkiel affirming that

if there had been only these, whereas there were several others equally pointing out future events published with them, they would ever remain undeniable monuments of the author's skill and of the substantial truth of the science of astrology.

Americans cannot but be struck by a recent extraordinary coincidence. In Zadkiel's Almanac for 1886 occurs the following prediction:

Shocks of earthquake in the 77th degree of west longitude may be looked for. Great thunder-storms and waves of intense heat will pass over the States. There will be great excitement in America.

What are the facts? The terrific shocks of earthquake which visited Charleston, S. C., Washington, Richmond, Augusta, Raleigh, etc., on the night of August 31, many lives being lost, took place in longitude 76 to 78 degrees west. Waves of intense heat passed over the States in July and August, the thermometer in the middle of the latter month in St. Louis rising to 104 in the shade. Coincidences more or less striking can be multiplied indefinitely, and it was by observing them that the system of astrology was constructed.

ITS PROBLEMS MERE PUZZLES

HAVING traced the influence of astrology upon literature, stated the principles of the science, and given an impartial outline of the supposed evidences of its truth which its professors advance, it is now necessary to subject those evidences to examination. Fortunately the cases adduced are of historical interest, and a discussion which otherwise might be tedious is closely connected with the progress of both ancient and modern civilization.

The ancients knew nothing of the two great planets Uranus and Neptune. Yet the "Text-book of Astrology" asserts that "the influence of Uranus is found to be very powerful in nativities, when he is angular or in aspect to the luminaries." Shortly after this planet was discovered, an astrologer called on an astronomer to secure his calculations of the periodical motions of Uranus, stating that it was very probable "that the want of a knowledge and use of its motions was the cause that, in judicial astrology, the predictions so often failed." The planet Neptune was discovered in 1846. The "Text-book of Astrology" affirms that "sufficient time has not elapsed to enable astrologers to determine the exact nature of Neptune's influence in nativities"; yet, the writer says, "until more experience has been gained as to his influence in nativities, it may be accepted that his general character is fortunate, and that persons born under his sway are healthy, good-natured, and romantic." When Mr. Proctor remarked, a number of years ago, "astrologers tell us now that Uranus is a very potent planet, yet the old astrologers seem to have gotten on very well without him," all that the standard authorities of the "Science" could reply was that "Democritus maintained that more planets would be discovered in succeeding ages." This is no answer to the proposition that the ancients seemed to succeed in total ignorance of the "very powerful" influence of Uranus, and the possible mighty influence of Neptune.

There are three fatal defects in the proofs they offer: (a) The number of instances investigated is too small to establish a law of cause and effect. (b) In the more remarkable predictions, reasoning upon existing conditions and tendencies, a shrewd guess or a mere coincidence can account for the fulfilment. (c) In the most striking cases there was ample time for the culmination of the operation of causes.

When William Lilly was examined by the British Parliament on his prophecies concerning the plague and the fire, he was thus addressed by Sir Robert Brooke:

Mr. Lilly, this Committee thought fit to summon you to appear before them this day, to know if you can say anything as to the cause of the late fire, or whether there might be any design therein. You are called the rather hither, because, in a book of yours long since printed, you hinted some such thing by one of your hieroglyphicks.

Unto which Mr. Lilly replied:

May it please your Honors: After the beheading of the late King, considering that in the three subsequent years the Parliament acted nothing which concerned the settlement of the nation's peace; and seeing the generality of the people dissatisfied, the citizens of London discontented, the soldiery prone to mutiny; I was desirous, according to the best knowledge God had given me, to make enquiry by the art I studied, what might, from that time, happen unto Parliament and the nation in general. At last, having satisfied myself as well as I could, and perfected myself as well as I could, and perfected my judgment therein, I thought it most convenient to signify my intentions and conceptions thereof in forms, shapes, types, hieroglyphicks, etc., without any commentary, that so my judgment might be concealed from the vulgar, and made manifest only unto the wise; I herein imitating the examples of many wise philosophers who had done the like. Having found, Sir, that the city of London would be sadly afflicted with a great plague, and not long after with an exorbitant fire, I framed these two hieroglyphicks, as represented in the book, which, in effect, have proved very true.

"Did you foresee the year?" said one. "I did not," said I, "nor was desirous; of that I made no scrutiny." I proceeded: Now, Sir, whether there was any design of burning the City, or any employed to that purpose, I must deal ingenuously with you; that, since the fire, I have taken such pains in the search thereof, but cannot or could not give myself any the least satisfaction therein I conclude that it was the finger of God only; but what instruments he used thereunto, I am ignorant.

Those were troublous times; plagues were common in Europe, fires of frequent occurrence, and modern methods of extinguishing them had not been invented.

Lilly did not pretend to have foreseen the year, or to reflect any light upon the instruments; yet he was constantly ascertaining "who stole fish" and what had become of lost dogs, and affirms that he never failed in questions of that sort. His hieroglyphics could have been applied to a variety of events. It would have been easy to interpret that which he afterward declared foretold the Great Plague as signifying murders and the hasty concealment of bodies, or the burial of soldiers after a battle. The hieroglyphic typifying the fire could have been applied to any other of a hundred things, as falling into a fire might be made to illustrate most catastrophes.

The coincidences in English history, it is to be noted, consist of certain events drawn from a period of six hundred years, which events occurred during the progression of Saturn through Aries. Saturn remains long in that sign, and his returns are separated by a considerable time. In the confused history of England during those six centuries there were hundreds of battles, and great events were numerous; yet but thirteen of these having an evil character are produced. English history furnishes scores of disasters which occurred when Saturn was *not* in Aries. In like manner, Jupiter is in Aries every twelve years or thereabouts; yet but seven prosperous events are produced from 1196 — nearly seven hundred years!

Those mentioned are great occurrences, but during the seven centuries more than a hundred occurred when Jupiter was *not* in Aries.

It will be observed that the American Revolution did concur with the transit of Uranus through the sign Gemini, and also that the next time that planet passed through Gemini, from 1859 to 1866, the great American civil war raged four years. But the period from 1784 to 1859 was just long enough for the causes growing out of slavery and different views of State sovereignty to culminate in a rebellion. Had the planet's orbit been smaller there would not have been time enough. This is all that appears. The astrologer declares that during the same time the west of England suffered fearfully from the cotton famine. This is not wonderful, as the cotton came from the South and its ports were blockaded. Had there been no cotton-mills in the west of England, or had the war begun sooner or later, they would not have suffered at that particular time.

DEATHS OF PRESIDENT GARFIELD AND LOUIS NAPOLEON

THE death of President Garfield, considered in connection with the appearance of comet B in his horoscope and also in the year of his death, is merely a proof that between the appearances of that comet sufficient time elapsed for the infant to grow to manhood and become President and for such modifications of political parties as then existed.

To give the statements concerning mental diseases value, thousands of cases should be adduced, and it should be proved that the majority of those who were insane were born under such aspects of the heavens, and that comparatively few born under other signs lost their reason. A score or five hundred coincidences of this kind are not sufficient to lay the foundation for a law.

The prediction of Zadkiel that earthquakes would occur in the 77th degree of west longitude, followed immediately by the earthquakes in this country, appears at first sight very remarkable. Yet to read all the predictions in Zadkiel's Almanac for 1886 and compare them with subsequent events is sufficient to dissipate belief that there was a foreseeing of those events. The Almanac for 1886 predicted for England that an effort would be made to abolish hereditary peerages; that the revenue would not be satisfactory; that theaters would suffer; that the school-board would be in bad odor, and that certain of its members would find their chances of reëlection very perilous; that some public buildings would be destroyed in Paris by fire; that German affairs would become entangled; that socialistic proceedings would cause trouble (a thing that has been true for several years, and no more true during 1886 and 1887 than it had been). An astounding prediction was made that there would be "some trouble in the Western States and a good deal of sickness, and that the President would find his office a burdensome one." The financial condition of Mexico was to be bad. In Australia there would be trouble connected with railroads, and serious accidents were only too probable. There would be a great outbreak of epidemic diseases, and naval forces would be increased. In Ottawa the Canadian government would find it difficult to maintain peace at home and abroad; and in Paris the Communists would resort to violence and the streets would be stained with blood. There is scarcely a fulfilment transcending the results of ordinary sagacity in conjecturing future events.

Much was made of the prediction of Zadkiel in his Almanac for 1853 of the fate of Louis Napoleon. That prediction was in the following words:

But let him not dream of lasting honors, power, or prosperity. He shall found no dynasty, he shall wear no durable crown, but in the midst of deeds of blood and slaughter, with affrighted Europe trembling beneath the weight of his daring martial hosts, he descends beneath the heavy hand of fate, and falls to rise no more.

Some of this language is extravagant, but as a whole it may be considered a correct description of the career and doom of Louis Napoleon. Yet Zadkiel was not alone in this prediction; for students of French history, and every one acquainted with the events of the preceding thirty years, anticipated the speedy downfall of the Empire. The observations of writers, statesmen, and philosophers concurred in the opinion that the career of Louis Napoleon would be terminated by revolution or foreign war. The world was not surprised at his overthrow, for all perceived that he lacked the genius of his great uncle, and that he had lost the power to fire the heart of his country; while the condition of France financially and morally for years was not such as to promise success in any serious conflict with any one of the great Powers. At the time of his fall, "affrighted Europe" did not tremble beneath the weight of his daring martial hosts.

From time immemorial the different characters and histories of twins have been alleged against astrology. Cicero quotes the stoic Diogenes, who, when contending against the Chaldean astrologers, says:

For instance, two twins may resemble each other in appearance, and yet their lives and fortunes be entirely dissimilar.

The characters and careers of Jacob and Esau are brought against them by Mr. Proctor and others. They answer ingeniously that a difference of five minutes in the time of the birth of twins may imply such a difference in the position of the planets as to indicate great dissimilarity in their careers.

They state this as follows: "It is well known to *accoucheurs* that the intervals between the births of twins vary greatly; in some cases three or four minutes, in other cases hours and even days. Every four minutes' interval brings another degree of right ascension on the meridian, consequently a difference of half an hour in the times of birth would make a great difference in the part of the sign of the Zodiac ascending (as one degree in arc represented one hour of life in directions) and would alter the periods of occurrence of the subsequent events. The whole sign of Aries only takes (in the latitude of London) about fifty-two minutes in ascending; hence it is evident that a difference of half an hour might give Aries at the birth of one child and Taurus at the birth of the second."

If they adhered to this proposition it would be more consistent; but they advance in proof of the truth of astrology, in all their books, many instances of twins having similar careers when it was impossible for them to procure infallible data as to the precise moment of birth, and when they knew there must have been some difference.

This subject has of late been made interesting by the manner in which the astrologers of England have made use of Francis Galton's monograph on the "History of Twins." Mr. Galton sent out circulars to persons who were either twins or near relatives of twins. He received "about eighty returns of close similarity, many of which entered into instructive

8

details." From these replies he draws various conclusions, such as that "extreme similarity and extreme dissimilarity between twins of the same sex
are nearly as common as moderate resemblance." He
says that when twins are a boy and a girl they are
never closely alike. In the thirty-five cases of great
similarity, there were seven in which both twins suffered from some special ailment or some exceptional
peculiarity. They were liable to sickness at the same
time in nine out of thirty-five cases. Eleven pairs
out of this number were remarkably similar in the
association of ideas, making the same remarks on the
same occasion. In sixteen cases their dispositions
were very similar. He affirms that only a few retain
their close resemblance through life, either physically
or in disposition. Again, he says that it is a fact
that "extreme dissimilarity, such as existed between
Jacob and Esau, is a no less marked peculiarity in
twins of the same sex than extreme similarity."

Since his views were published I have observed
various twins, and have seen some instances of astonishing similarity, but in other children of the
same parents, not twins, more instances which could
readily be accounted for by heredity and the influence
of similar surroundings and nurture. A number of
instances could be given of distinguished men, now
living or but recently deceased, where the physical
and mental resemblances between them and their
twin brothers are no greater than ordinarily exist
between brothers. Is it not important in a general
examination to collect with equal care instances of as
great similarities between children who have the same
parents but who are not twins? If not, no light can be
shed on an extraneous cause. Harmonies of disposition, similarity of personal appearance, and devotion
to each other through life have been seen between

brothers and sisters, not twins, more frequently between sisters, and occasionally between brothers.

Driven to concede these things, astrologers in modern times have been compelled to say:

> We do not deny the existence of many difficulties and anom-
> alies, and fully admit that astral science is incompetent to ex-
> plain the divergences in the human constitution and character
> without a free use of the doctrine of heredity. Our contention
> is that the two theories complete each other, the latter account-
> ing for the element of stability, the former for the element of
> variability.[1]

An illustration of the wild manner in which a person competent to edit Zadkiel's Almanac may reason
can be found in the "Text-book of Astrology," p. 164:

> Astrologers find that unless Mars afflicts either the ascendant
> or luminaries at birth (or in the fatal train of directions) there
> is no liability to take the smallpox.

How this can be ascertained without an acquaintance with the nativities of an immense number of
persons and their histories in relation to smallpox is
not set forth. The investigation is so difficult that
they could not possibly show that every person who
ever took smallpox was born when Mars was in a
certain relation to the birth. They are not kind
enough to inform us whether the vaccination of persons born under these circumstances would or would
not "take." They may hereafter carry it a little
farther, and dispose of the liability to hydrophobia,
cholera, yellow fever, etc., in a similar way!

Here is another case from the same source. An
individual was born when the sun and moon were
evilly configurated with Saturn and had no assistance from Jupiter. In harmony with theories of

---

[1] Wilson, "Dictionary of Astrology."

astrology, he did not prosper in Great Britain, but afterward went to Australia, where he became one of the wealthiest and most highly respected citizens of Melbourne. How is this explained? It is sufficiently easy:

> At his birth the planets Mercury, Venus, and Jupiter were located in the fourth house (the northern angle). By crossing the equator, and pitching his tent in a southern latitude (38°), *he inverted his horoscope* and thereby brought the *benefics* nearly to zenith.

When one declines to believe in astrology, he is disposed of without difficulty. For example, Luther condemned astrology. The "Text-book" says, perhaps this was owing to the very evil horoscope assigned to him by the great Cardan, and observes that Melanchthon believed in it, and that "*phrenologists* [!] will understand that Melanchthon's judgment on a scientific subject is entitled to far greater weight than Luther's."

DIVINATION

ASTROLOGERS maintain that if the coincidences had not been sufficient in number and character to prove an intimate connection between the stars and the fate of men, it would have been impossible to maintain faith in their system through so many ages. This claim is shown to be worthless by an examination of divination in general. In all countries and times this superstition has been practised, and to this day maintains itself in Asia and in various parts of the continent of Europe.

Divination was practised in almost innumerable ways, such as by observing the flight of birds, called Augury; the living human body, as Palmistry; dead bodies, as Aruspicy, the inspection of animals slain in sacrifice; Anthropomancy, the examination of a dead human being; by fire, Pyromancy, of which there were six varieties; by natural phenomena, thunder and lightning, air and winds and water; by mirrors and glasses; by letters and figures; and by direct appeals to chance. Besides these, salt, laurel, dough, meal, verses, dreams, and consulting the dead were used.

All these and many other methods were practised and held in highest reverence by many poets, philosophers, and warriors of Greece and Rome and other ancient nations. Coincidences as remarkable as any that astrologers boast followed the predictions of the diviners, and by these faith was maintained. In case of failure they quibbled and equivocated, after the manner of astrologers.

Cicero's treatise " On Divination," though written so long ago, exhausts the subject. That renowned work is frequently so misquoted as to place the authority of Cicero in favor of divination. There is an introduction, in which Cicero declares that—

It is an old opinion derived as far back as from the heroic times, and confirmed by the unanimous agreement of the Roman people, and indeed of all nations, that there is a species of divination in existence among men which the Greeks call μαντική; that is to say, a presentiment and foreknowledge of future events. A truly splendid and serviceable gift if it only exists in reality.

In testing this opinion, he represents a discussion between his brother Quintus and himself. Quintus affirms that all nations have believed in divination. He asserts that when the statue of Plato, which stood on the top of the temple of Jupiter, was struck by lightning, and the head of the statue could not be found, the soothsayers said that it had been thrown down into the Tiber, and it was found in that very place; and that King Deiotarus never did anything without taking the auspices. An instance which he emphasizes is told of Tiberius Gracchus, an augur of the highest reputation, who, when two snakes were caught in his house, convoked the soothsayers. The answer which they gave him was that "if he let the male escape, his wife would die in a short time; but if he let the female escape, he would himself die: accordingly he let the female escape, and died in a few days."

One of the most striking passages concerns the oracle at Delphi:

Would that oracle at Delphi have been so celebrated and illustrious, and so loaded with such splendid gifts from nations and kings, if all ages had not had experience of the truth of its predictions?

Some theologians, who should know better, to this day quote this passage for their own purpose, and attribute it to Cicero.

When Cicero replies he opens with metaphysical considerations, maintaining that if things come by chance they cannot be divined, and if by fate they cannot be changed. He then considers the inspection of the entrails of victims, and says:

Could you persuade any man in his senses that those events which are said to be signified by the entrails are known by the augurs in consequence of a long series of observations? How long, I wonder? For what period of time have such observations been continued? What conferences must the augurs hold among themselves to determine which part of the victim's entrails represents the enemy, and which the people; what sort of cleft in the liver denoted danger, and what sort presaged advantage?

On the subject of the ox without the heart he asks:

> How is it that you think it impossible that an animal can live without a heart, and yet do not think it impossible that its heart could vanish so suddenly, no one knows whither? For myself I know not how much vigor is necessary to carry on vital function, and suspect that if afflicted with any disease, the heart of a victim may be found so withered, and wasted, and small as to be quite unlike a heart.

He then tells him that in trying to prove the truth of the auguries he is overturning the whole system of physics, and concludes his argument in these words:

> After having thus destroyed divination by the inspection of entrails, all the rest of the science of the soothsayers is at an end.

Of the head which was discovered he says:

> Oh! But a head was found in the Tiber. As if I affirmed that those soothsayers had no skill! What I deny is their *divination*.

He quotes the old saying of Cato, familiar enough to everybody, that

> he wondered that when one soothsayer met another he could help laughing. For of all the events predicted by them, how very few happened! And when one of them does take place, where is the proof that it does not take place by mere accident?

Cicero had little respect for the oracle of Delphi. He thus attacks it:

> I now come to you,
> Apollo, monarch of the sacred center
> Of the great world, full of thy inspiration,
> The Pythian priestesses proclaim thy prophecies.

For Chrysippus has filled an entire volume with your oracles, many of which, as I said before, I consider utterly false, and many others only true by accident, as often happens in any common conversation. Others, again, are so obscure and involved that their very interpreters have need of other interpreters; and the decisions of one lot have to be referred to other lots. Another portion of them are so ambiguous that they require to be analyzed by the logic of dialecticians. Thus, when Fortune uttered the followed oracle respecting Crœsus, the richest king of Asia,

> When Crœsus has the Halys crossed,
> A mighty kingdom will be lost,

that monarch expected he should ruin the power of his enemies; but the empire that he ruined was his own. Whichever result had ensued, the oracle would have been true.

The use I make of divination is to show that in its diversified forms it was sustained by means similar to those employed by astrologers, and exerted the same kind of influence over the minds of men. Its supports were the occasional occurrence of striking coincidences which the superstition of the people accepted, while they were prevented from carefully examining the whole subject, both by fear of the consequences of unbelief to themselves personally, and by their habit of mind, which was in all respects the reverse of scientific. Also, many of the most powerful intellects were paralyzed by the opinion that if divination were given up belief in the gods must be renounced, and from that they shrank.

Many astrologers and diviners were undoubtedly wise men, acquainted with the laws of physics so far as they had been discovered, and with the progress of war and current events. They were as able to form rational conjectures of the future as any of their contemporaries. Some were masters of magic, skilful in sleight-of-hand, and were also capable of practising ventriloquism. When they exercised this knowledge and these powers they credited it to astrology or to the method of divination which they employed. As Lilly acknowledges, they saw by "*discretion* as well as art." The knowledge which they possessed in common with others of equal attainments, and the peculiar skill gained by long practice in observing the probable course of events, together with coincidences with casual but no causal connection, account for the apparent fulfilment of astrological and similar predictions.

To those who deny this there exists the same reason for believing in the various forms of divination as in astrology.

COINCIDENCES

Suspicion may arise that this theory places a burden upon the possibilities of fortuitous coincidence which it is not able to support. It is therefore necessary to show that coincidences are far more frequent and astonishing than is generally supposed.

Coincidences in names are of such frequent occurrence as to be familiar; but some of them are surprising. Daniel Webster married Catherine Le Roy. Not very long ago in Boston a suit was noticed, the parties to which were Daniel Webster and Catherine Le Roy. The First Unitarian Church of the city of Baltimore was attended for more than forty years by a gentleman recently deceased. From that pulpit he heard discourses by Doctors Furness, Bellows, Sparks, Burnap, and Greenwood. Two were settled pastors; the others, eminent men who appeared on various occasions. In Guilford, Conn., till within a few years, the Second Congregational Church had had but three pastors in its entire history — Root, Wood, and Chipman. This society resulted from a disturbance in the First Church, and when Mr. Root was about to be installed, one of the members of the First Church, with equal bitterness and wit, suggested a text, "And I saw the wicked taking root." Not many years since the city of New York had attention drawn to the names of four great criminals whose names contradicted their characters — Charles Peace, who had personated a clergyman, was hung for murder in England; Angel was the name of a defaulting cashier; John Hope, of one of the robbers of the Manhattan Bank; and the Rev. John Love was deposed for crime. On the day that the Hon. John P. Hale died, the schooner *John P. Hale* ran ashore on a reef called Norman's Woe.

Superstitions concerning dates sometimes exhibit remarkable coincidences. Thirty-three sovereigns have ascended the English throne since the time of William the Conqueror, every month except May witnessing the coronation of one or more; that month, not one. In the lives of men extraordinary coincidences often occur on particular days of the week. Friday, commonly counted unlucky, in the early history of the United States seems to be a day of good fortune. The "Norfolk Beacon," many years ago, gave the following list of fortunate events in early American history which occurred on Friday:

On Friday, August 3, 1492, Christopher Columbus sailed on his great voyage. On Friday, October 12, 1492, he first discovered land. On Friday, January 4, 1493, he sailed on his return to Spain, which, if he had not reached in safety, the happy result would never have been known which led to the settlement of this vast continent. On Friday, March 15, 1493, he arrived at Palos in safety. On Friday, November 22, 1493, he arrived at Hispaniola, on his second voyage to America. On Friday, June 13, 1494, he, though unknown to himself, discovered the continent of America. On Friday, March 5, 1496, Henry VIII. of England gave to John Cabot his commission, which led to the discovery of North America. This is the first American state paper in England. On Friday, September 7, 1565, Melandez founded St. Augustine, the oldest town in the United States. On Friday, November 10, 1620, the *Mayflower* made the harbor of Provincetown; and on the same day was signed that august compact, the forerunner of our present glorious Constitution. On Friday, December 22, 1620, the Pilgrims made their final landing at Plymouth Rock. On Friday, February 22, 1732, George Washington, the father of American freedom, was born. On Friday, June 16, Bunker Hill was seized and fortified. On Friday, October 7, 1777, the surrender of Saratoga was made, which had such power and influence in inducing France to declare for our cause. On Friday, September 22, 1780, the treason of Arnold was laid bare, which saved us from destruction. On Friday, October 19, 1781, the surrender of Yorktown, the crowning glory of the American arms, occurred. On Friday, June 7, 1776, the motion in Congress was made by John Adams, seconded by Richard Henry Lee, that the United Colonies were, and of right ought to be, free and independent. Thus, by numerous examples, we see that, however it may be with foreign nations, Americans never need dread to begin on Friday any undertaking, however momentous it may be.

Impressive coincidences have occurred in the words of parts performed by actors in their last appearance on the stage previous to death or attacks of fatal illness. The same is true of clergymen whose texts for their last sermons, and frequently the very words which they uttered before being stricken with paralysis or apoplexy, have been singularly appropriate. An appalling instance occurred in a certain church near New York. Nearly fifty years ago, its pastor stood in the pulpit reading the stanza,

> Well, the delightful day will come
> When my dear Lord shall take me home,
> And I shall see his face.

At this point he was smitten with paralysis and soon ceased to breathe. Thirty-three years afterward, another pastor standing in the same pulpit, reading the same stanza, was also smitten and removed to die.

In marriages, both in the beginning and progress of the attachment, opportunities that are called casual, or coincidences in times, places, and circumstances of meeting, have to all appearance in many, if not in most cases, influenced the fate of the "high contracting parties" more powerfully than anything which they had intentionally arranged. Indeed, many persons troubled with misgivings concerning a proposed marriage, encourage themselves, by recalling such circumstances, in the belief that it was "meant to be," or that it was "providential."

How often resemblances of persons in no way related confuse the question of identity! Detectives frequently unravel difficult problems by their skill and sagacity, but owe their success in many cases to chance coincidences. Such happenings are of assistance to lawyers, and by them desperate causes are saved. Every lawyer of large practice has a list of anecdotes of this sort with which he delights young "limbs of the law."

In an unsigned article appearing in the "Cornhill Magazine" in 1872, which is now known to have been written by Richard A. Proctor, from the fact that he incorporated it nearly all verbatim, without quotation, in his last work, is given a case which "relates to a matter of considerable interest apart from the coincidence." I condense the account.

Dr. Thomas Young was endeavoring to interpret the inscription of the famous Rosetta Stone. Sir George Francis Grey placed in Dr. Young's hands some of the most valuable fruits of his researches among Egyptian relics, including fine specimens of writing on papyrus, which he had purchased from an Arab at Thebes in 1820. Before this reached Young, a man named Casati had arrived in Paris bringing with him from

Egypt a parcel of Egyptian manuscripts, among which Champollion observed one which bore in its preamble some resemblance to the text of the Rosetta Stone.   Dr. Young procured a copy and attempted to translate it; then Sir George gave him the new papyri.   He discovered that this document was a translation of the enchorial manuscript of Casati, and says: "The most extraordinary chance had brought unto me the possession of a document which was not very likely ever to have existed, still less to have been preserved uninjured, through a period of nearly two thousand years; but that this very extraordinary translation should have been brought safely to Europe, to England, and to me, at the very moment when it was most of all desirable to me to possess it, as the illustration of an original which I was then studying, but without any other reasonable hope of comprehending it—this combination would, in other times, have been considered as affording ample evidence of my having become an Egyptian sorcerer."

Mr. Proctor regards this as most extraordinary.

Such coincidences are not uncommon.   About fifteen years ago seven old friends, who had casually met, were dining together at a hotel in the city of New York.   The subject of spiritualism was introduced; the extraordinary "manifestations" given by Charles Foster were discussed, and one said, "I don't believe in spiritualism, but the blood-red writing which Foster shows upon his arm, in which the name of a deceased friend of the visitor appears, confounds me."   Having investigated the subject, I ventured to say that was not difficult to explain; when another said, "Oh, yes, it has been exposed in the United States courts."   This excited attention.   He then stated that Colchester, a medium, was famous for producing the same phenomenon, and that the internal revenue officers had notified him to take out a license as a juggler.   He put in a defense that he was not a juggler, but a spiritual medium; and that those things were done, not by his own personal procurement, but by supernatural beings.   Prior to this

9

time, Colchester had made an arrangement with a famous prestidigitator to travel with him in Europe and give exhibitions in which Colchester was to perform this feat. During their intimacy he explained to the professional wizard how it was done. Afterward Colchester became too intimate with alcoholic spirits, and the tour abroad was abandoned. The revenue officers had become aware of this, and the wizard was summoned as a witness for the Government. He not only explained how it was done, but did it in the presence of the court and jury.

Now comes the strangest part of the story. Three years afterward, while I was in a furniture store in a city which had not been visited by me for several years, a gentleman entered on business and the proprietor excused himself for a few minutes. On his return he said, "That was rather singular business on which I was called away. The gentleman you saw is the famous wizard ——. He wishes to rent furniture for use in his performances here." I recognized the name of the man, whom I especially wished to see, to ascertain whether Colchester's methods and those of Foster were similar, and whether the results of my investigation were confirmed. At my request he was recalled and performed the feat — first with such rapidity of action as to invest it with all the mystery which perplexed most and appalled some of Foster's visitors; afterward more slowly, explaining the successive steps.

Such coincidences occur with more or less frequency to every student, investigator, or professional man.

The science of medicine affords many examples. Ancient remedies, deemed of utmost importance, are now utterly discarded; but they were long supported by coincidences. Men took them and recovered, the

inference being that they were cured by them.   Now
wider generalization and more accurate induction establish either that they were inert, or that the patient
recovered in spite of them.   Great modifications have
taken place in the most enlightened medical opinion
in regard to the use of water in different diseases, and
the relative value of bleeding and the occasions in
which it is indicated.   The growth of the idea that
one or two remedies are sufficient for every disease
is one, and the list of thousands of specifics for ten
times that number of symptoms another, illustration
of deception by coincidence.   In 1813 Sir Benjamin
Brodie published a work on diseases of the spine and
joints, lauding the advantages of calomel, setons,
blisters, and bleeding, with long confinement to a
recumbent position.   In 1834, in a new edition, he
confirmed what he had enforced twenty-one years
before.   In 1850 he thus recants:

A more enlarged experience has satisfied me that, in the very
great majority of instances, this painful and loathsome treatment is not only not useful, but absolutely injurious.   For
many years I have ceased to torment my patients thus afflicted
in any manner.

SO-CALLED "LAWS OF CHANCE"

In the realm of pure chance it is impossible to fix
the limits of coincidence.   Mr. Proctor's recent work,
"Chance and Luck," quotes from Steinmetz this
fact:

In 1813 a Mr. Ogden wagered one thousand guineas to one
that *seven* could not be thrown with a pair of dice *ten* successive
times.   The wager was accepted (though it was egregiously
unfair); and, strange to say, his opponent threw *seven* nine times
running.   At this point Mr. Ogden offered four hundred and

seventy guineas to be off the bet. But his opponent declined, though the price offered was far beyond the real value of his chance. He cast yet once more and threw nine, so that Mr. Ogden won his guinea.

Commenting on this, Mr. Proctor says:

Now here we have an instance of a most remarkable series of throws, the like of which has never been recorded before or since. Before they had been made it might have been asserted that the throwing of nine successive sevens with a pair of dice was a circumstance which chance would never bring about; for experience was as much against such an event as it would seem to be against the turning up of a certain number ten successive times at roulette. Yet experience now shows that the thing is possible, and if we are to limit the action of chance we must assert that the throwing of seven ten times in succession is an event which will never happen.

The late Astronomer Royal of England, Prof. Airy, once devoted a considerable part of every day for a week to tossing pennies with special reference to coincidences. During the time he had a run of twenty-eight successive "tails." By the law of chance this could not occur more than once in many hundred millions of times.

I will present one more, which I think will justify the assertion that no coincidence more wonderful has been recorded. The article was found by me in an Italian paper while Louis Napoleon was in prison at Wilhelmshöhe.

THE LETTER M AND THE NAPOLEONS

Marbœuf was the first to recognize the genius of Napoleon at the École Militaire, Marengo was the greatest battle gained by Bonaparte, and Melas opened to him the way into Italy. Mortier was one of his first generals, Moreau betrayed him, and Murat was the first martyr in his cause. Marie Louise partook

5688

of his highest destinies, Moscow was the abyss in which he was engulfed. Metternich conquered him on the field of diplomacy. Six marshals (Massena, Mortier, Marmont, Macdonald, Murat, Moncey) and twenty-six of his generals of divisions had names beginning with the letter M. Murat, Duke of Bassano, was the counselor in whom he placed the greatest confidence; his first great battle was that of Montenotte, his last that of Mont-Saint-Jean. He gained the battles of Moscow, Montmirail, and Montereau. Then came the assault of Montmartre. Milan was the first enemy's capital and Moscow the last in which he entered. He lost Egypt through the blunders of Menou, and employed Miollis to make Pius VII. prisoner. Malet conspired against him; afterward Marmont. His ministers were Maret, Montalivet, and Mollien. His first chamberlain was Montesquieu, his last sojourn Malmaison. He gave himself up to Captain Maitland. He had for his companion at St. Helena Montholon, and for his valet Marchand.

If we examine the history of his nephew Napoleon III. we find that the same letter has no less influence, and we are assured that the captive of Wilhelmshöhe attaches still more importance to its mysterious influence than did his uncle. The Empress, his wife, is a Countess Montijo; his greatest friend was Morny; the taking of Malakoff and of the Mamelouvert the principal exploits of the Crimean war, — exploits due chiefly to the French. His plan in the Italian campaign was to give the first battle at Marengo, but this was not fought until after the engagement of Montebello at Magenta. McMahon received for the important services rendered by him in the battle the title of Duke of Magenta, as Pélissier received for a similar service that of Duke of Malakoff. Napoleon III. now made his entry into Milan and repulsed the Austrians at Melegnano.

After 1866 the letter M seems to have become for him a presage of misfortune. We pass over Mexico and Maximilian, and take the present war, in which he had founded a vain hope on three M's — Marshal McMahon, Montauban, and the Mitrailleuse. Mayence was to have been the base of operations for the French army, but, repulsed on the Moselle, his fate was decided upon the Meuse at Sedan. Finally we have to mention the fall of Metz. All these disasters are due to another M, the enemy of Napoleon — and this is a capital M — Moltke.

THESE incidents must be sufficient to show that, excluding wise forecasts and self-procured fulfilments, we do not place too great a burden upon coincidences when we attempt by them to account for the specious evidences of astrology and divination.

INTERPRETATION OF COINCIDENCES

THE following principles concerning coincidences will be found reliable as working laws:

First. As a general proposition, the law of coincidences is that when two phenomena always coincide they are either connected as "cause and effect" or are the "effect of a common cause." But if they do not always coincide, neither of these is proved. They may then be the effects of separate causes working in their respective planes.

The first question is, Do the phenomena always coincide? The importance of a wide generalization is often lost sight of, and erroneous conclusions are asserted with all the confidence of demonstration. A physician who lives near the sea says that during the past five years he has noted the hour and minute of death of ninety-three patients, and that each has "gone out with the tide" save four, who died suddenly by accident. Yet about thirty-two years ago, a writer in the English "Quarterly Review" claimed to have ascertained the hour of death in 2880 instances of all ages. His observations show that the maximum hour of death is from 5 to 6 o'clock A. M., when it is 40 per cent. above the average; the next during the hour before midnight, when it is 25 per cent. in excess. Between 9 and 10 o'clock in the morning it is $17\frac{1}{2}$ per cent. above, but from 10 A. M. to 3 P. M. it is $16\frac{1}{2}$ per cent. below the average. From 3 to 7 in the afternoon the deaths rise to $5\frac{1}{2}$ per cent. above the average, and then fall from that hour to 11 P. M., averaging 6½ per cent. below mean. It is probable that both these observations are worthless in view of the small number of instances covered. It is clear that they do not concur; yet, taken separately, each would seem conclusive.

Second. Astronomical predictions are based upon a series of unvarying coincidences, in most cases in harmony with laws whose operations can be tested at any time. If these phenomena were irregular and unclassifiable such predictions would be wholly uncertain; but because they usually coincide,— and when they do not, interfering causes can be traced,— eclipses can be foretold for thousands of years in advance, and discoveries such as those of Uranus and Neptune be made.

Third. Chemistry and cognate sciences also work with fixed phenomena, so that when the most diverse elements are combined and effects observed, formulæ can be deduced by which at all times the same effects can be produced.

Fourth. Many of the most wonderful inventions have been made by seeming accident; for example, photography. But reflection upon the accident reveals the cause; the cause and the effect are seen to be *scientific* coincidences, and the art with its principles and practice is the result.

Fifth. The performances of jugglers are in harmony with the established methods of nature. The charm of their exploits is in successful concealment of the causes, rapidity of motion, distraction of attention, and shrewdly contrived illusions of the senses.

Sixth. It is essential to remember that so-called "laws of chance" reflect no light on the order of sequence. It may be rendered probable by those laws that a certain event will not occur on the average more than *once* in a *million* of times; but this gives no assistance in determining the order in which any two occurrences will take place. Thus, if it be shown that an event will occur once in a million of times, in the first million it may be the last in the series, and in the second it may be the first; and that will bring them side by side. Many years ago there was a famous lawsuit in New England. A wealthy woman died, leaving large sums for benevolent purposes, and to her niece—already very rich—almost a million of dollars. The niece made strenuous efforts to break the will. A codicil was produced, the signature of which was found to be exactly like another signature of the testatrix. It was hinted, if not explicitly charged, by the counsel for the will that it was a forgery. Professor Peirce of Harvard University was brought in as a witness. He testified that not more than once in many millions of times would two signatures of the same person be written precisely alike. From this it was designed to raise the presumption that where there is an exact coincidence it must have been done by tracing. The court sustained the will on other grounds, and declined to decide that question. But the force of a presumption of this kind is much weakened, if not destroyed, by the fact that all to which Professor Peirce testified might be true, yet the two similar signatures might occur in the same month. Mr. Proctor states it thus:

The balance is restored just as chance directs. It may be in the next thousand trials, it may not be before many thousands of trials. We are utterly unable to guess when or how it will be brought about.

The business of life insurance can be carried on with certainty, provided the system be constructed upon averages deduced from a sufficiently large number of lives; but the employment of a smaller number would make it ruinous. It is clear that "expectation of life," so called, cannot give the slightest hint as to the probable duration of the life of any man insured under a perfectly reliable system.

Seventh. When a phenomenon is seen with which human beings are not directly connected as actual or possible agents, and which appears to be unlike the course of nature, it should be studied scientifically to ascertain its cause. By such investigations everything now attributed to natural forces has been wrested from the domain of superstition. The work began almost contemporaneously with the beginning of the historic period. Its results are now the inheritance of the school-boy. He understands the causes of many things which were formerly attributed, even in classic Greece and Rome, to supernatural interferences.

Eighth. When phenomena are presented by human beings for which no natural cause is assigned and none appears, the first philosophical inquiry is, Is this deception or jugglery? Here the question of moral character comes into view. Has this person a motive to deceive? Is his character such as to raise doubts whether he be honest? The peculiar influence of that phase of human nature which loves to startle, to be regarded as extraordinary, either in action, knowledge, or susceptibility, and the strange opinions and morbid conditions which give fascination to the exercise of the ability to deceive, must not be ignored. When pay is received for such performances, the probability of dishonesty is strong. The possible paralleling of the phenomena by confessed jugglers is also an important consideration.

Assuming, however, that no ground to suspect jugglery or deceit can be found, the next question is,

Do the phenomena go beyond what is known of the possibility of chance coincidences? Not until it is shown that legerdemain cannot produce the effects; that most painstaking investigation can find no explanation and no antecedent in the order of nature; and, further, that the phenomena transcend the possible bounds of coincidences, is there the least presumption that the cause is supernatural. Yet comparatively few of the investigators of occult phenomena have taken pains to comprehend the facts and principles of natural science or the tricks of jugglers,— some of whom have been masters of science,— or to comprehend the vast possibilities of coincidence.

It should not be supposed that common sense and learning, without special experience, qualify persons to investigate these things. Yet physicians who would sneer with just contempt at a non-professional person who should attempt to give an opinion on a difficult question in medical science, and lawyers who would despise a layman presuming to appear as a judge of abstruse legal questions, and ministers who have given no attention to methods of deception or to the "night side of nature," will join with merchants, teachers, and farmers to pronounce upon subjects much further removed from their spheres than are the pursuits of those whom they call "laymen" from their own; and, because they cannot see how these things can be performed or explained, will give support by testimonials and affirmations of mystery to every new, or renewal of an ancient, superstition. Thus astrology and divination were maintained, and so vast structures of deception at the present day are upheld.

DREAMS, NIGHTMARE, AND SOMNAMBULISM

A COMPANY of intellectual and cultivated men and women were conversing upon some of the more unusual phases of human nature. Various thrilling incidents had been narrated, when a dream was related of such remarkable detail — with which, as was alleged, subsequent events corresponded — that it seemed as though it were not "all a dream"; and during the remainder of a long evening similar tales were told, until it appeared that all except two or three had dreamed frequently. Finally it was proposed to ascertain the opinions of every one present on the subject.

One bluntly said that he did not believe in dreams at all. When he was suffering from indigestion, or was over tired, or had much on his mind, he dreamed; and when he was well and not overworked, he did not, and "that is all there is in it." But he added that there was something he could never quite understand, and gave an account of a dream which his brother had had about the wrecking of a steamer, which led him not to take passage on it, and the vessel was lost, every one in the cabin being either seriously injured or drowned. At this a lady said that she had been in the habit of dreaming all her life, and nearly everything good or bad that had happened to her had been foreshadowed in dreams.

It was soon apparent that three out of four did not believe dreams to be supernatural, or preternatural, or that they have any connection with the events by which they are followed; but nearly every one had had a dream or had been the subject of one, or his mother, or grandmother, or some other relative or near friend, had in dreams seen things which seemed to have been shadows of coming events.

One affirmed that he had never dreamed: he was either awake or asleep when he was in bed; and if he was asleep, he knew nothing from the time he closed his eyes until he awoke.

Some expressed the belief that minds influence each other in dreams, and thus knowledge is communicated which could never have been obtained by natural means. One gentleman thought that in this way the spirits of the dead frequently communicate with the living; and another, a very devout Christian, remarked that in ancient times God spoke to his people in dreams, and warned them; and for his part he could see no good reason why a method which the Deity employed then should not be used now. At all events, he had no sympathy with those who were disposed to speak slightingly of dreams, and say that there is nothing in them; he considered it but a symptom of the skeptical spirit which is destroying religion. Another agreed with this, and, turning to one of those who had stoutly ridiculed dreams, said, "There are more things in heaven and earth, Horatio, than are dreamt of in your philosophy."

HISTORY AND PHENOMENA OF DREAMS

IN this paper, by *dreams* is meant the visions which occur in natural sleep; by *nightmare*, a dream unusually intense, involving a terrifying sense of danger and a physical condition to be more fully described; and by *somnambulism*, talking, walking, or performing other actions under the influence of a dream attending natural sleep.

Dreams are frequently spoken of, and in almost every possible aspect, by the oldest books of the world. In the Bible, God speaks in a dream to Jacob of the increase of the cattle, and warns Laban not to obstruct Jacob's departure. The dreams of Joseph, unsurpassed in description from a literary point of view, and of Pharaoh, with a history of their fulfilment, occupy a large part of the first book. The dream of Solomon and the dreams of Nebuchadnezzar, the warning of Joseph to take the young Child into Egypt, are parts of the history of the Christian religion. These, being attributed to supernatural influence, can reflect no light upon ordinary phenomena.

But the Bible distinguishes between natural dreams and such as these. It states very clearly the characteristics of dreams. The hypocrite "shall fly away as a dream, and shall not be found: yea, he shall be chased away as a vision of the night." David says, "As a dream when one awaketh," the Lord shall despise the image of the proud. Solomon speaks of the character of dreams thus: "For in the multitude of dreams and many words there are also divers vanities"; of their general causes he says, "For a dream cometh through the multitude of business."

Cicero says that men of greatest wisdom among the Romans did not think it beneath them to heed the warnings of important dreams, and affirms that in his time the senate ordered Lucius Junius to erect a temple to Juno Sospita, in compliance with a dream of Cecilia. Scipio's dream, philosophical, imaginative, grand, published in the works of Cicero, called

10

the most beautiful composition of the kind, has from its origin until now been the subject of discussion as to whether it was written by Cicero for a purpose or is the veritable account of a dream.

Almost all the famous characters described by Herodotus believed that dreams are of supernatural origin. Kings resigned their scepters; Cambyses assassinated his brother; priests attained greatness as commanders; cities which had been destroyed were restored by men who changed their plans and performed these acts because warned, as they supposed, in dreams; and with the invasion of Greece by Xerxes such night visions had much to do. Plato and Socrates believed in dreams, and even Aristotle admitted that they might have a supernatural origin.

There are those who affirm that they have never dreamed. It is obvious that they can testify only that they have never remembered a dream. Their evidence is therefore untrustworthy as to the fact of dreaming; for it is known that recollections of dreams, as a general rule, are very imperfect. Countless details have fled away; the scenes have been inextricably interwoven. A dreamer may be confident that he has dreamed hundreds of dreams, during any given night, yet not be able to recall with distinctness more than one or two. Besides, observation of some who declare that they never dream has demonstrated the contrary; for not only have they moved in ways which indicated that they were dreaming, but talked, and even responded to questions.

Upon only one phase of the subject is there substantial agreement among investigators; namely, the general characteristics of dreams. Time and space are annihilated, and all true estimates confounded. As a rule, to which there are occasional exceptions, nothing appears strange, and impressions which would accompany similar events in the waking state are not made; or, if at all, so slightly as not to produce their customary effects. Identity being often lost, no surprise is produced by a change of sex, age, name, country, or occupation. A young lady dreamed of seeing herself in her coffin, of listening to the observations of the mourners, and was not astonished to find herself dead, nor that, being dead, she could hear. She was not even surprised when the funeral services closed without the coffin-lid being shut down; nor when, in a very short time, she dreamed of being alive and engaged in her usual pursuits.

But the moment we pass beyond general statements of this character, opinions most incongruous and even contradictory are held, and strenuously advocated, by representative writers in every profession. [1]

Nightmare is something so terrible that its very name attributes its origin to the devil. The meaning

---

[1] Those who desire to see the opinions of leading writers, ancient and modern, down to the year 1865, and have not time to consult them in their own works, may find in Seafield's "Literature and Curiosities of Dreams" a very extensive collection. This work has been criticized as containing a large amount of valuable but *undigested* information. The criticism is not just, for it does not profess to have digested, but to present all for the digestion of others. The author expressly declares that he has "foregone such chances of greater credit and importance as would have been open to him if he had seemed to claim the whole as original, by incorporating the several theories and anecdotes with textual commentary of his own."

More recent investigations of great presumptive importance have introduced an immense amount of new matter into the literature, and considerable into the "curiosities," of dreams, or at least of dream investigations. Also I have found that some of the passages quoted by Seafield, read in their original setting, or compared with all the authors have said, require important modifications, if taken as expressions of mature opinion.

of "mare" is an incubus, as of a spirit which torments persons in sleep. In nightmare the mind is conscious of an impossibility of motion, speech, or respiration, a dreadful pressure across the chest, and an awful vision of impending danger. The victim sometimes realizes his peril, gathers all his forces, struggles vainly, and endeavors to shout for help. At last, by a desperate effort, he succeeds in screaming. If then some friendly touch or voice awakens him, the vision flees, and he is left stertorously breathing, perspiring, and more tired than if he had broken stone or worked in a tread-mill for as many hours as the nightmare lasted minutes. If not aroused, he may be awakened by his own screams; otherwise the incubus may not depart for a period, which, though short in actual time, seems like ages to him.

A young man under the writer's care was subject to attacks so harrowing that it was excruciating to be in the room with him during the paroxysm. Sometimes after he was awakened the terrifying vision would not wholly fade away for three quarters of an hour or more, during which his shrieks, groans, appeals to God, and the expression of unutterable agony upon his face were terrible. In the city of Philadelphia, a lad, having been exceptionally healthy from birth. was attacked with nightmare when fourteen years old. After a few seizures his father slept with him, for the purpose of awakening him should there be occasion. One night the father was startled by the voice of his boy calling in terrified tones, "Pop! Pop! I'm afraid!" He felt the hand of his son nervously clutching his wrist. Then the boy fainted, and died instantly. The post-mortem examination showed a large clot of blood about the heart, caused by paralysis due to fear. There is reason to believe that such instances are numerous enough to make nightmare worthy of serious medical investigation.

In nightmare, as A. Brierre de Boismont shows, the incubus takes different forms. Sometimes the subject fancies he flies in the air. He gives the case of a distinguished writer, whom he had seen in that state, uttering inarticulate sounds—his hair bristling, his countenance full of terror. At such times he would exclaim, "How surprising! I fly like the wind! I pass over mountains and precipices!" For several seconds after awaking he still imagined himself floating in the air. Others skim over the ground, pursued or threatened by dangers.

In childhood and youth, according to the same author, the individual is upon the edge of precipices, about to fall. In later years, robbers are breaking into the house, or the victim supposes himself condemned to death. Occasionally cats, or other animals or monsters, place themselves upon the stomach. "The weight of this imaginary being stifles, while it freezes the blood with horror." While not every case of nightmare is attended with motion or sound, nightmare passes into somnambulism when the victim shrieks or leaps from his bed, or makes any motion.

Somnambulism, in its simplest form, is seen when persons talk in their sleep. They are plainly asleep and dreaming; yet the connection, ordinarily broken, between the physical organs and images passing through the mind is retained or resumed, in whole or in part. It is very common for children to talk in their sleep; also many are liable to mutter if they have overeaten, or are feverish or otherwise ill. Slight movements are frequent. Many who do not fancy that they have ever exhibited the germs of somnambulism groan, cry out, whisper, move the hand, foot, or head, plainly in connection with ideas passing through the mind. From incipient manifestations of no importance somnambulism reaches frightful intensity and almost inconceivable complications.

Somnambulists in this country have recently perpetrated murders, killed their own children, carried furniture out of houses, wound up clocks, and ignited conflagrations. A carpenter not long since arose in the night, went into his shop, and began to file a saw; but the noise of the operation awoke him. The extraordinary feats of somnambulists in ascending to the roofs of houses, threading dangerous places, and doing many other things which they could not have done while awake, have often been described, and in many cases made the subject of close investigation. Formerly it was believed that if they were not awakened they would in process of time return to their beds, and that there would not be any danger of serious accident happening to them. This was long since proved false. Many have fallen out of windows and been killed; and though some have skirted the brink of danger safely, the number of accidents to sleep-walking persons is great.

Essays have been written by somnambulists. A young lady, anxious about a prize for which she was to compete, involving the writing of a composition, arose from her bed in sleep and wrote about a subject upon which she had not intended to write when awake; and this paper secured the prize. The same person, later in life, while asleep selected an obnoxious document from among several, put it in a cup, and set fire to it, and in the morning was entirely unaware of what she had done.

Intellectual work has sometimes been performed in ordinary dreams not attended by somnambulism. The composition of "Kubla Khan" by Coleridge while asleep, and of the "Devil's Sonata" by Tartini, are paralleled in a small way frequently. Public speakers often dream out discourses: there is a clergyman who, many years ago, dreamed that he preached a powerful sermon upon a certain topic, and delivered that identical discourse the following Sunday with great effect. Such compositions are not somnambulistic unless accompanied by outward action at the time of dreaming them.

SEARCH FOR ANALOGIES

THREE different views of dreams are possible, and all have been held and strenuously advocated. The first is that the soul is never entirely inactive, and that dream-images proceed all the time through the mind when in sleep. Richard Baxter held this view, and attempted to prove it by saying, "I never awaked, since I had the use of memory, but I found myself coming out of a dream. And I suppose they that think they dream not, think so because they forget their dreams." Bishop Newton says that the deepest sleep which possesses the body cannot affect the soul, and attempts to prove it by showing that impressions are often stronger and images more lively when we are asleep than when awake. Dr. Watts held the same view, and devoted a great deal of attention to it in his philosophical essays. Sir William Hamilton inclined to the same belief, because, having had himself waked on many occasions, he always found that he was engaged in dreaming.

Baxter's theory is an assumption of which no adequate proof can be offered; and Sir William Hamilton's test is inadequate, because an instant, even the minute fraction that elapses between calling a man's name or touching his body for the purpose of awaking him and resumption of consciousness, may be long enough for a most elaborate dream. Sir Henry Holland fell asleep while a friend was reading to him. He heard the first part of a sentence, was awake in the beginning of the next sentence, and during that time had had a dream which would take him a quarter of an hour to write down.

Lord Brougham and others have maintained that we never dream except in a state of transition from sleeping to waking. Sir Benjamin Brodie, in speaking of this, says:

> There is no sufficient proof of this being so; and we have a proof to the contrary in the fact that nothing is more common than for persons to moan, and even talk, in their sleep without awaking from it.

The third theory is that in perfect sleep there is little or no dreaming. This is supported by various considerations. The natural presumption is that the object of sleep is to give rest, and that perfect sleep would imply cessation of brain action; and it is found that " the more continuous and uninterrupted is our dreaming, the less refreshing is our sleep." Recent experiments of special interest appear to confirm this view. The effects of stimuli, whether of sound, touch, smell, sight, or hearing, in modifying the dreams without awaking the sleeper—or in awaking him— all point in the same direction; and though there is always a sense of time when awaking, which proves that the mind has to some extent been occupied, in the soundest sleep it is so slight as to seem as if the person had just lain down, though hours may have passed. Whereas, just in proportion as dreams are remembered, or as the fact of dreaming can be shown by any method, is sense of time longer. I do not speak of the heavy, dull sleep which, without apparent dreams, results from plethora, accompanies an over-loaded stomach, is the result of over-exhaustion, or occasionally supervenes after protracted vigils, but of the sound sleep enjoyed by the working-classes when in health, or by vigorous children.

The most interesting question is, Can a theory of dreams be constructed which will explain them upon natural principles, without either the assumption of materialism, or an idealism akin to superstition? It is to be understood that no phenomena can be ex-plained at the last analysis; but a theory which will, without violence, show the facts to be in harmony with natural laws, or so bring them within the range of things natural that they are seen to belong to a general class, and to the relations of antecedents and consequents, is an explanation. For example, electricity defies final analysis; but its modes of action are known, and even the greatest of mysteries, the form of induction which now surprises the world in the recently invented process of telegraphing from moving trains, is as susceptible of this kind of explanation as the action of steam in propelling a train.

We begin with analogies, and find these in the ef-fect of *drugs*, such as opium, alcohol, nitrous-oxid gas, hashish, etc. De Quincey describes all the ex-periences of dreams, both before and after he entered into a state of sleep, as resulting from the use of opium; and the peculiar sleep produced by that drug is attended by dreams marked by all the characteris-tics of those which occur in natural sleep. The effect of alcohol in setting up a dream state in the mind while the senses are not locked in sleep is, unfor-tunately, too well known. When a certain point is reached in intoxication the will is weakened, the auto-

matic machinery takes control, the judgment is de-
throned, and images — some grotesque and others
terrible — having the power of exciting the corresponding emotions, hurry through the mind until
frenzy is reached, subsequent to which a heavy stupor ends the scene. When a drunken man becomes
sober, his recollections of what he has done are as
vague and uncertain as those of dreamers; and a
similar inability to measure the flight of time, to perceive the incongruity of images, the moral character
of actions, and the value and force of words, charac-
terizes this state which attends dreaming. Ether,
chloroform, and nitrous-oxid gas, when the amount
administered is not sufficient to produce unconsciousness, cause similar effects. The writer, being compelled to undergo a surgical operation at a time when
he was greatly absorbed in the then impending civil
war, by the advice of physicians took ether, the effect
of which was to lead to a harangue upon abolitionism,
in which profane language was used. As the effect
deepened, though it was at no time sufficient to produce absolute unconsciousness, the scene changed,
devotional hymns were sung, and a solemn farewell
taken of the physicians and surgeon, who were warned
to prepare to die. Of all this the remembrance was
like that of dreams.

The influence of hashish has received much attention, and has been outlined in scientific works and
literary compositions. The most striking account of
its effects is that of M. Théophile Gautier, originally
published in "La Presse" and quoted in many works.
Under the influence of hashish his eyelashes seemed
to lengthen indefinitely, twisting themselves like
golden threads around little ivory wheels. Millions
of butterflies, whose wings rustled like fans, flew
about in the midst of a confused kind of light. More

than five hundred clocks chimed the hour with their flute-like voices. Goatsuckers, storks, striped geese, unicorns, griffins, nightmares, all the menagerie of monstrous dreams, trotted, jumped, flew, or glided through the room. According to his calculation this state, of which the above quotations give but a feeble representation, must have lasted three hundred years; for the sensations succeeded each other so numerously and powerfully that the relative appreciation of time was impossible. When the attack was over, he found that it had occupied about a quarter of an hour.

These drugs operate only upon the circulation, the nervous system, and the brain. They are physical agents, operating upon a physical basis, and yet they produce phenomena resembling those of dreams, with the exception that they do not in every case divorce the motor and sensory nerves from the sensorium as perfectly as in ordinary dreaming sleep.

Delirium is analogous in most respects to the conditions produced by these drugs. Its stages are often very similar to those of intoxication; so that it requires a skilled physician to determine whether the patient is under the influence of delirium, insanity, or intoxication. Delirium results from change in the circulation, or a defective condition of the blood; and in most instances there is no difficulty, when the disease is understood, in assigning the approximate cause of the delirium. The partial recollection or forgetfulness of what was thought, felt, said, or done in the delirium, and similar recollection or forgetfulness of dream-images, is well known by all who have experienced both, or closely observed them. The analogy between delirium and intoxication loses nothing in value from the fact that the drug is administered. Disease in the human system can engender intoxicating poisons as well as others.

Revery is a natural condition, so common to children that they are hardly able to distinguish between reports from the external world and images presented by their imagination. But revery is a common experience of the human race in all stages of development. It differs from abstraction in the fact that the latter is the intense pursuit of a train of reasoning or observation, which absorbs the mind to such an extent that there is no attention left for the reports of the senses. Hence the abstracted man neither looks nor listens, and a noise or an impulse, far greater than would suffice to awaken the same man if asleep, may be insufficient to divert him from the train of thought which he pursues. Revery is literally day-dreaming. It is not reasoning. The image-making faculty is set free and it runs on. The mind is scarcely attentive, hardly conscious, and the tear may come to the eye, or the smile to the lip, so that in a crowded street-car, or even in an assembly, attention may be attracted to one who is wholly unconscious of the same. A person may imagine himself other than he is, derive pleasure from the change, and thus pass an hour or morning. In revery we frequently become practical somnambulists; that is, speak audible words that we would not have uttered on any account, strike blows, move articles, gesticulate, and do many other things, sometimes with the effect of immediately recalling us to a knowledge of the situation, when we, as well as others, are amused, but often without being aware of being noticed. In extreme cases the only distinctions between revery and dreaming sleep are regular breathing and the suspension of the senses which accompany the latter.

The passage from revery into dreaming sleep is to be scrutinized, as the line of demarcation is less than the diameter of a hair. When persons lie down to sleep, their thoughts take on the dream character before they can lose consciousness. "Look," says Sir Henry Holland, "to the passage from waking to sleeping, and see with what rapidity and facility these states often alternate with each other." Abstract reason gives place to images that begin to move at random before the mind's eye; if they are identified and considered, wakefulness continues. But at last they become vague, attention relaxes, and we sleep. It is possible to realize that one is sleeping, and to make an effort to awake and seize the mental train. But the would-be sleeper resumes the favorable position, the head drops, the senses lose their receptivity, and he who spent the last hour of the evening in revery in a darkened room has undergone but a very slight change when he passes into sleep. The images still run on while the body reposes, until, according to his temperament and habits, the brain becomes calm, and the soporific influence penetrates, we cannot tell how far, into the higher regions of the sensorium.

In considering the passing *from the dream state into the waking state*, several analogies are to be noted. Sometimes an amusing sense of the last dream occupies the attention deliciously for a few moments. Again, it is not uncommon to pass out of a dream into a perception of the hour of the night and of the situation, sink back into sleep, and take up the thread of the dream where it had been left at the moment of returning consciousness. More frequently the dream, if resumed, will be modified by physical conditions. At other times the painful consciousness of a frightful dream remains.

From these analogies the conclusion is reasonable that dreaming is a phenomenon of the mind, dependent upon changes in the circulation of the blood, and

11

in the condition of the brain and nervous system, whereby the higher powers of the mind, including judgment, conscience, and will, are prevented from exercising their usual jurisdiction, the senses from reporting events of the external world by which to a great extent time is measured and space relations determined, while the image-making faculty and animal instincts are to a less degree affected; and that the images constructed in dreams are the working up of the raw material of sensations, experiences, and ideas stored in the mind.

MORE DIRECT EVIDENCE

Of the truth of this view I will submit further evidence.

First. There is no proof that babes ever dream. The interpretation of the smile of the infant, which in former times led fond mothers to suppose that "an angel spoke to it," is now that the cause is "spirit" in the original sense of the word—internal gaseous phenomena. Aristotle says, "Man sleeps the most of all animals. Infants and young children do not dream at all, but dreaming begins in most at four or five years old."

Pliny, however, does not agree with Aristotle in this, and gives two supposed evidences that infants dream. First, they will instantly awake with every symptom of alarm; secondly, while asleep they will imitate the action of sucking. Neither of these is of any value as proof. As to the first, an internal pain, to which infants appear to be much subject, will awaken them; and as they are incapable of being frightened by any external object until they are some months old, the symptom is not of alarm, but of pain. The imitation while asleep of the action of sucking is instinctive, and an infant will do so when awake, and when there is obviously not the slightest connection between the state of mind and the action. The condition of the babe in sleep is precisely such as might be expected from its destitution of recorded sensations.

Second. Animals dream. Aristotle's history of animals declares that horses, oxen, sheep, goats, dogs, and all viviparous quadrupeds dream. Dogs show this by barking in their sleep. He says further that he is not quite certain from his observations whether animals that lay eggs, instead of producing their young alive, dream; but it is certain that they sleep. Pliny, in his natural history, specifies the same animals. Buffon describes the dreams of animals. Macnish calls attention to the fact that horses neigh and rear in their sleep, and affirms that cows and sheep, especially at the period of rearing their young, dream. Scott, in the "Lay of the Last Minstrel," says:

> The stag-hounds, weary with the chase,
> Lay stretched upon the rushy floor,
> And urged in dreams the forest race
> From Teviot-stone to Eskdale Moor.

Tennyson also speaks of dogs that hunt in dreams. Darwin, in the "Descent of Man," Vol. I., p. 44, says that "dogs, cats, horses, and probably all the higher animals, even birds, as is stated on good authority (Dr. Jerdon, 'Birds of India'), have vivid dreams, and this is shown by their movements and voice." George John Romanes, in his "Mental Evolution in Animals," says that the fact that dogs dream is proverbial, quotes Seneca and Lucretius, and furnishes proof from Dr. Lauder Lindsay, an eminent authority, that horses dream. Cuvier, Jerdon, Houzeau, Bechstein, Bennett, Thompson, Lindsay, and Darwin assert that birds dream; and, according to Thompson, among birds the stork, the canary, the eagle, and the parrot, and the elephant as well as the horse and the dog, are "incited" in their dreams. Bechstein holds that the bullfinch dreams, and gives a case where the dream took on the character of nightmare and the bird fell from its perch; and four great authorities say that occasionally dreaming becomes so vivid as to lead to somnambulism. Guer gives a case of a somnambulistic watch-dog which prowled in search of imaginary strangers or foes, and exhibited toward them a whole series of pantomimic actions, including barking. Dryden says:

The little birds in dreams the songs repeat,

and Dendy's "Philosophy of Mystery" quotes from the "Domestic Habits of Birds" in proof of this.

We have often observed this in a wild bird. On the night of the 6th of April, 1811, about ten o'clock, a dunnock (*Accentor modularis*) was heard in the garden to go through its usual song more than a dozen times very faintly, but distinctly enough for the species to be recognized. The night was cold and frosty, but might it not be that the little musician was dreaming of summer and sunshine? Aristotle, indeed, proposes the question—whether animals hatched from eggs ever dream? Macgrave, in reply, expressly says that his "parrot Laura often arose in the night and prattled while half asleep."

Third. The dreams of the *blind* are of great importance, and the fact that persons born blind never dream of seeing is established by the investigations of competent inquirers. So far as we know, there is no proof of a single instance of one born blind ever in dreams fancying that he saw. The subject has been treated in the "New Princeton Review" by Joseph Jastrow, who has examined nearly two hundred persons of both sexes in the institutions for the blind in Philadelphia and Baltimore. Thirty-two became blind before completing their fifth year, and not one of these thirty-two sees in dreams. Concerning Laura Bridgman, the blind and deaf mute, Mr. Jastrow says, "Sight and hearing are as absent from her dreams as they are from the dark and silent world which alone she knows."

Fourth. The testimony is the same with regard to those born *deaf.* The celebrated Harvey P. Peet, LL. D., in his researches, among the most philosophical ever made, places this fact beyond rational doubt; but other investigators furnish equally valuable evidence. In visiting institutions for the blind and the deaf, I have made inquiry, and have never found an instance of a person born deaf, or of a child who lost his hearing before he was four years of age, dreaming of hearing. Among the results of recent inquiries I present the following from the principal of the State Institution for the Blind and Deaf at St. Augustine, Florida:

I have closely questioned the deaf children here as to whether they have ever *dreamed* of *hearing*, and the invariable answer is *No.* I have asked the same question of upward of fifty deaf persons with the same result, except where the person interrogated had lost his hearing after learning to talk. These last mentioned are all persons of some education who understood the question fully and were very positive that they had never dreamed of hearing more than a rumbling sound.

Very sincerely,
PARK TERRELL.

I was one of the members of a committee of three to visit the State institution of Michigan for the blind and deaf, at Flint, where there were hundreds of pupils. The method of awakening them in the morning and of calling them to recitations and to chapel services was by beating a bass-drum, which, of course, the blind could hear. But it was curious to observe the deaf awaking from a sound sleep in the morning, or called to chapel and recitation at other hours of the day, by the beating of a bass-drum in the central hall. Those who could not have heard the reverberation of all the artillery in the world felt the vibration of the building produced by the beating of the drum, and obeyed the signal. Some of them dreamed of vibration; none born deaf of hearing.

In further elucidation of the subject, I addressed a letter to Professor J. W. Chickering, Jr., of the National Deaf Mute College at Washington, D. C., and under date of February 3, 1888, received the following:

Deaf mutes of all grades dream frequently, though they are not given to imagination. As to the question whether they dream about anything involving sound, I have made diligent inquiry, and have been answered in the negative except in the case of the Rev. Job Turner. He says that he once dreamed of being counsel for a prisoner, and being greatly delighted to find himself making a very eloquent speech in his behalf.

The question of dreaming about sounds in the case of semi-mutes was discussed in the "American Annals" some years ago by Professor Greenberger of New York, and some statistics were given; but he dismisses your inquiry (*i. e.*, whether persons born deaf ever dream of hearing) very abruptly by saying, "This question was put to a number of congenital deaf mutes, and, as might have been expected, their answers were all in the negative."

I may state to you, as a matter of fact, that one of our deaf-mute teachers, who has no memory of hearing, has waked from sleep in a fright by the report of firearms; but that would be accounted for by the concussion and consequent action upon the nerves of general sensation.

Truly yours,

J. W. CHICKERING, JR.

Upon the above letter I may remark that the single case of the Rev. Job Turner, an educated man, accustomed to read and imagine spoken oratory, can be accounted for without assuming that he dreamed of hearing sounds, the speech-making being a movement of his mind involving an act rather than a perception. The being wakened by the explosion of firearms is, as Professor Chickering justly says, explicable on the same principle as that which accounts for the awaking of the deaf and the communication of information by the rhythmical vibration of a building.

Leaving out of account the question of the dreamless state of infants and very young children, I deem the facts that animals dream, that the congenital blind and deaf never dream of seeing or hearing, conclusive proof that dreams are phenomena of the physical basis of mind, dependent upon changes in the circulation of the blood, and the condition of the brain and the nervous system; and that images constructed in dreams are automatic combinations of the sensations, experiences, ideas, and images stored in the mind.

Three further collateral evidences can be adduced. First, the modification of dreams by physical conditions. With this all are familiar. These are plainly, so to speak, efforts of the image-making faculty active in dreams to account without the aid of the judgment for a physical sensation. Every one knows that the condition of the digestive organs, the position of the head or any other part of the body, will affect dreams.

Another fact is that the dreams of the very aged, unless something unusually agitating is anticipated or occurs, generally recur to scenes of former years, and therein greatly resemble their conversation. Even when the intellectual faculties are unimpaired, and the aged person is much interested in current events, and pursues a train of study and reflection by day under the control of the will, when at night the imagination is set free, scenes of early life or childhood furnish the materials of the images much more frequently than contemporaneous events. This is in harmony with the known laws of memory.

In regard to the dreams of the insane, the "Medical Critic and Psychological Journal" of April, 1862, says:

The dreams of the insane are generally characteristic of the nature of the aberration under which they labor; those of the typho-maniac are gloomy and frightful; of the general paralytic, gay and smiling; of the maniac, wild, disordered, pugnacious; in stupidity they are vague, obscure, and incoherent; in dementia, few and fleeting; in hypochondria and hysteria the sleep, especially during indigestion, is disturbed and painful.

This is in accordance with all the indications.

ACCOUNTING FOR THE CHARACTERISTICS OF DREAMS

In dreams, time and the limitations of space are apparently annihilated. This is to be explained by the fact that the reports of the senses and the movements of external bodies by which we measure time are shut out, and the mind is entirely absorbed in a series of images.

I entered the South Kensington Museum in London, and saw a painting of an Alderney bull, cow, and calf in a field, which produced so extraordinary an illusion that I advanced several steps toward it in broad daylight, under the belief that I was looking out of a window into the park. The same phenomenon occurs under the spell of an orator of the highest grade; and it is the charm of a theatrical performance to make an audience think and feel that a series of events which would ordinarily occupy many years is taking place before them. That which, under these circumstances, is accomplished in part by abstraction or external means, in dreams is done entirely by cutting off all possibility of estimating time or space.

The mind is supposed to move more rapidly in dreams than in waking thoughts. Dreams without doubt are more diversified and numerous than the waking thoughts of busy men and women absorbed in a particular routine of work, or in the necessary cares of the body, or in conversation circumscribed by conventional laws, the slow rate of speech, and the duty of listening. But it is an error to think that dream-images are more numerous than those of revery. In a single hour of revery one may see more images than he could fully describe in a volume of a thousand pages. It is as true of the waking as of the dreaming state, that

> Lulled in the countless chambers of the brain,
> Our thoughts are linked in many a hidden chain;
> Wake but one, and lo! what myriads rise:
> Each stamps its image as the other flies.

Apparent loss of identity in dreams, and finding one's self in impossible positions, are the result of the entire occupation of the perceptive faculties with one image at a time. A dream that a man is a clergyman may change into one that he is a general commanding on the field of battle, and he will see no incongruity. He may even imagine himself to be two persons at the same time, as in Dr. Johnson's case when he contended with a man, and was much chagrined to feel that his opponent had the better of him in wit. He was consoled, however, when on waking he perceived that he had furnished the wit for both.

The vividness of dreams is to be explained in the same way. If a man sees that his own house is on fire, and his family in danger, he looks at the scene in such a way that he becomes for the time as unconscious of anything else as though there were nothing in his brain but the picture. So in the dream, as he sees nothing but the picture, it must be more vivid than any ordinary reality can possibly be; only from the most extraordinary scenes can an analogy be drawn.

In dreams circumstances often appear which had been known by the dreamer, but practically forgotten. Men have sworn that they never knew certain things, and maintained that they had been revealed to them in dreams, when subsequent investigation proved indubitably that they had known, but had forgotten them. The recurrence is precisely like ordinary waking experiences. Events which have not emerged into consciousness for a score of years, or longer, and phrases, parts of words, expressions of countenance, tones of voices, analogies stumbled upon in the most out-of-the-way places, may in a single moment bring an entire scene with several series of related events before the mind.

The testimony of the mind excited to a certain degree of activity by fear of death by shipwreck or fire, or, as Whymper has shown in his "Scrambles among the Alps," the immediate expectation of a fatal fall, is that it seems to see at a glance the whole of the past life. This is sufficient to show what it can do in an entirely normal state, and nothing can ever occur in dreams more vivid than this, though it is to be considered that we have only the statements of these persons in regard to what they think was their mental condition; nor in any case could they know that they saw everything.

When one dreams that he is dreaming, which occasionally occurs, he is approaching the waking state; but since he cannot at that time sit in judgment fully on what he dreams without waking, it is equally clear that his state resembles that of a delirious person who may perceive that he is delirious and acknowledge it, but in a few seconds be again absorbed in what he sees.

Some of the most interesting achievements of the mind in dreams are the composition of poetry and the working out of mathematical problems. Dr. Abercrombie says that his friend Dr. Gregory told him that thoughts and even expressions which had occurred to him in dreams seemed to him so good when he awoke that he used them in his college lectures. Condorcet, having gone to bed before finishing certain profound calculations, said afterward that sometimes the conclusions of the work had been revealed to him in dreams. Dr. Abercrombie relates that Benjamin Franklin, than whose a more well-balanced and self-controlled mind never existed, assured Cabanis that the bearing and issue of political events which puzzled him when awake were not unfrequently unfolded to him in his dreams. Dr. Carpenter attempts to explain this by the theory well known as "unconscious cerebration." Like the terms of the phrenologists, this may describe but does not explain the process; and what it describes occurs frequently while we are awake. Not only in questions of memory, but in the profoundest thought, how often, when we have been compelled to turn from one class of work to another, and are, so far as our consciousness reports, entirely absorbed in it, in an instant a thought germane to the first problem which was occupying the mind appears with such clearness as to surpass in pertinency and value anything which we had previously reached. We are compelled to take note of it, and in the case of defective recollection the best of all modes is to cease to think about the matter, and in a short time it will appear almost with the intelligence of a messenger bringing something for which he had been sent.

When one has wearied himself, and his perceptions have been somewhat obscured, even though nothing had occurred of the nature of unconscious cerebration, it would not be surprising if after refreshing sleep the first effort of his mind should classify and complete the undigested work of the day before. The dream imagery under which such things are done frequently invests the operation with a mysterious aspect, which, on analysis, appears most natural. I am informed by one of the participants that some time since two gentlemen in Pennsylvania were conversing concerning an intricate mathematical problem. One of them succeeded in its solution by algebraic methods. The other insisted that it could be done by arithmetic, but, after making many efforts, gave up the problem, and retired for the night. In the morning he informed his friend that in the night, while he was asleep, an old Scotch schoolmaster, who had been his instructor many years before, appeared to him and said, "I am ashamed of you that you could not do that sum. It can be worked out by arithmetic, and I will show you how now." And he added that he had immediately done so, and in the morning when he awoke he had put the figures on paper just as his schoolmaster had done in the dream; and there they were, a complete solution of the example.

It was a very impressive dream, but easily explained. It was a workable problem. The man, ashamed of himself that he could not do it and exhausted with his efforts, had sunk into a troubled sleep. His mind undoubtedly had recurred to his old teacher and the rule; and as he dreamed about the matter, the working out of the problem had to come in some form. What more natural than that the image of the teacher who taught him the greater part of what he knew of the subject of arithmetic, especially in difficult problems, should have come in to give bodily shape to the shame which he felt, and that his fancy should attribute the information to him? So that, instead of such a dream being extraordinary, it is the most natural method in which it could occur.

The mind when awake is capable, by an effort of the imagination, of conceiving most grotesque ideas. For example, a man sees before him a huge rock. He may conceive the idea that that rock is transformed into pure gold, and that upon it is a raised inscription, made of diamonds, promising the rock as a reward for the guessing of a conundrum. Being awake, he perceives both clearly—the rock in its original character, and the image of the gold rock with the raised letters in diamonds. Perceiving both, he knows the rock to be real and the other to be fantastic. If the faculties by which he identifies the granite rock were to be stupefied, leaving those by which he conceives the idea of the gold and diamonds in full exercise, it is clear that he would believe that the granite rock was gold. If awake, in this state, he would be insane; if asleep, he would be dreaming. So, if the dreamer be absorbed in images which seem to him real, if the faculties by which he would distinguish an ideal conception from an objective reality were restored, he would take cognizance of his surroundings, and though the image might remain it would not seem real. The statement of this self-evident fact is sufficient to show what all the evidence I have col-

12

lated combines to prove, that *Mercutio*, in "Romeo and Juliet," was scientifically correct when he said:

> True, I talk of dreams,
> Which are the children of an idle brain,
> Begot of nothing but vain fantasy.

Nightmare, with all its horrors, is but a variety of dream. The causes for its peculiarities are various — position; pressure upon the stomach, whereby the sympathetic nerves are affected, and through them the brain; extreme fatigue, etc. When one is awake and has precisely the same unfavorable physical sensations which would produce nightmare, he refers them to their proper source, changes his position, measures the probable consequences, resorts to medical aid, or absorbs himself in work; but when asleep, the mind attempts to account for the sensation, and will perhaps construct an image of Bunker Hill Monument pressing upon his chest to account for a sensation which, if he were awake, he would have no difficulty in explaining.

The relation to nightmare of sleeping on the back is so simple as hardly to need an explanation. Many persons never have an attack unless they get into this position.

Somnambulism differs from dreams in the fact that one or more of the senses may be in an active condition, and that one or more of the organs may respond to the idea which absorbs the mind. A merchant in New York, traveling on the Mississippi River, occupied the same state-room with a stranger of highly respectable appearance. In the morning the stranger, taking up his stockings, said sadly, "I see I have been at my old tricks again." "To what do you refer?" asked the merchant. "My stockings are wet, and I must have arisen in the night and traveled all over the ship."

As already remarked, talking in the sleep is the simplest form in which somnambulism appears. Usually dreamers do not move their limbs, and especially are incapable of rising or walking, because under ordinary circumstances the impulse to do these things is created by the will, and it requires a strong exertion thereof to overcome the inertia of the body and to begin the complex series of motions necessary to move from place to place. In sleep the image is not sufficiently vivid to take control of the muscles.

Cicero says that if it had been so ordered by nature that we should actually do in sleep all that we dream of doing, every man would have to be bound to the bed before going to sleep. The justice of this remark is illustrated in the case of somnambulism.

The peculiarity of somnambulism which identifies it with dreaming is complete absorption of all the powers and faculties in the image. A voice falling in with that may be heard; one speaking of other matters is unnoticed. Dreamers who have never been somnambulists could, by a process of training, be transformed into such; and, what is more important, the tendency can be destroyed if taken in time.

Sir Henry Holland says that it is an old trick to put the hand into cold water, or to produce some other sensation not so active as to awaken, but sufficient to draw the mind from a more profound to a lighter slumber; thus the sleeper may be made to answer questions.

Great light has been reflected upon natural by artificial somnambulism, known by the various names of mesmerism, animal magnetism, electro-biology, hypnotism, etc. It is an astonishing fact that in these states a particular sense may be exalted so as to give results which in a normal condition would be impossible; and which to a superficial observer, and even to an investigator if he be inexperienced, appear to transcend the bounds of the human faculty. Abnormal states, involving changes radically different from dream somnambulism, happen spontaneously when awake, occur in delirium, and at rare intervals the somnambulist may pass into them. They will be treated elsewhere.

MYSTERIOUS DREAMS ANALYZED

If the foregoing attempt at explanation covered all the actual phenomena of dreams, there is no reason to doubt that it would be satisfactory to readers of intelligence; but it is claimed by many that in dreams premonitions of future events are given, especially of death; that events which have taken place, of interest to the recipient of the communication, are made known; and that the knowledge of current events is frequently imparted when the dreamer is at a great distance.

An acquaintance of mine, a young man, nineteen years of age, a student in a large seminary about sixty miles from New York, was strongly attached to a teacher who died, to the great grief of the student. Some time afterward the young man dreamed that the teacher appeared to him and notified him that he would die on a certain day and hour. He informed his mother and friends of the dream, and expressed a firm belief that when that time came he should die. They considered it a delusion; and as no alarming change took place in his health, they were not anxious. When the day arrived they noticed nothing unusual; but after dining and seeming to enjoy the meal and to be quite cheerful, he went to his room, lay down, and died without a struggle.

The following case is said to be authentic: The father of a certain lady died. About a year afterward she aroused her husband by sobbing and trembling violently, while tears ran down her cheeks. She explained that she had just had a vivid dream, in which she had seen her father assemble all his children in his room in the old house, and tell them that the family heirlooms were being disposed of to strangers. The same dream recurred the next night. A day or two afterward this lady, while walking in the town where she lived, saw her father's walking-stick, with a gold band bearing an inscription, a gift from all his children, in the hands of a stranger. The sight so affected her that she fainted. Later inquiries proved that the stick had changed hands on the day previous to her first dream.

The case of William Tennent is in point. Mr. Tennent, a remarkable preacher of Freehold, N. J., zealous in promoting revivals, had a particular friend, the Rev. David Rowland, who was also exceedingly successful. A notorious man named Thomas Bell, guilty of theft, robbery, fraud, and every form of crime, greatly resembled Mr. Rowland. Passing himself off for him, he imposed upon citizens of Hunterdon County, N. J., robbed them and fled, everywhere representing himself as the Rev. Mr. Rowland. At the time he perpetrated this robbery in Hunterdon County, "Messrs. Tennent and Rowland, accompanied by two laymen, Joshua Anderson and Benjamin Stevens, went into Pennsylvania or Maryland to conduct religious services. When Mr. Rowland returned, he was charged with the robbery committed by Bell. He gave bonds to appear at the court of Trenton, *and the affair made a great noise throughout the colony.*

Tennent, Anderson, and Stevens appeared, and swore that they were with Mr. Rowland and heard him preach on that very day in Pennsylvania or Maryland. He was at once acquitted." But months afterward Tennent, Anderson, and Stevens were arraigned for perjury. Anderson was tried and found guilty. Tennent and Stevens were summoned to appear before the next court. Stevens took advantage of a flaw in the indictment and was discharged. Tennent refused to do that, or to give any assistance to his counsel, relying upon God to deliver him. The authorized "Life of Tennent" now gives the particulars:

Mr. Tennent had not walked far in the street (the bell had rung summoning them to court) before he met a man and his wife, who stopped him, and asked if his name was not Tennent. He answered in the affirmative, and begged to know if they had any business with him. The man replied, "You best know." He told his name, and said that he was from a certain place (which he mentioned) in Pennsylvania or Maryland; that Messrs. Rowland, Tennent, Anderson, and Stevens had lodged either at his house, or in a house wherein he and his wife had been servants (it is not now certain which), at a particular time which he named; that on the following day they heard Messrs. Tennent and Rowland preach; that some nights before they left home, he and his wife waked out of a sound sleep, and each told the other a dream which had just occurred, and which proved to be the same in substance: to wit, that he, Mr. Tennent, was at Trenton, in the greatest possible distress, and that it was in their power, and theirs only, to relieve him. Considering it as a remarkable dream only, they again went to sleep, and it was twice repeated, precisely in the same manner, to both of them. This made so deep an impression on their minds, that they set off, and here they were, and would know of him what they were to do.

On the trial the evidence of these persons, and of some others who knew Bell, and were acquainted with his resemblance to Mr. Rowland, was sufficient to secure Mr. Tennent's acquittal.

To explain such dreams as these some introduce a supernatural element, claiming that they are sent by God to warn his people; others adopt the hypothesis now known as telepathy; while still others content themselves with vague references to "clairvoyance."

Close investigation of a large number of alleged premonitions of death, revelations of current and past facts, and predictions of the future has afforded me no ground for a scientific presumption either of supernatural interference, of telepathy, or of clairvoyance. That is, authentic cases can be more reasonably explained without than with any of these assumptions.

The English Society of Psychical Research was founded in 1882, and has pursued its investigations since that time. The names of its president, vice-presidents, corresponding members, and council include men justly distinguished in various fields of scientific investigation, and some occupying high religious positions; the list of members is also imposing. The investigations, as usual in such cases, have been left to a few members whose tastes and opportunities are favorable, and many of the most learned and conservative members of the body appear, from the reports of all the proceedings, to have taken no active part in the work. President G. Stanley Hall, of Clark University, formerly Professor of Psychology and Pedagogics in Johns Hopkins University, who is one of the corresponding members, regrets, in an elaborate review of the experiments and their results, the absence from the investigations of the most celebrated alienists. Certain active members, by the frequency of their contributions, have practically, in the public mind, committed the Society to telepathy, or the ability of one mind to impress, or to be impressed by, another mind otherwise than by means of the recognized channels of sense. Of course dreams have a bearing upon this subject, and to them the Society has paid a great deal of attention.

The Society, as represented in the two bulky volumes entitled "Phantasms of the Living," edited by Edmund Gurney, Frederic W. H. Myers, and Frank Podmore, does not claim that the cases which they have presented, drawn from dreams, would be sufficient to prove the truth of telepathy. They confess that they are on doubtful ground, and say:

For (1) the details of the reality, when known, will be very apt to be read back into the dream, through the general tendency to make vague things distinct; and (2) the great *multitude* of dreams may seem to afford almost limitless scope for *accidental* correspondences of a dream with an actual occurrence resembling the one dreamt of. Any answer to this last objection must depend on statistics, which, until lately, there has been no attempt to obtain; and though an answer of a sort can be given, it is not such a one as would justify us in basing a theory of telepathy on the facts of dreams alone.

They acknowledge that, dreams being often somewhat dim and shapeless things, "subsequent knowledge of events may easily have the effect of giving body and definiteness to the recollection of a dream." They concede that "millions of people dream every night, and in dreams, if anywhere, the range of possibilities seems infinite." But when they come to present the subsequent cases, their reasoning upon them is in many instances unscientific in its destitution of rigor. For example, in cases of partial fulfilment where a person dreamed of death, and the dream did not occur until a number of hours after the death, they call that a deferment of percipience. They say that the impression when it first arrived "was unable to compete at the moment with the vivid sensory impressions and the crowd of ideas and images that had belonged to normal senses and waking life, and that it may thus remain latent until darkness and quiet give a chance for its development." The same sort of reasoning might be applied to account for the fact that such information is not universally communicated. It is flying about loose in the heavens and in the earth; but, not being able to compete with the crowd of images in any except few cases, does not generally materialize.

When they come to cases where the dreams contain the general feature of conversation between the dreamer and the agent, they say, "This is, of course, a clear instance of something superadded by the dreamer's own activity"; and when the circumstances of the death do not concur with it, they claim a fulfilment, and attribute a failure to agree to a death imagery superadded by the independent activity of the dreamer.

Where a woman dreams twice of death and it is fulfilled, and she also has the candor to state that on another occasion she dreamed of a death and nothing came of it, they say:

> The absence of any ascertained coincidence on the third occasion might be represented as an argument for regarding the correspondence on the two previous occasions as accidental, but it would be a very weak one; since even if the dream had recurred a thousand times, the chances against the accidental occurrences of two such coincidences would still remain enormous.

Many of the cases they cite depend upon vague memory, and others do not supply adequate particulars.

Their general method of writing about these dreams and of the whole theory of telepathy is that of an affectionate mother lingering over her child, and wherever coddling is necessary doing it *con amore*. There are two radical defects to be seen in the entire method: First, not a twentieth part of the care is taken in the investigation of the cases and their authentication which would be required for a case of ordinary importance in a court of justice; secondly, the use of the so-called doctrine of chances is so ludicrous as to be practically a burlesque of science. They sent to 5360 persons taken at random, asking them to state whether they had ever had a dream of the death of some person known to them, which dream was an exceptionally vivid one, and of which the distressing impression lasted an hour after arising in the morning, at any time within the twelve years 1874 to 1885 inclusive. Of these 173 answered "Yes." It would be difficult to believe, if it were not published to the world on the authority of the society, that any one should conclude that that number could furnish a basis upon which to ascertain an average to be applied to the whole population; yet they do so, and say that it is as satisfactory as the proof that a similar number of persons taken at random would afford on the average number of cases of short sight or color-blindness.

Short sight and color-blindness are physical conditions, depending upon physical causes; dreams are evanescent, irregular, depending upon phenomenal causes; and the dream-images of a single family in a single week may amount to hundreds of thousands, of which any one under the operations of laws not subject to statistics may be vividly remembered.

But of the whole number of 173 who had vivid dreams of death, there were only 24 where the event fell within 12 hours of the dream. By an application of the law of chance they endeavor to maintain that there would not be more than *one* such coincidence in that time, and that therefore "twenty-four is twenty-four times larger than the doctrine of chance would have allowed us to expect." As well might the law of chance be applied to the determination of the number of thoughts on any given subject that would naturally arise in one or more minds in a given period.

As shown in Chapter II, the "law of chance" is not capable of application to such subjects. Events are continually occurring, whether attention is directed to them or not. Of all possible occurrences, the time, place, and manner of death are most uncertain. Human lives revolve about a few central points—home, business, health, friends, travel, religion, country. Dream-images are about persons and things. That there can be millions of images portrayed in the gallery of dreams, and that the great majority deal with these pivotal points of human life and human thought, taken in connection with the fact that all the events of human history, past, current, and future, revolve about these same points, make it absolutely certain that the number of coincidences must be vast. It is, in fact, smaller rather than larger than might reasonably be expected.

It is natural that a large proportion of dreams of a terrifying nature should relate to deaths, because in death center all grounds of anxiety concerning one's self or one's friends. As death is the king of terrors and the dream state often a disturbed state, death would be also the king of dreams.

Of the 173 who declare that they have had distressing dreams, only 24 experienced fulfilment. An exact statement of the situation of the twenty-four persons dreamed about, or their physical condition and circumstances, would be as essential to a scientific estimate as the condition and circumstances of the dreamer.

The recollection of dreams depends much upon habit and upon the practice of relating them. I

found by experience that this had a tendency to per-
petuate a particular dream. For twenty-five years I
was visited at irregular intervals by a dream of the
death, by drowning, of my brother who is still living.
It frequently recurred soon after I had told it with
elaborateness of detail to another. The number of
appalling dreams that come to nothing is very great,
where the vividness of details sometimes fairly compels belief. In many instances a dream of one's death
originates in a profound derangement of the nervous
system, and the effect of such a dream upon that
weakened condition may be fatal. The young student
to whom reference has been made came of a family
peculiarly liable to instant death from heart-disease.
Since that period his only brother died without warning, when quietly, as it was supposed, reposing upon
his bed, and since the death of the brother, their
mother has died in a similar manner. The dream
was so vivid that the young man believed it, and
prepared himself for it in mind while his body was
depressed by the natural physical effect. Had he
been treated as was another young man who had a
similar dream, and believed it as implicitly, he might
have lived. In that case a sagacious physician, finding evidences that death was near, and believing the
symptoms to be caused wholly by the impression that
he was to die, administered a heavy dose of chloroform. When the young man became conscious and
found the hour fixed upon for his death long past, he
speedily recovered.

The repetition of dreams on the same night or on
other nights is explained by the impression which
they make; and doubtless the number 3 has literary
and religious associations which have an effect upon
some dreamers. If they have a notion that 3 is the number for significant dreams, when they have dreamed

the same thing thrice they are fully aroused and sleep no more. This is not always the case. A member of Congress who dreamed that his only daughter died awoke in great agitation, but on composing himself to sleep the dream returned. This continued for the fourth time, and even until the *ninth*, and after each recurrence he was awakened: in the morning, though not a believer in dreams, he hastened to his home in a western State, feeling assured that something terrible had happened or was about to happen. The first person whom he met was his daughter, in perfect health.

Coinciding dreams of two persons about a third are often not fulfilled. Abercrombie gives the case of a young man and his mother dreaming substantially the same dream the same night, in which he told her that he was going on a long journey, and she said, " Son, thou art dead." But nothing came of the dream. A young man not far from New York dreamed that his father was being burned to death in a hotel. The same night a lady, a friend of the family, dreamed the same. Nothing came of it.

In regard to the dream of William Tennent's witnesses, the following points may be noticed: First, "the affair made a great noise in the colony"; secondly, Tennent, Stevens, and Anderson all knew where they had been in Pennsylvania or Maryland, and it was easy for them to procure witnesses who could conclusively prove their innocence, and a supernatural interference was not necessary; thirdly, the delay between the trial of Rowland and that of Tennent at a period when information was principally distributed by word of mouth, taken in connection with the general interest in the subject of religion at that time and the excitement produced by the preceding trial, rendered it highly probable

13

that all of every community where Rowland had preached knew about these facts. The account cannot tell much about these witnesses, or even whether the preaching and the dream occurred in Pennsylvania or Maryland. The natural explanation of the whole proceeding is that they knew the facts and had talked, or heard others talk, about the trial; and so far as evidence goes they had themselves conversed about it, and the double dream was a mere coincidence. Whether this be true or not, the facts that the accounts are so defective, contradictory, and improbable, and that Mr. Anderson was allowed to be convicted and punished when he was as innocent as Mr. Tennent, greatly strengthen the natural explanation of the entire proceedings, for it is certain that fortunate coincidences have as often helped sinners as saints.

In the "Princeton Review" for July, 1868, the first article is a discussion of the trial of the Rev. William Tennent, by that eminent lawyer and Presbyterian, Chancellor Henry W. Green of New Jersey. After an elaborate and closely analytical investigation of the records, to which he had complete access, he shows that the events transpired in 1742; that they were first reduced to writing in 1805, more than sixty years after they had occurred; and that the narrative lacks precision and certainty in all its details. He closes the review in these words: "It will be perceived in what we have said we have taken as true every part of the narrative which is not shown to be erroneous by unquestionable record testimony, or by circumstances so strong as to compel the disbelief of a fair and impartial man. We fully admit the perfect integrity of all the witnesses, whose veracity is involved, the perfect integrity of Mr. Tennent, his unqualified belief in all the statements which he made.

. . . But from whatever cause the errors may have arisen, and whether our hypothesis as to the real facts be true or erroneous, certain it is that the narrative in all its material facts and circumstances is either established by the record to be untrue, or is rendered by the facts of the case utterly incredible. . . . We assert, therefore, with perfect confidence that his deliverance was not effected by supernatural means, and that the attendance of the witnesses was not procured by a dream."

The possibilities of coincidence in human affairs are incomputable. A gentleman residing near New York remarked to a friend on the 4th of February, 1888, "We shall have snow to-day." There was not a sign of it then, but before they separated snow began to fall. "How did you know that it would snow?" asked the friend. The sad and singular answer was, "Forty-three years ago to-day I buried my only son. It snowed that day and has snowed on the 4th day of February every year since, and I felt sure that it would snow to-day." Let those who fancy that the law of probabilities is of any value when applied to a particular day ascertain how many chances there were that it would snow for forty-three consecutive years in a certain part of the country on the 4th day of February.

Inquiry of the passengers on numerous ocean voyages has shown that not a ship crosses the sea upon which there is not some passenger who had a dream that the ship would be destroyed, which strongly tempted him to remain at home; or was warned by a friend, who, after such a dream, prophesied disaster; or which had not left behind some intending passenger deterred by a dream.

Many of the supposed cases of fulfilment of dreams, and where the coincidences are most startling, relate to events which neither man nor devil, disembodied spirit nor angel, could foreknow if true, since neither the events nor their causes were in existence in the universe; and the fulfilment depended upon actions involving juxtapositions which could not have been foreseen by any finite being, as they were themselves coincidences, and only conceivable as foreknown by God, because of the assumption of his infinity.

RATIONAL USE OF DREAMS

By some it is maintained that dreams are of great value in the argument for the immortality of the soul; the short method being that they prove the soul immaterial and independent of the body, and if immaterial then immortal. If this has any value it would apply equally to animals.

Others have held that we are responsible for our dreams. An article in the " Journal of Psychological Medicine" for July, 1849, says that we are as responsible for our dreams as for our waking thoughts; just as much so as we are told we shall be at the great tribunal for every idle word. And another writer affirms that in dreams each man's character is disintegrated so that he may see the elements of which it is composed. But few dreams are more absurd than such conceptions of them as these. Gluttony, evil thoughts, intemperance, vigils, and anxiety may affect dreams, but the responsibility is for the gluttony and other vices and sins; the dreams are simply the incidental results. Many most devout persons who have been unduly excited in religious work have been terrified and driven almost to doubt their acceptance with God by the fearful dreams of an impure or immoral character which have made their nights hideous. Religious biography abounds with such accounts. The sufferers have attributed them to the devil, of whom one of them naïvely said, "The evil spirit, having no hope of succeeding with me by day, attacks me in sleep." Intellectual persons of sedentary habits have also been troubled in this way. The explanation in such cases is simple. The "Journal of Psychological Medicine" for January, 1857, says:

When persons have been much engaged during the whole day on subjects which require the continued exercise of the intellectual and moral attributes, they may induce so much fatigue and exhaustion of those powers that when they are asleep, to their subsequent sorrow and surprise, they may have the most sensual and most vicious dreams.

The author of the foregoing proceeds to explain the fact upon the natural principle that the exhausted intellectual faculties, not being active and vigorous in the dream, the intellect received imperfect impressions; while the animal propensities, having been in a state of comparative inactivity, manifested greater activity.

In the case of great religious excitement, the principle embodied in the stern saying of a writer, that "When one passion is on fire, the rest will do well to send for the buckets," is a sufficient explanation. The intellect and the will being subdued by sleep, the generally excited condition of the brain and the nervous system produces a riot in the imagination.

Some rely upon dreams for evidence of acceptance with God, and of God's love. Where they have other evidences and sound reason, they do not need the help of dreams. When destitute of other evidences, it has been observed that their conduct is frequently such as no Christian, and sometimes as no moral person, could safely imitate.

One of the best observations in favor of dreams is by David Hartley, M. D.

The wildness of our dreams seems of singular use to us, by interrupting and breaking the course of our associations. For if we were always awake, some accidental associations would be so much cemented by continuance, as that nothing could afterwards disjoin them, which would be madness.

Nevertheless, I would prefer to take the risk of apparently dreamless sleep.

A marked increase in the number or change in the character of dreams should be seriously considered. They are sometimes the precursors of a general nervous and mental prostration. In such cases habits of diet and exercise, work and rest, should be examined. If dreams which depress the nervous energies and render sleep unrefreshing recur frequently, medical counsel should be taken. The habit of remembering and narrating dreams is pernicious; to act upon them is to surrender rational self-control.

A gentleman of Boston who travels much is in the habit of dreaming often of sickness and death in his family. He always telegraphs for information, but has had the misfortune never to dream of the critical events, and to be away from home when they came to pass. Still, like one infatuated with lotteries, he continues to believe in dreams. Another, whose dreams are equally numerous and pertinent, never so much as gives them a thought, and has had the good fortune to be near his family whenever urgently needed.

An extraordinary dream relating to probable or possible events may be analyzed, and anything which seems of importance in it from its own nature or the way things are stated, may wisely be made a subject of reflection. But to take a step upon a dream which would not be taken without it allies him who does it to every superstition that stultifies the godlike faculty of reason.

PRESENTIMENTS, VISIONS, AND APPARITIONS

One question more than others all
Of thoughtful minds implores reply:
It is, as breathed from star and pall,
"What fate awaits us when we die?"

IF these words are true, certainly next in importunate demand is whether men shall direct their conduct by practical wisdom and right motives, or look for and follow occult intimations which may either confirm or contradict the judgment.

Exclusive of the sphere of true religion,—which does not claim to be an infallible guide except to repentance, purity of motive, and the life beyond,—omens, premonitions, presentiments, visions, and apparitions have exerted the greatest influence over the decisions and actions of mankind.

Omens are extraordinary events which, on account of the opinions held of them, are thought to presage disaster. They are not true presentiments, but generalizations from imperfect data. Astrology and divination exhibit on a large scale the fallacies underlying such conclusions, belief in them being sustained by the observation of occasional coincidences between events and preceding actions or conditions that could have had no causal connection with them. Dreams often afford similar materials for erroneous

151

reasonings, and, as they originate in the mind, they are sometimes so similar to presentiments that it is impossible to decide whether a presentiment caused the dream, or a dream the presentiment.

WHAT IS A PRESENTIMENT?

A PRESENTIMENT in the strictly etymological sense is a previous conception, sentiment, opinion, or apprehension; but its secondary meaning, which has almost supplanted the primary, in both the French and the English use of the word, is an antecedent impression or conviction of something about to happen. Though presentiments of good are common and often fulfilled, as their results are not tragical they are seldom remembered or attributed to supernatural causes; and for this reason the word presentiment is confined almost exclusively to inward premonitions of evil, and is practically the equivalent of "foreboding" in such passages as Dryden's, "My heart forebodes I ne'er shall see you more."

Few would consider general forebodings of evil worthy of special investigation. To some temperaments they are peculiar, and prosperity, however great, cannot dissipate them. They may arise from overwork, old age, or from prolonged sickness of any kind except consumption; and as evil overtakes the majority of mankind, such general forebodings are certain of general fulfilment. It is only when time and events concur with the presentiment that it becomes a phenomenon requiring scientific treatment; and being a product of the mind allied to many other experiences, it is a philosophical problem of the first magnitude.

A writer in the "Cornhill Magazine" for October,

1886, attempts to lay down the essence of a true presentiment. He says that "it must be spontaneous; it must come at a time when you have no reason to look for it." He explains these conditions by saying that you must not be ill and think you have a presentiment that you will not recover; you must not be away from home and think that some calamity has happened there; you must not know that a friend is in danger and have a presentiment of his death; you must not have reason to suspect a man and have a presentiment that he will cheat you.

In laying down these conditions he justifies himself by saying that they are necessary, "because in all these instances there is a simple natural cause for fear or uneasiness." I cannot admit that all these conditions are exact. The person may indeed be sick, yet the illness may be slight, and its seat removed from any fatal possibility; and if in opposition to every indication he have a foreboding that he will not recover, which persists in defiance of reason, and does or does not end in death, it has the mental and emotional characteristics of a presentiment. Of course if a person have yellow fever, and a presentiment of his death, it is in harmony with popular belief; though, according to the statistics of the last epidemic in Jacksonville, the proportion of deaths is but one to ten cases, and the rational expectation would be that an ordinary person attacked had nine chances in ten for recovery. Again, if a person leaves his family in perfect health, knowing no cause of danger either to them or to his property, and has a presentiment impelling him to go back, and on arriving finds his worst fears realized, although his peculiar state of mind arose during an absence from home, it has the characteristics of a presentiment, both in its origin and the relation of time and events.

Conclusions drawn from reasoning and generalizations from data may produce convictions so strong that men would die for them. Under their influence they may risk their lives and fortunes in the pursuit of objects which cannot be attained, if at all, until after many years. These are not presentiments, for the sum of the reasonings and experiences of the man becomes the unconscious test which he applies to everything submitted to his judgment.

But if there be genuine presentiments which foretell future events, they must have an external source, human or extrahuman. That God could produce such impressions none who admit his existence can doubt. Whether other beings, in or out of human bodies, could do so is an unproven theory. Clairvoyance and telepathy do not apply to the subject of presentiments in the sense now under consideration. The clairvoyant theory of perception is the power to read the past, discern the present, and forecast the future; that of telepathy, a transfer of ideas and feelings spontaneously or intentionally from a living person called the agent to another called the percipient.

Most persons holding that God could at any time create a presentiment will incline to the comfortable belief that he sometimes does so, and that this is one of the means whereby he cares for those who put their trust in him. But the fact that God can produce presentiments is not in itself an evidence, nor does it even rise to the dignity of a presumption, that he will produce them. He could preserve all his servants from destruction by sea or by land; he could impart to all his people a knowledge of future events; but he does not. The righteous often die in the pestilence and in calamities at sea; the wicked may escape, while those who pray sink.

While it would be presumptuous to affirm that no

such presentiment as we are considering is ever imparted by the Spirit of God to human beings, two propositions may be supported without irreverence: first, that the human mind without special influence from God or other beings may originate presentiments; second, that the probability is that this is their true explanation.

UNSUSPECTED MENTAL RESOURCES

SELF-ESTEEM is common and self-conceit general, yet few persons have an adequate idea of the resources of their own minds. Most fancy that what they recollect is the measure of what they know; whereas, in addition to every fact or idea that any person remembers, there are countless others which have entered his mind, and are liable at any moment to cross the plane of his consciousness. He who, when a thought arises, will ask, "How came I to think of this?" in the effort to trace the successive steps by which the mind traveled from the last conscious thought or experience to that which is the subject of retrospection, will be compelled to conclude that these lightning-like movements of the mind have as often been directed by associations of which we are unconscious as by those whose significance and relations are perceived. Experiments to determine the rapidity of thought, by uttering a sentence or command and noting the time before the rational perception of it is manifest, are deceptive, because they involve the rate of motion of the senses, which is slow compared with the movement of ideas in the mind.

Revery frequently affects the emotions powerfully, and produces an influence which is felt for days, and even months, after the mind, calmly reflecting, rejects the idea that there is any cause for the depression. A common experience of foreign travelers is that the mind runs over the whole field of personal interest, illuminating it as with flashes, bringing before him who pursues his way "remote, unfriended, melancholy, slow," vivid thoughts of home and friends. Such pensive states are often accompanied by intense concern, which crystallizes into conviction, that death or some other calamity has already taken place. Thousands of letters and many telegraphic despatches inspired by such feelings cross the sea every summer, to elicit responses indicating that there is no occasion for anxiety. Many business men will also acknowledge that at different times in the course of their careers, for reasons which they have not been able to fathom, an impression of impending calamity has possessed them, which was so strong as to make them ready to dispute the truth of the trial balance showing them solvent and prosperous.

The observation of the reader will doubtless furnish instances of persons whose forebodings of calamity—sometimes confirmed by the event, but oftener otherwise— are recognized by their business partners and friends, and call for the exercise of patience and the use of every means to dissipate the mysterious, unwelcome, and paralyzing impression. A manufacturer whose name is known in every city in the Union, and in most foreign countries, whose riches are estimated at many millions, employees numbered by thousands, charities munificent, piety undoubted, and sanity unquestioned, has had presentiments of disaster a score of times within the last twenty-five years, not one of which has been fulfilled; but all, while they lasted, were as intense and overpowering as any could be.

Two other mental phenomena must be observed. No discipline, however protracted and rigid, can exclude thoughts which start mysteriously concerning life, business, home, friends, investments, etc. The mathematician may be engaged in solving the most intricate problems, the theologian in preparing discourses, the essayist in the flow of composition, the accountant in adding a column of figures, but none of these can be certain of fifteen consecutive minutes undisturbed by ideas or impressions almost as vivid as a living personality. The superiority of the disciplined to the undisciplined mind consists chiefly in ability to expel the intruder, and not in exemption from such visits.

The other phenomenon is, that the mind, in a voluntary or an involuntary review of the situation, will frequently pause upon one phase of it, which will predominate over others without any apparent reason. A parent absent from home may be particularly anxious about one of three children, and be for weeks under the shadow of a causeless fear. As every mental state must have a cause, in the labyrinth of associated ideas and feelings, some occasion must exist; but introspection may never reveal it. To demonstrate that the mind cannot originate presentiments is, therefore, impossible; and we are brought to the question whether, in the number or character of such presentiments, there be convincing evidence that they have a supernatural origin.

Many experiences called presentiments are not of that nature. Dr. Forbes Winslow's "Psychological Journal" gives a tragic account of a presentiment to the great master of kings, Talleyrand. Dr. Sigmond received it from the widow of the private secretary and friend of Talleyrand, M. Comache. It shows signs of having been written afterward and embel-

14

lished. Talleyrand said, "Upon one occasion I was gifted for a single moment with an unknown and mysterious power." He had fled from France with an intimate friend named Beaumetz. They had arrived in New-York together, and considering that they could not return to France, decided to improve the little money that was left by speculation, and freighted a small vessel for India. Bills were all paid and farewells taken; but there was a delay of some days for a fair wind, during which the time of the departure was uncertain. Beaumetz was irritated to an extraordinary degree, and unable to remain quietly at home. He hurried back and forth from the city with an eager, restless activity. He had ever been remarkable for great calmness and placidity of temper. One day he entered, evidently laboring under great excitement, though trying to seem calm. Talleyrand was writing letters to Europe. Beaumetz, with forced gaiety, said: "What need to waste time penning those letters? They will not reach their destination. Let us take a turn on the Battery. The wind may be chopping round; we may be nearer our departure than we imagine." The language in which the dénouement is described is graphic:

We walked through the crowded streets to the Battery. He had seized my arm and hurried me along, seemingly in eager haste to advance. We had arrived at the broad esplanade, the glory then, as now, of New-York. Beaumetz quickened his steps still more until we arrived close to the water's edge. He talked loud and quickly, admiring in energetic terms the beauty of the scenery, the Brooklyn Heights, the shady groves of the island, the ships riding at anchor, and the busy scene on the peopled wharf, when suddenly he paused in his mad, incoherent discourse, for I had freed my arm from his grasp, and stood immovable before him. Staying his wild and rapid steps, I fixed my eye upon his face. He turned aside, cowed and dismayed. "Beaumetz," I shouted, "you mean to murder me.

You intend to throw me from the height into the sea below. Deny it, monster, if you can." The maniac stared at me for a moment, but I took especial care not to avert my gaze from his countenance, and he quailed beneath it. He stammered a few incoherent words, and strove to pass me, but I barred his passage with extended arms. He looked vacantly right and left, and then flung himself upon my neck and burst into tears. "'T is true, 't is true, my friend. The thought has haunted me day and night like a flash from the lurid fire of hell. It was for this I brought you here. Look! You stand within a foot of the edge of the parapet. In another instant the work would have been done." The demon had left him. His eye was unsettled, and the white foam stood in bubbles on his white lips, but he was no longer tossed by the same mad excitement under which he had been laboring, for he suffered me to lead him home without a single word. A few days' repose, bleeding, abstinence, completely restored him to his former self, and, what is more extraordinary, the circumstance was never mentioned between us. My Fate was at work.

What there is in this narrative to imply anything extraordinary, in view of the extraordinary circumstances, I am unable to perceive. Beaumetz had been unusually calm; he became greatly excited. Every action he performed and every word he said, for several days, was sufficient to excite alarm as to his mental condition. He was on the verge of an attack of acute mania. That Talleyrand had recognized his condition to some extent is apparent; that his mind perceived the danger, and that he took the only natural course to escape, is also clear; and the history of lunatic asylums abounds in accounts by friends or attendants of their discerning at the right moment that the maniac meant to perpetrate a tragic deed. In some instances it has been foreseen, and the wife, after predicting her own death at his hands, has succumbed to the maniacal fury of the once loving husband rather than allow him to be placed under restraint. A case of this kind, originating in the highest circles of American society, and culminating in Europe, has startled the world within a few years.

IMPRESSIONS AND "IMPERATIVE CONCEPTIONS"

IMPRESSIONS are closely allied to presentiments, and many persons, both devout and undevout, yield to their influence. Baseball pitchers, prize-fighters, soldiers, and politicians are subject to them. The celebrated Dr. Nathan Bangs, a minister of great influence and strength of character, early in life was accustomed to believe in and follow impressions. The manner in which he was delivered from the fear of them is described in Stevens's "Life of Bangs," page 101:

On a certain occasion, when the weather was very cold and the snow deep, the mind of Dr. Bangs became more than usually impressed with the value of souls. As he rode along he came opposite a dwelling which stood quite a distance back in the field, and instantly he became impressed with the thought that he ought to go and talk and pray with that family. He was in a feeble condition, no path had been made to the house, and he knew it would be dangerous for him to wade that distance and expose himself to the cold. So he resisted the impression and passed on; but no sooner had he passed the house than it became doubly strong, and " he finally turned back, tied his horse to the fence, waded through the snow to the house, and *not a soul was there !*"

His friend and successor in Canada, Dr. Fitch Reed, who communicated these facts to Dr. Stevens, says, "From that time he resolved never to confide in *mere impressions*."

A ludicrous instance of an impression connected with a supposed answer to prayer was notorious in the city of New York forty years ago. A gentleman of excellent character prayed that he might receive an impression from God when he should come into the presence of the person who would make him a suitable wife. He received assurance that his prayer would be answered, and tried to maintain a devout and expectant frame of mind. The months passed without a sign, but one day, while walking up Broadway, he saw a lady walking before him whose motions were exceedingly graceful, and instantly came the impression, " This is the woman whom God hath chosen for thee." For a long time he followed her in silence. At last the object of his anxiety turned into a side street. He turned also, and at that moment she dropped her handkerchief. He hastened forward to take it from the ground, and as she lifted her veil to thank him he perceived that she was of African descent! In an instant his faith in impressions was forever destroyed, and it was his custom in speaking of the occurrence to say that he had learned that prayer could not be substituted for common sense.

The number of impressions of which nothing comes is so much greater than those which appear to be fulfilled as to satisfy rational minds that they are not to be relied upon; and this requires on moral grounds the further conclusion that they are not of supernatural origin.

"Imperative conceptions," known among the insane, often have parallels among the sane. It is common for lunatics who have committed some atrocious act to assign, and often with absolute truth, that "it had to be done," or that they "had to do it." Certain crimes committed by the sane under a powerful influence have also been excused upon that ground, when a just view would show that, though strongly impelled, they were not incapable of resisting the impression, and were therefore responsible. I venture to affirm that there are few who have not at some time in their lives felt almost irresistibly drawn to perform an act, make a decision, or utter a word which they knew was not expedient; but the conviction that "it had to be done" predominated, and in many instances they have yielded. Where the consequences are not serious the effects may still be evil, for when the "ego" yields contrary to the judgment its power of resistance is lessened. These imperative impressions, which in the purely insane absolve from guilt, are often seen in their germs in the conduct of children who are dominated by their imaginations and sensibilities.

These are all akin to the state of mind in which presentiments arise.[1]

ANALYSIS OF TYPICAL PRESENTIMENTS

PRESENTIMENTS concerning hours of death have sometimes been defeated by deceiving their subjects. Well-authenticated instances exist of chloroforming those who had made preparation for death, but whose gloomy apprehension was dispelled when they found that the time had passed and they were still living.

[1] Dr. Henry M. Hurd, long the justly distinguished superintendent of the Eastern Michigan Asylum for the Insane at Pontiac, and now superintendent of Johns Hopkins General Hospital, Baltimore, Md., in speaking of imperative conceptions says: "By this term is understood a mental concept or impression, arising in the mind without external cause, or an emotional basis, or logical connection with any previous train of thought, which dominates the will and often compels to actions which are known to be ludicrous or improper, or contrary to the judgment of the individual. The imperative conception differs from the delusion in the fact that it is not elaborated by any process

The case of the dissipated Lord Lyttleton, who was subject to "suffocating fits," and who claimed that his death had been predicted to occur in three days, at twelve o'clock, midnight, is easily explained. On the evening of that night some of his friends to whom he told the story said, when he was absent from the room, "Lyttleton will frighten himself into another fit with this foolish ghost story"; and thinking to prevent it they set forward the clock which stood in the room. When he returned they called out, "Hurrah, Lyttleton! Twelve o'clock is past, you 've jockeyed the ghost; now the best thing to do is to go quietly to bed, and in the morning you will be all right." But they had forgotten about the clock in the parish church tower, and when it began slowly tolling the hour of midnight he was seized with a paroxysm and died in great agony. The opinion of those who knew the circumstances was that the sudden revulsion of feeling caused such a reaction as to bring on the fit which carried him off. This is a rational view, for when one nearly dead believes that he is about to die, the incubus of such an impression is as effective as a dirk-thrust or poison.

Many extraordinary tales are told of presentiments on the eve of battle, and the particulars are given; but this is not wonderful. Soldiers and sailors are

of reasoning, and does not commend itself to the reasoning or to the judgment. . . . *It is not necessarily an evidence of insanity*, unless it persists and dominates the conduct habitually. All persons have imperative conceptions arising spontaneously in the mind, which momentarily influence action and compel attention." He gives as illustrations the common experience of an overpowering impression that a watch has not been wound, or a window fastened, or that some other regular duty has not been performed, which is enough to destroy a person's peace of mind after he has retired, and compels him to leave his bed only to find that there is no foundation for the impression.

proverbially superstitious. The leisure they frequently have favors the recital of marvelous experiences; and battles depend upon so many contingencies, and are liable to be controlled by such inexplicable circumstances, as to give to even the bravest of men a tinge of superstition. It has been observed that most unrighteous battles, fought against an oppressed people, have been attended by victories turning upon circumstances that may have been accidental; and that the most heroic patriotism has been defeated in the same way. That soldiers should have presentiments is not strange; and that those who have been exceedingly fortunate through a score of battles should sometimes in moments of depression conclude that they would die in the next battle is not extraordinary. In these voluminous narratives we find little or nothing of presentiments of certain escape, though they too are often fulfilled and as often disappointed.

A correspondent of "Notes and Queries," second series, thirty-fourth volume, having spent several months in the Crimea during the severest period of the bombardment, says: "I can state that many cases of presentiment were fulfilled; as also that some were falsified. There were also many deaths without any accompanying presentiment having been made known." The great Turenne exclaimed, "I do not mean to be killed to-day"; but a few moments afterward he was struck down in battle by a cannon-ball.

The possibilities of chance in the fulfilment of presentiments are incomputable, as a fact which occurred in this country during the civil war, and which is known by thousands yet living to be true, may serve to show. Joseph C. Baldwin, a young gentleman residing in Newark, N. J., was a journalist of more than local fame. He wrote under several pseudonyms, one of which was "Ned Carrol," and another "Frank Greenwood." The articles written under the latter name were unlike any of his other productions, being personal and censorious in character; and Frank Greenwood was in consequence most unpopular in Newark and vicinity, while Ned Carrol was a general favorite. Early in the war Mr. Baldwin enlisted in the 11th regiment of New Jersey Volunteers, and after arriving at the seat of war wrote several letters for publication, in one of which, sent to the Newark "Courier," he described the death of the mythical Greenwood in these words:

ARMY OF THE LOWER POTOMAC,
GENERAL HOOKER'S DIVISION.

MR. EDITOR:

I only fulfill the dying request of a beloved comrade in apprising you of his sad fate. Two months ago Frank Greenwood joined our company (C, 5th regiment), and soon became a general favorite, owing to his great sociability and undaunted courage. He received his death-wound from a shell, which was thrown from the Cockpit Point rebel battery, and burst within twenty feet of him, while holding the signal halyards at a review on the 3d inst. We mourn him as a brother.

NED CARROL.

On the 15th of May, 1864, Lieutenant Baldwin, who had been in the battles of Bull Run, Gettysburg, Fredericksburg, Chancellorsville, Antietam, and the Wilderness, and a score or more of skirmishes, who had had many narrow escapes and many wounds in the active service, sat in camp knowing of no danger near, when a piece of iron from a shell "thrown from a rebel battery," which "burst within twenty feet of him," struck him in the back of the head, killing him instantly.

Let those who propose to prove supernatural portents by mathematics determine what the "probability" was that in a mere spirit of jest he should describe in detail the manner of his own death months afterward.[1]

Soon after the civil war I concluded to go South by steamer, and took passage from St. Louis on the steamship *Luminary* for New Orleans. Navigation on the Mississippi River at that time was uncertain. Many old vessels were employed, the condition of the river was dangerous, and during the preceding twelve or fifteen months nine steamers had been blown up, or otherwise destroyed, resulting in great loss of life. Nearly all the accidents had been caused by the explosion of what are known as tubular boilers, and strong prejudice arose against vessels having boilers of that kind. The *Luminary* was of the old-fashioned sort, and a number of passengers had taken it solely on that account.

I was accompanied to the vessel by my brother, who up to that time had traveled with me, and was about to return by rail to the coast. As he was upon the point of bidding me farewell, I was seized without a moment's thought or preparation with an appalling impression that the vessel would be lost, and that I was looking upon my brother for the last time. For some time I seemed to behold with almost the vividness of an actual perception the explosion, to hear the shrieks of the passengers, and to feel myself swallowed up in the general destruction. Composing myself as much as possible, I said to my brother: "If ever a man

---

[1] Dreams without any proper authentication of detail, are published and republished. "The night that President Lincoln was murdered, a neighbor of mine," writes a physician, "declared that the President was killed, and by an assassin. It was several hours before the news reached the town."

The wife of a New York clergyman made a similar statement just before the news arrived of the assassination of President

had a presentiment of death, I have it now; but you know I have for years held that presentiments spring from physical weakness, superstition, or cowardice. Would you yield to these terrible feelings?" He replied, "No! If you do, you will always be a slave to them." After some further conversation he went ashore, and the boat started.

For several hours the dread of disaster overhung me, but gradually wore off, and late at night I fell asleep. The distance from St. Louis to New Orleans is about twelve hundred miles. The time taken by the *Luminary* was seven days. It was in all respects, after the first day, a delightful voyage. After remaining in New Orleans a few days, I reëmbarked on the same vessel, continuing up the river eight hundred miles, making in all more than two thousand miles without accident.

Since that experience, in many voyages I have made it an object to inquire of travelers and others concerning presentiments, and have found that they are very common, occasionally fulfilled, generally not so; and that it is the tendency with practically all persons who have had one presentiment come true to force themselves into all conversations, and to become tyrants over those dependent upon them or traveling with them. It is to be frankly admitted that no matter how vivid a supposed presentiment might be, its nonfulfilment would not demonstrate that there are no presentiments which must have originated external to

Garfield, and said that she saw him in a railway station, surrounded by ladies and others.

But we hear nothing of the seventeen persons who communicated to Andrew Johnson, in the course of the three years that he was President, dreams describing his death by assassination; nor of similar communications made to the late President Arthur.

the mind of the subject; but having been led by my experience to induce many persons to defy such feelings without a single instance of reported evil results, it confirms strongly the hypothesis of their subjective origin.

That presentiments are governed by no moral principle in the characters of the subjects to which they are applied, or of those who receive them, the occasions upon which they are given, and their effects, is apparent. The most immoral have claimed to have them, have communicated them to others, and they have sometimes been fulfilled by events from which those having them have derived great advantages. A few of the best of men have had presentiments that seemed to correspond with subsequent events, but the great majority of good people have not; and the calamities which have befallen most have come without any warning, except such as could be inferred from existing situations. Experience, foresight, and guidance by ordinary sagacity have been all that mankind have had to rely upon; and to be governed only by these, combating or disregarding presentiments, impressions, and powerful impulses for which no foundation can be found in the nature of things, is the only safe and stable rule.

VISIONS

VISIONS are appearances to the mind's eye without a corresponding reality. Of the hallucinations of the insane it is necessary to say but little, as there is no doubt as to their nature and source. Generally the insane think them to be true perceptions, and endeavor to conform their conduct to them. Yet in some instances, and very often in the beginning of insanity, they admit them to be morbid and contend against them.

A question of deeper interest, and of closer relation to the subjects treated in this volume, is whether subjective visions are possible to the *sane;* and, if so, whether they are at all common, and liable to occur as isolated circumstances. On a full survey of the subject, both these questions must be answered in the affirmative. To say nothing of the visions produced by alcohol, opium, hashish, fever, blows upon the head, prolonged abstinence, deep anxiety, or those which precede attacks of epilepsy or of apoplexy, it is certain that hallucinations often arise without assignable cause or subsequent effect; and the subjects of them demonstrate their sanity by recognizing the unreal character of their perceptions.

Griesinger, one of the most eminent and discriminating writers on mental diseases, says: "Nothing would be more erroneous than to consider a man to be mentally diseased because he had hallucinations. The most extended experience shows rather that such phenomena occur in the lives of very distinguished and highly intellectual men, of the most different dispositions and various casts of mind, but especially in those of warm and powerful imagination." In illustration he speaks of Tasso, who, in the presence of Manco, carried on a long conversation with his protecting spirit; and of Goethe's well-known blue-gray vision, and his ideal flowers with their curious buds. He speaks briefly also of the hallucinations of Sir Walter Scott, Jean Paul, Benvenuto Cellini, Spinoza, Pascal; of Van Helmont, who saw his own soul in the form of a light with a human countenance; of Andral, the great physician, who experienced an hallucination of sight; and of Leuret, an investigator, thinker, and writer whose testimony may be implicitly trusted,

15

who, in his "Fragments of Psychology," gives an account of a phantasm of hearing which he experienced.

A. Brierre de Boismont divided hallucinations that are compatible with sanity into two kinds — those which are corrected by the understanding, and those which, on account of superstition, sluggishness of thought, love of the marvelous, inability to interpret them correctly, or because the emotions which they excite make calm consideration impossible, are not corrected. The cases which he adduces are numerous and striking. One is that of Talma, who, when he trod the stage, could by the force of his will make all the brilliant dresses of his numerous audience disappear and substitute skeletons for the living characters. When he had thus filled the theater with these singular spectators, his emotions were such as to give to his playing a force which produced the most striking effects. The case of an intelligent lady who would see a robber enter her chamber and conceal himself under her bed is in point. Though the spectacle produced violent palpitation of the heart and universal trembling, she was aware of its falsity, and after some moments her judgment and reason would triumph so that she could approach the bed and examine it without fear.

Another case was communicated by a physician of acknowledged reputation to Sir Walter Scott. The first hallucination was that of the presence of a great cat. After a few months the cat disappeared, and a phantom of a higher grade took its place — that of a gentleman usher dressed as though he was in the service of a lord lieutenant, or of some great functionary of the Church. But after some months he disappeared, and a phantom horrible and distressing — a skeleton — appeared. The fact of these visions was concealed by the subject of them, who was an important officer in a department of justice, for several years. Though he knew that they were of subjective origin, they wore him out, and he died a victim to the agony in which his life was passed.

Dr. Abercrombie gives a case of a man who had been all his life beset by hallucinations: when he met a friend in the street, he was uncertain whether he was a real person or a phantom, but by paying close attention he could distinguish between them. Dr. Abercrombie declares that he was at the time of writing in good health, of a clear intellect, and occupied in business.

Many forcible instances, the most valuable of which are those personally attested by Boismont, or by the authorities whom he quotes, are given where the mind was *sane*, though the hallucinations were *not* corrected by it. It must not be supposed that these hallucinations of the sane are confined to persons of distinction, sedentary habits, or poetic temperaments. Many have had once or twice in their lives spectral illusions, or instances of hallucination; and among plain men, mechanics, laborers, and the peasantry of all nations, they are very common. Griesinger, after giving a list of distinguished men who, though sane, had hallucinations, says: "Judging from what we have heard and observed on this subject, hallucinations doubtless occur also in men of very average minds, not as *rare* but as *frequently overlooked* phenomena."

I suggested, more than twenty years ago, the importance of a census upon a large scale of hallucinations of the sane. Within the last four or five years a somewhat systematic attempt has been made on both sides of the Atlantic. The results so far as tabulated show meager returns, though recently the Society of Psychical Research has given increased attention to the matter. Some of the most fruitful fields for such a census appear to have been neglected.

Down to within a few years a large proportion, if not a majority, of the converts in revivals in evangelical denominations, in the course of their religious exercises, experienced transient hallucinations, some of which were grotesque, some coherent, and others sublime. Thus, a business man who had fasted, prayed, and lost sleep for several days, was in his barn attending to his horses, when he saw before him in broad daylight a wheel revolving rapidly. It was about the size of a cart-wheel, and emitted radiant sparks and streams of light of various colors. He said to himself, "Am I dreaming, or have I lost my senses?" Recognizing the different objects around him, he concluded that he was in his right mind, and fixed his eyes upon the wheel, which still whirled with inconceivable speed. Suddenly he discerned standing upright and immovable in the midst of it, unaffected by the motion of the rim, the form of the Saviour, who pronounced his sins forgiven. The hallucination continued some minutes. He believed it a divine evidence of conversion; its origin was undoubtedly subjective.

Another person, now a minister in New England, was so wrought upon at the moment he felt the sense of guilt and perplexity removed that he mistook the long stove-pipe in the country church for Jacob's ladder, and essayed to climb it. Not until restrained for some minutes by bystanders did he recognize the situation.

Such hallucinations occur still; among the negroes they are almost the rule. Yet these persons are not insane, and resume their ordinary vocations as before.

Spectral illusions are very common in children, and

are most frequently, though not always, perceived in the night between waking and sleeping.

The persistence of dreams after one is fully awake is also a suggestive occasional experience. After the appearance of an article on "Dreams, Nightmare, and Somnambulism," in "The Century," the editor of that magazine received a letter written by a gentleman of the city of New York describing a dream which he had had a few weeks before, in which he dreamed that he was lying on his back in his own room and saw a frightful black hobgoblin, well defined in shape, which stood by the side of his bed and acted as if about to attack him. In the midst of the horror produced by the specter, he awoke, found himself lying on his back just as he had dreamed, looked around the room, and recognized the furniture and other things in the room, but continued to see the hobgoblin as plainly as he saw anything else, heard him growl, and distinctly saw him going on with his hostile demonstrations. Reasoning upon what he should do, he struggled to move, was unable to stir hand or foot for some time, but finally did move, and that instant the uncanny specter vanished. He says: "I had my eyes on the hobgoblin at the moment when I made the movement, and at once tried to see whether there was any object in the room which I could have mistaken for it, but could find none."

Books of marvels contain narratives which sometimes afford the evidence of their explanation, but frequently omit details which a person not disposed to the marvelous would be sure to examine if he had the opportunity. In Stilling's "Pneumatology," translated from the German and edited by Dr. George Bush, there are many of these. Stilling endeavors to show that people who see themselves are generally likely to die soon afterward. He says: "When a person sees himself out of himself, while others who are present observe nothing, the apparition may be real, or it may be merely imaginary; but when it is also perceived by others it is no fantasy, but something real." He then gravely adds, "I myself know of persons having seen themselves and dying shortly afterward."

He tells of one of the Government secretaries who went, as he was wont to do, to the archives to look for a paper which was very important. On arriving there, he saw himself sitting on a chair. Much terrified, he went home and sent a woman servant to fetch the documents. It is asserted that the woman found him there also. Dr. Stilling does not say that this man died "shortly afterward"; but that he did die some time after is probable, as the book is nearly a hundred years old.

Another case is that of a professor who was having a theological dispute with a number of his friends. Having occasion to go to the library for a book, he saw himself sitting on a chair at the table where he usually sat. Going nearer, he looked over the shoulder of the person and saw that this figure of himself pointed with one finger of the right hand to a passage in the Bible. He looked at the passage indicated, and saw that it was, "Set thine house in order, for thou shalt die." Full of astonishment and fear, he went back to the company and related the occurrence; and in spite of all they could say he was firm in the opinion that this apparition betokened his death, and accordingly took leave of his friends. "The day after, at six o'clock in the evening, he expired, *being advanced in years*." Many not advanced in years would be killed by such an experience as this.

The origin of such visions is readily traced. To imagine one's self in a familiar place with almost the vividness of life is not uncommon. Whether the vision shall be that of one's self or of another, when the mind is in such a state as to develop visions, depends much on the general belief at the time. The same principle is illustrated where it seems impossible not to see, in his accustomed seat at the table, a person who has died; and when worn with anxiety and long watching, even strong-minded men have been for a moment almost certain that they saw the familiar figure pass through the room. They have felt "the touch of a vanished hand" and heard "the sound of a voice that is still." Add a belief in the marvelous to such impressions, and the vision is complete.

Sudden flashes of the imagination may develop the phenomenon instantaneously. Thus a sea captain engaged in his duty saw in the mist the figure of a boyhood companion beckoning to him. He was certain that it portended his death or that of the friend whose figure he saw, but nothing came of it. A gentleman passing along the street suddenly saw his brother whom he had not seen for twenty-five years. The figure was plain, and he was about to speak to him when he disappeared. Some time afterward the news came of his death at about the time of the vision. Taken alone, it might seem as if there was some connection between the two circumstances; but so many have such occasional experiences which seem remarkably real, and yet are not followed by any noteworthy event, that the natural explanation is adequate to cover the cases.

The visions and hallucinations of hypnotism and animal magnetism require special examination.

HABITUAL VISIONS

HALLUCINATIONS may become frequent, and to a certain extent systematic, especially if a belief in their supernatural origin exists; in which case a person may be for a long period of sound and discriminating understanding, except when in a trance, or beholding a vision.

The visions of St. Theresa have, for three hundred years, formed an important chapter in religious literature, and another in pathology. At twelve she was devoutly pious, becoming so after the death of her mother. About the age of fifteen she fell off into a very worldly state, and against her will was placed by her father in a convent. She was frequently ill, and finally, after a year and a half, owing to a dangerous sickness, returned home. Some time afterward she was seized with a violent fever, and upon recovery determined to devote herself to a religious life, and in opposition to her father's wishes entered a Carmelite convent and took the veil. This was in her twentieth year. Her biographer, as translated by Dr. Madden, says that she was attacked "with frequent fits of fainting and swooning, and a violent pain at her heart, which sometimes deprived her of her senses." Her first trance was in 1537, in her twenty-third year; it lasted for four days, and during it through excess of pain she bit her tongue in many places—a phenomenon common to fits of various kinds. At last she was reduced almost to a skeleton, had a paralytic affection of her limbs, and remained a cripple for three years. Her first vision was three years later, when she had allowed herself some dissipation of mind. "The apparition of our Lord was suddenly presented to the eyes of her soul, with a rigorous aspect testifying to the displeasure occasioned by her conduct."

There were great differences of opinion as to the source of her visions. Several very learned priests and confessors judged her to be deluded by the devil. One of them instructed her to make the sign of the cross, and to insult the vision as that of a fiend. In one of her visions, according to her statement, the Lord appeared angry at her instructions, and bade her tell them it was tyranny. She acknowledged that she frequently saw devils in hideous figures, but she drove them away by the cross or by holy water. She also claimed to see St. Joseph, the blessed Virgin, and other saints; had visions of purgatory, and saw a great number of souls in heaven who had been there.

There is no difficulty in explaining her visions on natural principles. She was a religious woman, in such a state of health as to be subject to trances, and they took their character from her conventual and other religious instruction. Visions of this kind have been common in the excitable of all sects. The early Methodists had many of them, which Mr. Wesley could not understand; and he expelled some persons from the society because they persisted against his commands in narrating visions which even he could not accept as of divine origin.

Luther suffered from hallucinations of a religious character for a considerable period of his life. The opposition he encountered and his sedentary life, taken in connection with the extraordinary powers attributed to Satan in the middle ages, fully explain his visions. Luther thought that the devil removed a bag of nuts, transformed himself into a fly, hung on his neck, and lay with him in bed. His visions would sometimes come on after nightmare. Here is his own account: "I awoke in the middle of the night. Satan appeared to me. I was seized with horror. I sweated and trembled. My heart beat in a frightful manner. The devil conversed with me. His logic was accompanied by a voice so alarming that the blood froze in my veins."

Zuinglius had a similar experience when he was half asleep. A phantom, black or white, he could not say which, appeared before him, called him a coward, and stirred him up to fight. This is explained by Forbes Winslow as a case of overheated sensorium, "during the transient continuance of which the retina became so disturbed as to conjure up a phantom which the patient not only mistook for a reality, but, what is still worse, acted upon his mistaken or diseased imagination."

Swedenborg's visions were of the same class. He was educated, devoted himself for many years to science, and up to his fifty-fourth year had the reputation of a scientific and philosophic student; was a professor in the mineralogical school, and believed to be a simple-minded man of the world. About 1743 he had a violent fever, in which for a little time he was mad, and rushed from the house stark naked, proclaiming himself the Messiah. After that period a change took place in him, and he lived twenty-nine years in the firm conviction that he held continual intercourse with angels and also with deceased human beings. He says that he conversed with St. Paul during the whole year, particularly in reference to the text Romans iii. 28. He asserted that he had conversed three times with St. John, once with Moses, a hundred times with Luther, and with angels daily "for twenty years."

Swedenborg had an elevated style of thought, and when reasoning upon the fundamental principle which underlies his theological views, he is acute and profound. Attention has frequently been called to his shrewdness in explaining why, when he claimed to hear the voices of angels, those who stood by could not, by his declaring that he was accustomed to see and hear angels when perfectly wide awake, and adding: "The speech of an angel or of a spirit sounds like and as loud as that of a man, but it is not heard by the bystanders. The reason is that the speech of an angel, or of a spirit, finds entrance first into a man's thoughts, and reaches his organs of hearing from within." It is necessary only to read his literal statements to perceive the subjective character of the visions. He gives detailed accounts of the habits, form, and dress of the angels. He sends his opponents mostly to Gehenna and sees them there. The chief representatives of the reformed churches go to heaven, but Catholics and some of his Protestant opponents he sees in vision elsewhere.

Visions and hallucinations of men of this class are quoted against each other in the ecclesiastical conflicts of the middle ages, and more lately, as proofs of the doctrines held by them. But as proofs they are mutually destructive, exist in all religions, true or false, and are liable to occur apart from religion. In the revivals which occurred in the early part of this century in the United States, and which sometimes take place now, visions are not infrequently connected with religious experience. When men pray without attending to the necessary cares of the body days and weeks together, the result is faintings and trances accompanied by visions. Where they are believed to be of divine origin they produce profound impressions, but there is no reason to think their cause different from those already discussed, nor have unbelievers in Christianity always escaped them.

The autobiography of Lord Herbert of Cherbury relates a remarkable vision, which is a noteworthy illustration of inconsistency. Lord Herbert did not believe in the divine origin of Christianity, and wrote a book against the credibility of the accounts of miracles in the Bible. When the manuscript was completed he exhibited it to Grotius and Tilenus, whom he met in France. They praised it much and exhorted him to publish it; but he foresaw that it would encounter opposition, and hesitated for some time. The history of what followed is given in his own words:

One fine day, about noon, my windows being open, I took my book, knelt down, and pronounced aloud these words: "O eternal God, creator of the light which illuminates me, thou who enlightenest souls when thou wouldst, tell me by a celestial sign if I should publish or suppress my work." I had hardly uttered these words than a loud but agreeable sound proceeded from heaven, which impressed me with such great joy that I felt convinced that my request was granted. Howsoever strange this may appear, I protest, before God, not only that I heard the sound, but saw, in the clearest sky on which I ever gazed, the spot whence it came. In consequence of this sign I published my book, and spread it throughout all Christian lands, amongst all the learned capable of reading and appreciating it.

This circumstance is of great importance. No doubt has ever been thrown upon the truth of the recital, which shows how a person not subject to hallucinations, under circumstances of deep meditation, or under the influence of strong desire and expectation, may generate an hallucination, which may be the only one that he will experience in the course of a lifetime, and leave no evil effects except the false inferences which, supposing it to be of supernatural origin, he will draw from it. It demonstrates also that the absence or the presence of any particular form of faith is not essential; and it is obvious that Lord Herbert might easily have passed into a state of habitual visions in all respects analogous to those of Swedenborg or St. Theresa.

VISIONS OF THE DYING

THE visions which the dying are supposed to see are regarded by many with reverence bordering upon awe. The explanation given by Dr. Edward H. Clarke, a devout physician of Boston, in his "Visions: a Study of False Sight," is strictly physiological. After a long and suggestive philosophical exposition, he says:

Should a bright ray of light falling from some object in the chamber on the retina of a dying person excite the visual apparatus and cells, the hieroglyphic of a departed child, husband, lover, or friend be brought into the field of subjective sight, the beloved one would be reproduced, and at once projected into space. Intense emotion, engendered by such a sight, would for an instant break through the stupefying power of nature's anæsthetic, as the surgeon's knife sometimes momentarily breaks the spell of ether, and the dying individual, springing, with eyes intent, features transfigured, and arms outstretched, toward the vision, would naturally pronounce the long-remembered name, and then fall back and die. Such scenes have occurred. Few could witness them without an overwhelming sense of awe, oppressed "with thoughts beyond the reaches of our souls," at beholding for a moment the apparent lifting of the veil and the glory within. To the dying such a vision would not be false. It would not be imagination. It would be real to him. The well-known features would be there, and yet they would be a creation or reproduction of a dissolving brain, and not a messenger from the opened heavens. The vision would be a physiological effect, not a supernatural intervention.

Dr. Clarke is not willing to say that it is impossible that there should be to the dying a revelation of the future into which they are about to enter. He says:

16

"Probably all such visions as these are automatic. But yet, who, believing in God and personal immortality, as the writer rejoices in doing, will dare to say *absolutely all ?*—will dare to assert there is no *possible* exception?" The single case given by Dr. Clarke appears insufficient to raise a presumption, much less to support a conclusion.

During the past thirty years I have seen many die, and many who thought themselves to be dying who afterward recovered, but I have no ground to suppose any of the visions supernatural, nor have I seen any indication of the development of a faculty of cognizing another world.

Some years ago I was visiting at the house of a citizen of Brooklyn, now one of the editors of a leading scientific publication. The father of his wife was very ill, the disease being consumption complicated with extreme age. It was thought that he could not survive the day. For several days he had been in a state of stupor bordering upon coma, and had not spoken for some hours. During the absence of his daughter from the room I sat by his bedside watching his painful breathing and anticipating the end, which could not be long delayed. Suddenly the dying man opened his eyes and said, "Old Virginia! old Virginia! old Virginia!" I immediately summoned his daughter, but he neither uttered another syllable nor showed any sign of consciousness, and died in a few hours. On asking members of the family if he had been connected in any way with Virginia, they said he had not, but was a native of Kentucky. Three months afterward his son-in-law informed me that inquiry suggested by the circumstance revealed the fact that he was born in Virginia and lived there until he was ten years old. The sufficient explanation was that the vital force was so nearly exhausted as to be incapable of stimulating any of the brain cells, except those early impressed: a vision of the lovely scenes of his childhood rose in his mind, and his intelligence was sufficient only to recognize it as in a dream.

The following facts cannot be disregarded in elucidating the subject:

First. Such visions occur in all parts of the world, under every form of civilization and religion; and when the dying appear to see anything, it is in harmony with the traditions which they have received.

Second. Such visions are often experienced by those whose lives have not been marked by religious consistency, while many of the most devout are permitted to die without such aid, sometimes experiencing the severest mental conflicts as they approach the crisis.

Third. Where persons appear to see angels and disembodied spirits, the visions accord with the traditional views of their shape and expression; and where wicked persons see fiends and evil spirits, they harmonize with the descriptions which have been given in the sermons, poems, and supernatural narratives with which they have been familiar.

Fourth. Many of the most remarkable visions have been seen by persons who supposed themselves to be dying, but were not; and who when they recovered had not the slightest recollection of what had occurred. When a student I was called with others to witness the death-bed scene of the most popular young man in the institution. He had professed during his illness a religious conversion, and was supposed to be dying of typhoid fever. Never have I heard more vivid descriptions or more eloquent words. It seemed as though he must see another state of being. After the scene he sank into a lethargic state, in which he remained for some days, afterward gradually recovering. Both his conversion and visions were utterly forgotten, and not until many years later did he enter upon a religious life.

Fifth. A consideration of great weight is this: the Catholic Church confers great honor upon the Holy Virgin; Protestants seldom make any reference to her. Trained as the former are to supplicate the sympathy and prayers of the mother of our Lord, I am informed by devout priests and by physicians that when they have visions of any kind she generally appears in the foreground. Among the visions which dying Protestants have been supposed to see I have heard of only two in which the Virgin figured, and these were seen by persons trained in their youth as Catholics.

APPARITIONS

THE passage most frequently quoted on the subject of apparitions is that which Dr. Johnson, in "Rasselas," puts into the mouth of the sage Imlac:

That the dead are seen no more I will not undertake to maintain against the concurrent testimony of all ages and all nations. There is no people, rude or unlearned, among whom apparitions of the dead are not related and believed. This opinion, which prevails as far as human nature is diffused, could become universal only by its truth; those that never heard of one another would not have agreed in a tale which nothing but experience could make credible. That it is doubted by single cavilers can very little weaken the general evidence; and some who deny it with their tongues confess it with fears.

All authorities agree that Dr. Johnson was superstitious and credulous, and this passage when critically examined does not seem to be entitled to the weight which its clearness of statement and his great name have gained for it. The concurrent testimony of all ages and nations can hardly create a presumption, unless it be assumed that there have been no universal errors. The assertion that the opinion could become universal only by its truth compels the assumption that all universal opinions are true. To prove that the dead are seen no more, or cannot appear to living beings, is of course impossible. But that a thing cannot be proven impossible is not a reason for believing it actual. No one can demonstrate that the spirit of Mahomet is not now embodied in the present Sultan of Turkey, but no one believes it.

Belief in apparitions, common in all ages, generally dying out in the middle of the last century, was revived in the antagonisms created by the excesses of materialistic and infidel opinions, which denied the truth of the miracles recorded in the Christian Scriptures. John Wesley says, "It is true that the English in general, and indeed most of the men in Europe, have given up all accounts of witches and apparitions as mere old wife's fables." He expresses great sorrow at this, and adds, "If but one account of the intercourse of men with superior spirits be admitted, their whole castle in the air (deism, atheism, materialism) falls to the ground."

The discussion of Mr. Wesley's views of the relation of witchcraft to true Christianity is not in place here. His testimony as to the opinions of men of his time is the best of which the case admits, and the assertion quoted concerning the value of proof of that kind in the then pending conflicts with the free-thinkers justifies the use made of it by Dr. Hibbert in his "Philosophy of Apparitions," published not more than forty years after Wesley's death.

Two subjects which have a bearing upon any theory of apparitions, telepathy and modern spiritualism, are also postponed. Telepathy does not bear directly upon apparitions in the sense of the direct manifestations of the dead only so far as it is connected with alleged perceptions by living persons of others who have just died or are in the very article of death at the time when it is alleged that they are perceived by the said living persons remote from them. At the close of the second part of "A Theory of Apparitions," published by the Society of Psychical Research, the writer says, "Of apparitions after death we say nothing here," and makes use of telepathy merely for the purpose of analogy. Modern spiritualism has so many phases, and its alleged and real phenomena are many of them so dissimilar in matter and manner to the spontaneous apparitions referred to by Lord Byron in

> I merely mean to say what Johnson said,
>   That in the course of some six thousand years,
> All nations have believed that from the dead
>   A visitant at intervals appears,

as to make it necessary to consider it separately.

What I design is to show that when the evidence is rigorously though fairly examined, the Scotch verdict "Not proven" must be rendered concerning the reality of apparitions; and that the presumptions of their natural origin are so strong as to leave little doubt in minds not intoxicated by a love of the marvelous, or who do not desire to find by sensuous evidence an "Elysian road which will conduct man undoubtingly to such beliefs as his heart most craves."

Before the development of the scientific spirit belief in apparitions was universal. Scarce an instance can be given from antiquity of a tale of supernatural events carefully investigated, because to be told of the appearance of a ghost excited no more surprise than to be informed of a storm at sea, or of an extraordinary flash of lightning. In Greece and Rome such narratives furnish the materials of poetry, and for ages after the hold of the marvelous upon ordinary writers was broken the impression of primeval superstitions was so strong that the questions which science now asks—nay, more, the questions which practical men now ask—were not propounded.

To believe merely because antiquity believed is but to tighten the swaddling-clothes of the infant about the grown man and force him once more into the cradle.

The testimony of a single witness to an apparition can be of little value, because whatever he thinks he sees may be a spectral illusion or a hallucination. The state of mind of one who thinks that he sees an apparition is unfavorable to calm observation; and after he has seen it he has nothing but his recollection of what he saw, unsupported by analogies or memoranda taken during the vision. To say that immediately after he witnessed such a thing he made a note of it, is at best to say only that he wrote down what he could remember at that time.

Identification of the dead by a living person must be a matter of great difficulty, particularly as in many of the ghost stories the deceased had not been seen for twenty or twenty-five years, or perhaps was never seen by the individual to whom he is alleged to appear. In view of the mental excitement, not to say trepidation, induced by the belief that he sees a spontaneous and unexpected apparition, one who fancies that he sees the dead can hardly be competent to determine whether it be a subjective vision or an actual object.

It has frequently been laid down as indisputable that if two see a vision at the same time its objective and authentic character is conclusively demonstrated. This by no means follows; on the contrary, a hundred may be confident that they see an apparition, and the proof that they do not may be conclusive. In the middle ages thousands believed in Vampyrism. Less than two hundred years ago in Hungary, Moravia, Silesia, and Lorraine it was prevalent. "Some dreamed that these malicious specters took them by the throat, and, having strangled them, sucked their blood." Others believed that they actually saw them. At times when the imagination is greatly excited, and a belief in ghosts exists, they can be manufactured by the thousand, and thousands can see them. The colored people in the South have no trouble on this point. It is not an unusual occurrence for the ghosts of men hanged to appear to the prisoners in the jail, and though the officers may look at midnight, or whenever the ghost is said to appear, and can perceive nothing, scores of the prisoners are certain that they see the dreadful vision. An instance of this kind within a few years led to the permanent reformation of several persons.

Sailors, naturally superstitious, have great powers as ghost-seers. A vessel that sailed from Newcastle-upon-Tyne had on board a cook one of whose legs was shorter than the other, so that he walked in that way which in the vulgar idiom is called "with an up and a down." He died on the trip and was buried at sea. A few nights afterward the captain was told by the mate that the cook was walking before the ship, and that all hands were on deck to see him. Angry at being awakened, the captain told the mate to let the cook alone and race with him to see whether the ship or he would get first to Newcastle. But being further importuned the captain finally turned out. I will now quote the words of Mr. Ellis (who published them in " Brand's Popular Antiquities ") as they were received from the captain :

He honestly confessed that he had like to have caught the contagion, and on seeing something move in a way so similar to that which an old friend used, and withal having a cap on so like that which he was wont to wear, verily thought there was more in the report than he was at first willing to believe. A general panic diffused itself. He ordered the ship to be steered toward the object, but not a man would move the helm. Compelled to do this himself, he found on a nearer approach that the ridiculous cause of all their terror was part of a maintop, the remains of some wreck, floating before them.

If he had really caught the contagion the evidence would have been complete ; the Society for Psychical Research might make much of it, and it would be declared to be convincing proof of a future state.

Dr. Tuke gives an instance of a general misapprehension of vision. At the conflagration in the Crystal Palace, in the winter of 1866–67, when the animals were destroyed by fire, it was supposed that the chimpanzee had succeeded in escaping from his cage. Men saw the unhappy animal holding to the roof and writhing in agony while trying to grasp one of the iron ribs. They watched its struggles with sickening dread — but there was no animal there. " It was a tattered piece of blind, so torn as to resemble, to the eye of fancy, the body, arms, and legs of an ape ! "

When Brigham Young asserted that he saw the angel of the Lord from Ensign Point, making signs that this was the place where the great city and tabernacle of the Latter Day Saints should be established, Mormons surrounding him thought they beheld the angel, and nothing could shake their conviction of its reality.

Mistakes of identity account for many apparitions. Resemblances between persons in no way related are much more numerous and striking than is generally supposed. Lord Byron, who was superstitious, in speaking of ghosts wrote:

> And what is strangest upon this strange head
> Is that, whatever bar the reason rears
> 'Gainst such belief, there 's something stronger still
> In its behalf, let those deny who will.

Yet he occasionally laughed at apparitions. In 1811, writing to Mr. Murray, he says, "My old school and form fellow Peel, the Irish Secretary, told me he saw me in St. James street; I was then in Turkey. A day or two afterward looking across the way, he said to his brother, 'There is the man I took for Byron.' His brother answered, 'Why, it is Byron, and no one else.' I was at this time *seen* to write my name in the Palace book. I was then ill of a malaria fever. If I had died, here would have been a ghost story." According to the telepathic theory, Byron's self might have left his body in Turkey, where he was sick, and made an excursion to London. It would be interesting to have an account of the state of his body on that day; whether much agitated, or enjoying a calm and refreshing sleep in the absence of the perturbed spirit of the poet, who must have been an uneasy tenant at the best of times. But these details were omitted, and the natural explanation would be "mistaken identity."

A whole city was excited by the appearance of a person known to be dead — a silent man, who entered a hotel, registered his name, and looked wistfully about, speaking to no one, and not willing to explain his business. Terror seized upon the people. Every one who looked at him affirmed that he was the dead man. He was compelled after a few days to account for himself, and had no difficulty in proving, not only that he was a living man, but that he had never seen the man whom he so strongly resembled. A remarkable fact about this case was, that both the dead man and his double had three moles on the left cheek.

Jugglery and intentional deception, subsequently confessed, have explained many cases of apparition which within a short period previous to the exposure had been generally believed real in the communities where they were reported. One of the most common sources of supposed supernatural interference with ordinary laws is unexplained noises, especially those that appear to respond to questions. Many of these have been afterward explained by chemical conditions; others by the wind shrieking through bottles, down chimneys, and occasionally by pendulum motions caused by gravitation, shakings, or motions by the movements of distant bodies; one famous case by changes that had taken place, the result of mining operations beneath the ground upon which the house stood. The ringing of bells when it was obvious no one was pulling the wires — occasionally the result of electricity, at other times of the actions of cats—has terrified some ordinarily intelligent persons almost out of their senses. Disturbances produced by dogs, cats, and even rats, magnified by large rooms, immense fire-places, the transformation of innocent objects on nights when the moon is at the full, and deep shadows produced by movements of the limbs of trees reflected in mirrors, have all contributed to the production of awful impressions.

In a certain rectory within forty miles of the city of New York stood an old-fashioned candlestick surrounded by prisms of glass which were pendent from the top. On several occasions the family were awakened by the ringing of these in the night, the effect of which was to terrify the servants and all the inmates of the house, except the wife of the rector, who determined to solve the mystery. For a long time the sounds were not produced except in total darkness, but by gradually introducing the practice of burning a light at night the ringing was finally heard one night when there was a light in the room. The lady of the house then went quietly down to the dining-room and saw a large rat with every expression of pleasure leaping forward and with his fore legs striking the prisms so as to make them ring, evidently taking the keenest delight in the sound thus produced. My informants were the rector and his wife.

In an article on Apparitions written by Andrew Lang, in the second volume of the "Encyclopædia Britannica," ninth edition, he says:

> The writer once met, as he believed, a well-known and learned member of an English university who was really dying at a place more than a hundred miles distant from that in which he was seen. Supposing, for the sake of argument, that the writer did not mistake some other individual for the extremely noticeable person whom he seemed to see, the coincidence between the subjective impression and the death of the learned professor is, to say the least, curious.

To determine whether or not it was a case of mistaken identity is very important, but no opportunity is given in the passage quoted. If it was a subjective impression, the coincidence would be curious and nothing else; though not more so, as I have shown abundantly, than many coincidences in trifles, and other circumstances absolutely disconnected, and many subjective impressions without coincidences. Mr. Lang, in the article referred to, has written like one who has crammed with the literature of the subject without being at the pains to reason closely upon the alleged facts. He refers to the superstitious horror shown by a dog at the moment of a supposed apparition to his master. That the dog exhibited horror when his owner thought he saw an apparition may be readily believed. All familiar with dogs know that nothing will terrify them more than an appearance of alarm on the part of their masters without visible cause. Of the same nature is the remark concerning the mysterious disturbances at the house of the Wesleys: "The mastiff was more afraid than any of the children." The volatile imaginations of children have never shown great horror of mysteries; they were sustained, too, by confidence in their parents. But the dog heard mysterious noises which naturally greatly agitated him.

Mr. Lang closes his remarks on this part of the subject by naïvely saying, "The case of Balaam's ass is sufficiently well known." This is not pertinent. Balaam's ass, according to the record, not only saw a supernatural appearance, but engaged in a process of reasoning in which he called up his past life to vindicate himself from abuse, and further engaged in a conversation with his master in the latter's vernacular. Indeed, he exhibited a cogency of reasoning which, applied to most of the tales adduced to prove the reality of apparitions, would effectually "lay" the ghosts.

Many persons fancy that mysterious noises which will appear to respond to questions, to make raps or answer raps, conclusively prove that they are directed by intelligence. Sometimes they may, and the intelligence is quite likely to be of human origin; but noises of atmospheric, chemical, or electrical origin may furnish astonishing coincidences, as fissures in the rocks are extremely difficult to be distinguished from hieroglyphics. Some years ago an alphabet based on the spiritualistic alphabet was applied to

17

successive gusts of wind of a stormy autumn day, and the coincidences were astonishing. Short sentences of a very significant character at times appeared to respond to the arbitrary standard. In any case the conclusion that a noise the cause of which is not yet understood must be supernatural is a process of reasoning *ab ignorantia*.

That ghosts do not come to those most interested in them, and seldom or never to any who long for them, has been a matter of note from the earliest times. Wordsworth's words, often quoted, state the conclusion drawn from this in language natural and almost convincing:

> 'T is falsely said
> That there was ever intercourse
>   Betwixt the living and the dead,
> For surely then I should have sight
> Of him I wait for day and night
>   With love and longings infinite.

The ceremonies practised by the Christian Church in the middle ages in the successful exorcising of ghosts are not less striking than the sort of evidence on which the ghosts were accepted. Two or three clergymen are necessary and the ceremony must be performed in Latin, "the language which strikes the most audacious ghost with terror." According to history and tradition the ghost may be laid for any term less than a hundred years, "in any place or body, filled or empty." But what a ghost hates most is the Red Sea. It is related on the most indisputable authority that the ghosts have earnestly besought exorcists not to confine them in that place; nor is any instance given of their escaping before the time!

When we consider the injustice frequently inflicted upon orphans whose estates are squandered by trustees; the concealment or destruction of wills; the ingratitude to destitute benefactors; the diverting of trust funds for benevolent purposes to objects abhorrent to those who with painful toil accumulated them and with confidence in the stability of human laws bequeathed them; the loneliness and despair that fill human hearts; and the gloomy doubts of the reality of a future existence,— all of which would be rendered impossible if actual apparitions took place,— the conclusion gathers almost irresistible force that neither in the manner of the alleged comings nor in the objects for which they come is there any evidence to be found of their reality.

If it be assumed that the testimony of one or of one hundred to a supernatural event is not sufficient to prove that it occurred, the question, "What becomes of the testimony of the Apostles and the five hundred brethren to the resurrection of Christ, and of Stephen to his seeing the heavens open," arises again. It admits of but one answer. If they had nothing to communicate but the assertion that they saw a human being alive who had been dead, it would be necessary to reject it on the ground that it is far more probable that they were deceived than that such a thing occurred.

But this is not the whole case. They present to us the whole body of Christian doctrine, declaring that it was received from that person who predicted that he would rise from the dead, whom they believed they saw, and with whom on various occasions they conversed after his resurrection. If Christianity in its relation to, and effect upon, the moral nature of the thinker does not convince him of the divine origin and consequent truth of the record, I know of no means of doing so.

WITCHCRAFT

The art is old and new, for verily
All ages have been taught the matter.
GOETHE.

ADDISON says that among all the poets who deal
with fairies, witches, magicians, demons, and
departed spirits, the English are much the best, "and
among the English Shakspere has incomparably ex-
celled all others. There is something so wild and yet
so solemn in his speeches of his ghosts, fairies, witches,
and the like imaginary persons, that we cannot for-
bear thinking them natural, . . . and must confess, if there are such beings in the world, it looks
highly probable that they would talk and act as he
has represented them."

As Addison saw his fatal day thirty years before
Goethe's natal star arose, he could not compare the
prince of German poets with others; but if the ruling
sentiment of modern critics may be accepted, Shakspere's ghosts and witches still maintain their superiority. These are "the secret, black, and midnight
hags" that brewed the charm for Duncan's murder,
and the familiar but ever awe-inspiring ghost of
Hamlet's father:

I am thy father's spirit,
Doomed for a certain time to walk the night.

But the fancies of poets can give no help to him
who deals with one of the darkest tragedies of

humanity, the only stain on the ermine of Sir Matthew Hale,—whose fame without it would rival that of Daniel for wisdom, as it does for integrity,—and the chief stigma upon the early history of New England. Nor is witchcraft of the past only: for by many theologians it is believed to reappear in modern spiritualism, and by a multitude of Christians to be a reality, because, as they suppose, it is plainly asserted in the sacred Scriptures; and its baleful spell still holds four fifths of the fifteen hundred millions of the human race "fast in its slavish chains."

DEFINITION OF WITCHCRAFT

FROM the earliest ages religions, true and false, claimed divine aid, and their production of effects by other than natural causes was considered by all except avowed unbelievers to be lawful. The supernatural is occult; but the latter word is used only to apply to the illegitimate, and to the imaginary sciences of the middle ages. As the terms at first employed were descriptive, rather than definitive, they came naturally to be used promiscuously, one word sometimes standing for everything preternatural exclusive of religion, and at others for a single form of such action. In an English book dating from the middle of the sixteenth century most of these ancient terms are included in a single sentence: "Besides the art magyck, sortilege, physnomye, palmestrye, alcumye, necromancye, chiromancy, geomancy, and witchery, that was taught there also." (Bale, "English Votaries.")

Magic, applied by the Greeks to the hereditary caste of priests in Persia, still stands in the East for an incongruous collection of superstitious beliefs and rites, having nothing in common except the claim of abnormal origin and effects. Astrology, divination, demonology, soothsaying, sorcery, witchcraft, necromancy, enchantment, and many other systems are sometimes included in magic, but each term is also employed separately to stand for the whole mass of confused beliefs which, outside of the sphere of recognized religion, attempt to surpass the limitations of nature. For this reason the title of a work on this subject seldom indicates its scope.

But witchcraft has been restricted by usage and civil and ecclesiastical law until it signifies a voluntary compact between the devil, the party of the first part, and a human being, male or female, wizard or witch, the party of the second part,— that he, the devil, will perform whatever the person may request. The essential element in witchcraft as an offense against religion and civil law is the voluntary nature of the compact. Possession by the devil against the will, or without the consent of the subject, belongs to a radically distinct idea. The sixth chapter of Lord Coke's "Third Institute" concisely defines a witch in these words: "A witch is a person which hath conference with the *devil*, to consult with him to do some act." English laws in 1665 define witchcraft as "Covenant with a familiar spirit, to be punished with death."

CURRENT BELIEF

WITCHCRAFT is at the present time believed in by a majority of the citizens of the United States. The larger number of immigrants from the continent of Europe are more or less in fear of such powers. To these must be added no inconsiderable proportion of persons of English and Scotch descent; for a strong vein of superstition is discernible in many Irish, Scotch, and some English, whose "folk-lore," diffused in nursery tales and neighborhood gossip, has entwined itself strongly about the fibers of spontaneous, subconscious mental imagery. Among the more ignorant members of the Catholic Church of every nationality the belief produces a mysterious dread, against which men and women cross themselves, and resort to various rites supposed to be efficacious.

Where colonies of immigrants have remained isolated, retaining the use of their own language, the influence of witchcraft is more easily traced. The interior of Pennsylvania affords better illustrations of this, and on a larger scale, than any other State. It has been but two or three years since suit was brought by a man against his mother, in one of the counties of Pennsylvania, to recover damages for a dog which he charged her with having killed by witchcraft; and he not only brought suit, but obtained judgment from a justice of the peace. Various witnesses testified as to their experiences in witchcraft, and only one said that he had never had a friend or relative who was bewitched.

In divers villages in Pennsylvania are women who are supposed to be witches. Some are shrewd enough not to apply their arts for strangers, but to those whom they know, as stated in an article in the New York "Sun" some years ago, they will sell charms to ward off lightning from buildings, dry up the wells of the enemies of applicants, force cows to give bloody milk, cause sickness in the family, destroy beauty, separate man and wife, and reunite estranged lovers.

In the interior parts of the Southern States, where a large proportion of the white population cannot read, and there is little admixture of society, there are "witch-doctors," who, assuming that all disease is caused by witches, secure thriving practice in counteracting their influence. The Philadelphia "Times," on the authority of a reputable correspondent, who gives many facts to sustain his representations, says: "For generations the poor whites have believed in witches, and the belief is deep-seated and incurable."

The African population brought this belief from the Dark Continent, and it persists among them, though the progress of religion and education is doing something to check it.

I have recently noted more than fifty suits instituted in the United States by persons against those who they claimed had bewitched them; but under existing laws the accused could not be prosecuted except where money had been obtained under false pretenses, or overt acts of crime suggested or committed.

During pedestrian tours in New England, in various parts of the West, and in every Southern State, I have frequently stayed for the night at the houses of poor farmers, laborers, fishermen, and trappers. In such journeys I have invariably listened to the tales of the neighborhood, stimulating them by suggestion, and have found the belief in witchcraft cropping out in the oldest towns in New England, sometimes within the very shadow of the buildings where a learned ministry has existed from the settlement of the country, and public schools have furnished means of education to all classes. The horseshoes seen in nearly every county, and often in every township, upon the houses, suggested the old horseshoe beneath which Lord Nelson, who had long kept it nailed to the mast of the *Victory*, received his death-wound at Trafalgar.

In Canada the belief is more prevalent than in any part of the United States, except the interior of Pennsylvania and the South. In the French sections, exclusive of the educated,—a relatively small number,—

the belief, if not universal, is widely diffused. But it is by no means confined to Canadians of French extraction. Until within a few years the descendants of the English and Scotch in many parts of British America were more widely separated from each other and from the progress of modern civilization than the inhabitants of the United States, or the settlers of Australia, excepting certain sections of New Zealand and Tasmania. In all these regions the educated generally dismiss it as a mystery, or repudiate it as an ancient superstition. Nevertheless it is often found in the more secluded communities, hamlets, and rural districts, liable on slight provocation to manifest itself in credulous fears, insinuations, and accusations.

In the West Indies this belief prevails among the negroes, and is not unknown among the more ignorant whites. Of South America and Mexico travelers, missionaries, and foreign residents bring similar accounts.

In Italy those of the people who are not Protestants or free-thinkers generally believe in the possibility of witchcraft, and to the peasants it is a living reality. Nor are all who reject the Catholic Church or avow irreligion free from credulity as regards occult influences. Modern Greece, Bulgaria, Servia, and the neighboring States abound in similar superstitions. The common people of Hungary and Bohemia fear witchcraft, and it still dominates a considerable part of the rural population and the allied classes of Germany, and particularly of Austria.

French peasants are afraid of evil eyes, warlocks, ghosts, spells, omens, enchantments, and witches; not in every part of the country, but in the more primitive sections. In France their persistence is promoted by dialects, kinship, and various influences peculiar to the country. It has been but a few years since the world was shocked by the burning of an old woman as a witch in the district of Sologne, cupidity and fanaticism leading to the crime. Having softening of the brain, she did and said strange things, from which her children concluded that she was a witch and determined to burn her to death. When the time decided upon arrived, they sent for a priest, who confessed her. Soon after his departure her daughter screamed, "It is greatly borne upon me that now is the time to kill the hag; if we delay she may commit a sin in thought or deed, and the confession will go for nothing." As she burned, two of her children cried, "Aroint thee, witch!" I do not refer to this to intimate that the French people sympathize with such things, for France was filled with horror, and the murderers were brought to justice, but as an illustration of the persistence of the belief.

In Norway, Sweden, and Denmark witchcraft yet throws a spell over many of the sailors, fishermen, and solitary farmers. In Lapland sorcerers and witches abound, the latter claiming the power of stilling winds and causing rain to cease. It has been a comparatively short time since English seamen trading in Archangel were in the habit of landing and buying a fair wind from the witches.

But it is in Russia that the popular belief more generally resembles that of the whole world many centuries ago. Ralston, in "Songs of the Russian People," states: "But a little time ago every Russian village had its wizard, almost as a matter of course, and to this day it is said there is not a hamlet in the Ukraine that is not reported to keep its witch." When traveling in the interior of that country, accompanied by a master of the Russian language, I found that the peasants still believe that witches and wizards can steal the dew and the rain, send whirlwinds, hide the moon and the stars, and fly through the air on brooms and tongs. Their chief meetings take place three times a year, on "bald hills," and there are thousands of stories of witches going up chimneys and flying through the air; an analogy exists between these and ancient German legends on the same subject. They chalk crosses on their huts and windows, hang up stove-rakes for protection, tie knots, and wear amulets. Plagues in men and cattle are popularly attributed to witches. Epileptics, and those afflicted with St. Vitus's dance, are supposed to be bewitched. According to popular belief in Russia, witches assume the form of dogs, cats, and owls; but the shape they like best is that of a magpie. The Metropolitan Alexis solemnly cursed that bird, "on account of the bad behavior of the witches who have assumed its plumage."

In Scotland, Ireland, and England belief in witchcraft lingers, and only those who are at the pains to inquire how far it extends, and how strong the impression is, can form an adequate idea of either.

LOOKING BACKWARD

It is important to notice how late in the Christian era individual belief, popular excitements, and judicial proceedings have been sufficiently conspicuous for permanent record.

In "Reports of Trials for Murder by Poisoning," by Browne, a barrister at law, and Stewart, senior assistant in the laboratory of St. Thomas's Hospital, a standard work for physicians, chemists, and jurists, published in London in 1883, I find the case of Dove; and in the said trial various references were made to the prevalence of the belief in witchcraft among persons of the prisoner's class. It appears from the evidence that his interviews with the witch-man on the subjects of lost cattle, removing strange noises from his house, the bewitching of his live stock, and the deaths of persons inimical to him, and the promise of the witch-man to get him out of all difficulty, which led to the murder, were in the summer and autumn of 1855 and the spring of 1856.

In 1846 in England, and in 1845 in Scotland, cases of witchcraft attracted much attention.

The following series of incidents occurred in England about fifty years ago, and the son of the subject, now one of the most highly respected and well-informed clergymen west of the Alleghany Mountains, noted for his devotion to the physical sciences, writes me concerning it:

My father, like many others, fully believed in witchcraft. In a little ancient cottage about a mile from my father's lived an old woman who had the reputation of being a witch. One spring, as my father was planting potatoes in his field, the old lady came to him to beg a piece for a garden. This he said he could not grant, as he needed all for himself. She left the field muttering something, which I suppose my father understood to mean mischief. That evening, when still in the field, he was seized with a strange nervous sensation, and an utter inability to speak. Later in the evening he had a severe fit. This state of things continued for some years. Mother always sent one of the boys with him to render help or report his condition. Another phase of the witchcraft superstition was a belief in white witches, or those who could neutralize or destroy the work and influence of witches. My father heard of one living many miles away, and at once went to see him. I shall ever remember the interest with which we listened to his story. He said the white witch told him that he had been bewitched, as he supposed, by the old woman, but that her influence could be entirely destroyed. He then gave my father a little piece of paper upon which was written a charm which would in all future time protect him from all influence of witches. This paper must be worn over the breast, suspended by a piece of tape from the neck. It must never be opened, never touch wood, stone, or iron, nor be handled by any one but himself. Said my father in concluding his story: "The white witch told me to always wear this over my breast, and that inside of three days I shall have one fit more, but after that I will never have another symptom of the kind." The following evening when at supper he had another severe attack of his old trouble, but sure enough it was the last. He lived more than twenty years after that, but never had another symptom of fits, or nervous difficulty of any kind. He was absolutely cured, as I know.

In March, 1831, the case of an old woman in Edinburgh came before the court on account of her being attacked.

In 1827 a man was burned as a wizard in south-western Russia; and in 1815 a person in northern Russia was sentenced by a legal tribunal to undergo thirty-five blows of the knout, as well as a public church penance, for witchcraft.

In 1815 Captain Samuel Wardwell of Maine, captain of the schooner *Polly,* desiring to excel all his competitors in the number of trips made between Boston and Penobscot in one season, hired Mrs. Leach, a reputed witch, for a bushel of meal a trip, to guarantee him fair winds.

"Moll Pitcher," so famous that for more than fifty years "to her came the rich and the poor, the wise and the ignorant, the accomplished and the vulgar, the brave and the timid," died April 9, 1813, in Lynn, Massachusetts, aged seventy-five years.

Contemporary with her was a woman in Newburyport, who came from Scotland in 1759 or 1760. Her career for many years was such as to command the respect and fear of the people. Mr. Samuel L. Knapp, who wrote in 1825, speaks of another supposed witch in Massachusetts named Danforth, who lived in a gloomy, hollow glen. On this Mr. Samuel G. Drake, writing in 1869, says:

The writer is not as old as he from whom the above extracts are made; but it was his fortune in youth to be acquainted in many towns, in nearly all of which there was a reputed witch.

18

In 1751, in Hertfordshire, two harmless people were mobbed, the woman beaten to death, the man nearly so. A similar incident happened as late as 1776 in Leicestershire. In Burlington, New Jersey, in January, 1731, a man and woman suspected of bewitching cattle were tried in the presence of the governor, by being weighed against a large Bible.

In 1728 Rhode Island reënacted its laws against witchcraft, which implies some agitation upon the subject; in 1720 there was a case in Littleton; prosecutions occurred in South Carolina in 1712; in 1706 there were disgraceful scenes, persons being subjected to ordeals and various barbarous tests; and in the year 1700 an execution for witchcraft took place in Albany, New York.

In noting these events we have reached the period of the dreadful outbreak in New England, separated by only a few years from a yet more dreadful frenzy of human nature in England, Scotland, and on the continent of Europe.

REVERSING THE POINT OF VIEW

WHENCE came witchcraft? Writings, pictures, monuments, ruins, and traditions preserve the history of mankind; but man himself, in color, configuration, unconscious gesture, language, rites, customs, and unwritten laws, is a true encyclopedia of humanity more valuable than the contents of libraries.

As a general proposition, the uncivilized tribes of the world may be said to have been, from prehistoric times, what they are now. Mounds and other remains of uncertain date indeed often show a higher degree of development than at present exists among the in-

habitants of particular regions; but this is not conclusive proof of degeneration, because of the vastness
and complexity of ancient migrations of which no
adequate history remains. The state of primitive uncivilized mankind, when widely scattered and numerous in population, may therefore be inferred from the
present condition of barbarous tribes. In all these
witchcraft is believed in, producing a mortal dread,
and its practice is punished by death in the most
horrible forms. In China, India, and Japan it has
always existed and still prevails.

In the ancient empires, the Magism of the Median
court, with its incantations, divining-rods, omen-read-
ing, and dream-expounding, became closely allied to
witchcraft, as in Scythia in previous ages, and subsequently in Persia. Many of its practitioners openly
avowed the aid of evil spirits. While both Magism
and Zoroastrianism had an essentially religious basis,
witchcraft hung upon their skirts continually endeavoring to rival them. In Babylon the Magi included
the scientists and philosophers of the age; but as
quacks are parasites upon modern scientists, deriv-
ing from general names, such as "physician" or "professor," held in common with those entitled to them a
particular reputation with the common people while
practising the most shameless impostures, so many
of the Babylonian astronomers were astrologers, and
others of the Magi dealt avowedly with spirits.

In Egypt, notwithstanding the sublimity of the religion which taught a system of morality founded upon a final judgment, a swarm of basest superstitions
and most demoralizing influences counteracted its influence; and witchcraft prevailed among the people
at the very time that Egypt was surpassing other
nations in science. In Benjamin's sack was found
Joseph's cup, "whereby, indeed, he divineth"; and

his own words, " Wot ye not that such a man as I can certainly divine ? " reveal the custom in Egypt.

The various forms of consulting evil spirits, of seeking illegitimately preternatural help and knowledge, were all practised by the Canaanites and their descendants the Phenicians. Isaiah traces the existence of such things back to the Chaldeans and the Babylonians.

The answer of the Chaldeans to Nebuchadnezzar showed that throughout the world such a class existed; for they said, " There is not a man upon the earth that can show the king's matter; therefore there is no king, lord, nor ruler that asked such things at any magician, or astrologer, or Chaldean."

THE ISRAELITES AND WITCHCRAFT

THE Israelites came from a people surrounded by idolatry, and addicted to sorcery. They appear to have believed for a long time in the reality of the gods of the heathen, considering them inferior, however, to the God of Abraham, Isaac, and Jacob, and were continually lapsing from the true faith into paganism and sorcery. During the hundreds of years that Jacob's descendants were in Egypt their faith was greatly corrupted; when Moses tarried long in the Mount, they compelled Aaron to make a golden image to represent God. Surrounded by the Egyptians, and in the midst of the Canaanites, who were not wholly driven out for centuries, their kings and many of their people frequently relapsed into witchcraft and idolatry.

Solomon, according to all the traditions of antiquity, as well as the testimony of the Bible, turned both to idolatry and magic. In D'Israeli's " Curiosities of

Literature" (Rabbinical Stories) it is said, "He is a favorite hero of the Talmudists, and the Arabs also speak of him as a magician." The son of the godly Hezekiah, Manasseh, "practised augury, and used enchantments, and practised sorcery, and dealt with them that had familiar spirits, and with wizards." There never was a time in the history of Israel that among its people were not those who practised every form of divination, astrology, magic, and witchcraft.

WITCHCRAFT AND CHRISTIANITY

CHRISTIANITY originated among the Hebrews, who were firm believers in the reality of witchcraft. It was immediately brought into contact with the Romans, of whose empire Syria was a province; and with the Greeks, among whom it spread during the apostolic age. Among the Greeks and Romans the same general belief, with the corresponding practices, existed. Homer is said to have derived many of his verses from Daphne, the daughter of Tyreseis the Soothsayer, who was considered to surpass all women in the art of divination. Scot, in his "Discoverie of Witchcraft," gives extended extracts, among others the passage in Ovid:

> Witches can bleed our ground by magic spell,
> And with enchantment dry the springing soil;
> Make grapes and currants fly at their command,
> And strip our orchards bare without a hand.

Virgil and Horace make similar references. Lecky affirms that "Sorcery could say with truth that there was not a single nation of antiquity, from the polished Greek to the rudest savage, which did not admit a real art enabling men to foretell the future."

In Asia Minor and adjacent Oriental countries Christianity was saturated with superstitions of every kind, the entire mass directly or indirectly affecting Christians of every nation. The New Testament shows that Christianity did not at once eradicate preëxisting superstitions. It required a renunciation of the worship of idols, faith in God as superior to all antagonistic forces, natural and supernatural, and obedience to the precepts of Christ and his Apostles; but there is no reason to believe that it distinguished concerning the natural or supernatural origin of many superstitious beliefs not essentially incompatible with submission to the Gospel. The credulity of the early Christians is apparent in the writings of most of the ante-Nicene fathers. They believed in the supernatural origin of many of the alleged pagan miracles, some of them in the fable of the phenix, and were prepared to accept any tale of strange things which could be attributed to the devil or his agents. Extraordinary knowledge, devotion to philosophy, and the practice of arts not understood by the people, especially by persons suspected of heresy, were made the foundation of social persecutions and legal prosecutions for witchcraft.

Roger Bacon, in the thirteenth century, on account of his scientific attainments, was charged with witchcraft, denounced by the Pope, and several times imprisoned. From time to time trials for witchcraft are recorded in Roman history. In the fourth century ecclesiastical decrees against it were made, and at various periods trials took place under them. Europe was permeated with the superstition.

Early Christian laws partook largely of the nature and of the spirit of the enactments of the same races when in paganism. The Ostrogoths punished it with death; the Visigoths with stripes, shaving the head, and exposure. The pagan Saxons burned witches and sorcerers, and even ate them. The Anglo-Saxons placed them under penalty of death; the ancient law of Scotland burned them at the stake. In Hungary they were first handed over to the bishop, then branded on the forehead, neck, and back in the form of a cross.

The accusation of witchcraft was frequently used against societies, such as the Templars, from 1307 to 1313. It was on this charge that Joan of Arc was burned to death. Thus in 1429 the Stedinger, who had fought for nearly thirty years against the Archbishop of Bremen and the Count of Oldenburg, were, with the help of the Pope, suppressed.

In 1488 Pope Innocent VIII. issued a bull establishing commissions of inquisitors, and succeeding popes appointed other commissions. Sometimes the suspects were accused of heresy aggravated by witchcraft, and again of witchcraft leading to heresy. But witchcraft was the charge that especially inflamed the populace, and was pursued with the greatest zeal by the inquisitors. The epidemic raged in France so that by the end of 1320 fires for the execution of witches blazed in nearly every town. The more fires the more witches, accusations, and trials: the priests began to despair, wondering how it could be explained that it was impossible to commit "so great a number of the Devil's slaves to the flames, but that there shall arise from their ashes a sufficient number to supply their places." Seldom were there acquittals.

Luther and the reformers believed as firmly in the existence of witchcraft as the Roman Catholics, though the latter charged that the Hussites in Bohemia, and the followers of Luther, deceived the people by magic and witchcraft. A Jesuit theological professor declared that Albert of Brandenburg was the king of wizards, a famous magician who laid waste the country with fire and sword. The same Jesuit affirmed that wherever the heresy of Calvin went in England, Wales, or Ireland, the "black and diabolical arts of necromancy kept pace with it." Charlton T. Lewis, LL. D., in his history of Germany, says, "Protestants and Catholics alike carried on their judicial barbarities, which desolated whole tracts of country. Neither age, sex, nor rank was a protection against this persecution. Counselors and scholars were sent to the stake, though women were the especial objects of vengeance; and the trials did not end until the reign of Frederick the Great."

In England laws, both ecclesiastical and civil, were enacted against witchcraft. Various changes were made in the phraseology of the law down to the time of Elizabeth, when sorceries, enchantments, charms, and witchcraft were made punishable with death when death ensued from their practice; in other cases, for a first offense, a year's imprisonment, and for a second, death. James I. was not satisfied with any previous act, as he was "an expert and specialist in the matter." In his time a law was passed making various distinctions. In Scotland similar acts were passed, the chief of them dating from 1563. In Ireland trials took place as early as 1324 in ecclesiastical courts.

THE PROBLEM

THE history of witchcraft exhibits features common to all forms of mental and moral contagion, and its characteristics are similar everywhere; so that the study of its phenomena in New England, where the information is full, the date recent, and the habits, language, religion, and institutions analogous to those of all English-speaking races, will have special advantages.

The first settlers of New England brought across the Atlantic the sentiments which had been formed in their minds in Great Britain and on the Continent, as well as the tendencies which were the common heritage of such an ancestry. They were a very religious and also credulous people; having few books, no papers, little news, and virtually no science; removed by thousands of miles and months of time from Old World civilization; living in the midst of an untamed wilderness, contending against a climate unlike anything they had experienced, surrounded by Indians whom they believed to be under the control of the devil, and whose medicine-men and soothsayers they accounted wizards. Such mental and moral soil was adapted to the growth of witchcraft, and to create an invincible determination to inflict the punishments pronounced against it in the Old Testament; but the coöperation of various exciting causes was necessary to a general agitation and a real epidemic.

Samuel G. Drake's "Annals of Witchcraft in New England and Elsewhere in the United States, from their first Settlement," which is here epitomized, enables us to trace the sporadic manifestations of witchcraft step by step to the fearful explosion of 1692. The Pilgrims landed in Plymouth in 1620. In 1636 they included in the summary of offenses "lyable to death," "the solemn compaction or conversing with the Divell by the way of Witchcraft, conjuration, or the like." The colony of Massachusetts adopted the Body of Liberties, which contains a similar clause. In 1642 Connecticut included this in its Capital Code: "Yf any Man or Woman be a witch, that is, hath or conforteth with a Familiar Spirit, they fhall be put to death."

It is believed that the first actual trouble from witchcraft occurred in New Haven, and the first execution was in 1646 in Hartford. In 1647 Rhode Island made the penalty "Felone of Death."

The first execution for witchcraft in the colony of Massachusetts Bay was that of Mrs. Jones in Boston in 1648. Another woman was executed in Hartford in 1648.

From the settlement of Springfield in 1636 there was more or less trouble about witchcraft.

Mrs. Knapp suffered death in the New Haven colony in 1653. The troubles continued through 1654 and 1655. In 1656 Mrs. Ann Hibbens was executed in Boston. In the same year there was a trial at Portsmouth, but no conviction. In East Hampton, Long Island, in 1657, Mrs. Garlicke was tried for witchcraft.

There were troubles in 1659 at Saybrook, Connecticut, and Andover, Massachusetts. In 1660 at Scituate, Plymouth, and at Oyster Bay, Long Island, there were disturbances, but no convictions. In 1662 Mr. and Mrs. Green Smith were executed at Hartford, and in 1665 the Court of Sessions in the State of New York tried Ralph Hall and his wife Mary. They were finally acquitted after three years' imprisonment. In 1669 Susannah Martin was prosecuted. She was one of those afterward executed at Salem. Catharine Harrison of Wethersfield was convicted, but the special court reversed the decision.

Mrs. Mary Parsons, of the highest social standing in Northampton, was charged with witchcraft in 1674, kept in prison several months, and acquitted. At that time three of the most enlightened men of the age, Governor Leverett and Generals Gookin and Dennison, had charge of the administration.

In 1675 a queerly worded law was enacted to regulate the Pequot Indians: "Whofoever fhall Powau or vfe Witchcraft, or any Worfhip of the Devill, or any fals Gods, fhall be convented punifhed."

In 1681 and 1682 in Massachusetts there was much excitement, and cases arose in 1683 which show a descent to the lowest depths of barbaric superstition. In 1684 Margaret Matson was tried in Delaware County, Pennsylvania, before William Penn. Philadelphia was then only three years old. The court brought in the verdict that she was "guilty of having the common fame of a witch, but not guilty in manner and form as she stands indicted." Tradition says that Penn said to her, "Art thou a witch?" and "Hast thou ridden through the air on a broomstick?" When she answered yes, he said that she had a right to ride on a broomstick, that he knew no law against it, and thereupon ordered her discharge.

In 1685 Mary Webster, who had been acquitted in Boston in 1683, was accused of killing William Smith by sorcery. She was acquitted, but harassed by the people and often mobbed until her death in 1696. The famous case of the Goodwin children in Boston occurred in 1688. Mary Randall was arrested in Springfield in 1691, and kept in jail for a while, but there was no trial.

Thus it appears that, from the settlement of New England, wherever unaccountable events took place,— if horses and cattle were sick in an unusual manner or acted strangely; if adults or children were attacked by incurable or mysterious diseases; if lightning struck men, animals, or buildings, or storms disturbed sailors,— the cause was attributed to witchcraft. Under such circumstances any woman who had incurred the animosity of neighbors, especially if she had made threats against "afflicted" persons, was liable to the suspicion of complicity with the devil. But as there had been only two or three executions at most in any one part of the country, and intelligence of the trials spread slowly, no great excitement arose until 1692.

In view of the preceding history, the events in Salem, Salem Village, and vicinity might have been expected in any community in New England where many social feuds existed, and where strong superstition, great energy, and force of will, with an entire want of discretion, were united in the character of the minister of the parish. All these conditions existed in Salem Village, where the epidemic originated.

Upham, in "Salem Witchcraft," has portrayed in a graphic and convincing manner the influence of local feuds upon the investigation of charges. But if the people of New England had not believed in the reality of witchcraft, and if their laws had not decreed the penalty of death against those convicted of practising it, personal, social, and ecclesiastical animosities could not have caused such terrible deeds.

Salem witchcraft thus arose: The Rev. Mr. Parris, minister of the church in Salem Village, had formerly lived in the West Indies, and brought a few negro slaves back with him. These slaves talked with the children of the neighborhood, some of whom could not read, while the others had but little to read. In the winter of 1691–92 they formed a kind of circle which met at Mr. Parris's house, probably unknown to him, to practise palmistry and fortune-telling, and learn what they could of magic and necromancy. This circle consisted of two or three negro slaves; Elizabeth, daughter of Mr. Parris, aged nine; his niece Abigail Williams, eleven; Ann Putnam, twelve (Upham says that the last-named was the leading agent in all the mischief that followed); Mary Walcot, seventeen; Mercy Lewis, seventeen (she was one of the worst, and fairly reveled in murder and misery); Elizabeth Hubbard, seventeen (almost as bad); Elizabeth Booth and Susannah Sheldon, each eighteen; and two servants, Mary Warren and Sarah Churchill, each twenty years of age. These servants hated the families of John Proctor and George Jacobs, with whom they lived. With them met three married women, one the mother of Ann Putnam.

Before the winter was over some of them fully believed that they were under the influence of spirits. Epidemic hysteria arose; physicians could not explain their state: the cry was raised that they were bewitched; and some began to make charges against those whom they disliked of having bewitched them. In the end those of stronger mind among them became managers and plotters, directing the rest at their will. By the time public attention was attracted Mr. Parris had come to the conclusion that they were bewitched, and, having a theory to maintain, encouraged and flattered them, and by his questions made even those who had not believed themselves bewitched think that they were.

From March, 1692, to May, 1693, about two hundred persons were imprisoned. Of these some escaped by the help of friends, some by bribing their jailers, a number died in prison, and one hundred and fifty were set free at the close of the excitement by the proclamation of the governor. Nineteen were executed, namely: On July 19, Sarah Good, Sarah Wildes, Elizabeth Howe, George Jacobs, Susannah Martin (who had been tried and acquitted in Boston about twenty years before), and Rebecca Nurse; on August 19, John Proctor, Bridget Bishop, George Burroughs (minister of the gospel), Martha Carrier, and John Willard; on September 22, Martha Corey, Mary Eastey, Alice Parker, Mary Parker, Ann Pudeater, Willmet Redd, Margaret Scott, and Samuel Ward-

19

well. Giles Corey, a man eighty years of age, when charged refused to plead, and was pressed to death — the only instance of the application of this ancient law on the American continent.

When it is remembered that a number of these persons were among the most pious and amiable of the people of Salem, Salem Village, and other parts of Essex County; that they were related by blood, marriage, friendship, and Christian fellowship to many of those who cried out against them, both as accusers and supporters of the prosecutions, the transaction must be classed among the darkest in human history.

DOES THE BIBLE TEACH THE REALITY OF WITCHCRAFT?

Sir Matthew Hale, in his "Trial of Witches," 1661, basing the conclusion upon the Scriptures, affirms that there is a real supernatural operation of the devil at the request of a witch. John Wesley, who was born only twelve years after the scenes in Salem, wrote in May, 1768: "They well know [meaning infidels, materialists, and deists] — whether Christians know it or not — that the giving up of witchcraft is in effect giving up the Bible." In a letter to his brother, written some years afterward, he declares that he believes all Cotton Mather's stories. His opinions upon these subjects were those of the age, but did not convince his brother Charles, who frequently expostulated with him for his credulity. With the same spirit and in the same way he affirmed it a giving up of the Bible to question various ideas now rejected by the most devout Christians, and did on some points himself repudiate in later periods of his life what in similar language he had condemned others for disbelieving.

An examination of the references to witchcraft shows that only the existence and criminality of the *attempt* to practise it are to be concluded from the words of the Scriptures. The conclusion is not well founded that if there was no reality in witchcraft the prophets and apostles must necessarily have known it; for the Scriptures show that the prophets were limited in knowledge upon a variety of points, many of them closely allied to the religious truths which they taught. They drew illustrations from supposed facts of science, medicine, and natural history, which served their purpose for the time; and in *such particulars* wrote exactly as authors of to-day, who find their illustrations in the state of knowledge in the age in which they live. Moses declares that "the man or the woman who hath a familiar spirit, or is a wizard, shall be put to death"; and "thou shalt not suffer a witch [Rev. Ver. *a sorceress*] to live." It is clear that the same law would be needed and the same language would be employed if the *pretense* of having a familiar spirit, or the *attempt* to *practise* witchcraft, were in question. In Deuteronomy xviii., Moses attempts to enumerate all possible forms of occult practices, when he warns the Israelites against the practices of the nations whose land the Lord had given them, condemning "divination," one that practiseth augury, or an "enchanter," or a "sorcerer," or a "charmer," or a "consulter with a familiar spirit," or a "wizard," or a "necromancer."

In the forty-seventh chapter of Isaiah, the Israelites are taunted with the multitude of their enchantments and sorceries, and they are told to call upon "the astrologers, and the star-gazers, and monthly prognosticators" to save them if they can. The astrologers in this passage are "the dividers of the heavens"; the star-gazers, "the reviewers of the heavens"; the monthly prognosticators, "those who give predictions from month to month." The word translated "a consulter with familiar spirits" is from a term whose literal meaning is equivalent to that of our ordinary word ventriloquist, drawn from the fact that such persons chirp, mutter, speak as one from the ground, or from the abdomen. The only place where the word "witchcraft" occurs in the Authorized Version of the New Testament is Galatians v. 20, where among the works of the flesh are named "idolatry and witchcraft." Witchcraft is there translated from φαρμακεία, signifying "enchanters with drugs."

The laws of Moses and the maledictions of the prophets show an attempt to prohibit, punish, and extirpate the whole host of occult practices of Egypt, Babylon, and Media, Persia, Phœnicia, and every other nation with which the Israelites came in contact. The theocratic nature of the government of God as set forth by Moses could not allow any rival; the attempt was rebellion and treason, the punishment death.

Against the conclusion which we draw that the attempt, and the attempt only, was to be considered in the trial of a case, it is said, "How, then, could an Israelitish judge decide the case of a person arraigned under this law? Would not the whole issue of the case depend upon the proof that the accused really had an attendant spirit? And is not the law an express declaration, not merely of the possibility, but also of the actual occurrence of such connections?" Not at all. Unless the Israelitish judges had the power of supernatural perception, the only thing that they could take cognizance of would be the *attempt*.

Those who reject this conclusion, if they would be

consistent, must believe all the forms of imposture comprehended in the common law of Israel to be supernatural; they must believe in astrology, augury, and charms; and that the heathen gods were actual supernatural devils. St. Paul says, "We know that no idol is anything in the world"; and though, when warning the people to flee from idolatry, he says that "the things which the Gentiles sacrifice they sacrifice to *devils* and not to God," it is a strained and long-drawn inference that he means to say that beyond the heathen gods there are real demons which they worship. If that were so the prophet Jeremiah was himself deceived, and deceived the people, when he said, "Be not afraid of them [the heathen gods], for they cannot do evil, neither is it in them to do good."

THE WITCH OF ENDOR

THE account of the Witch of Endor is the only instance in the Bible where a description of the processes and results is given. Whether any one appeared to the witch, and if so who, has caused endless debate. Lange gives a summary of the different views. The Septuagint and the Apocrypha represent that it was Samuel, and Justin Martyr held the same; Tertullian that it was a *pythoness*, exclaiming, "Far be it from us to believe that the soul of any saint, much less a prophet, can be drawn forth by a demon"; Theodoret, Justin, Origen, Ambrose, Augustine, and some Jewish rabbis held that the "appearance of Samuel" was produced by God's power; and Delitzsch, Hengstenberg, and other moderns support it. Luther held that it was "the Devil's ghost"; Calvin that "it was not the real Samuel, but a spectre." Grotius thought that it was a deceptive spirit.

Amid the conflict I also will show "mine opinion." Saul, who was a man of strong passions, feeble judgment, and little self-control, had sinned, and God refused to hear him. With the Philistines visible at a distance of four miles, encamped in a better position than his own, being forsaken by God, his heart sank within him, and he determined to know the worst. Taking his servants into his confidence, he sought out a professed witch, or necromancer. Having received an oath that she would not be punished, she began in her usual way. "Whom shall I bring up unto thee?" This was her professed business. "Bring me up Samuel!" Immediately afterward the woman cried with a loud voice, and said to Saul, "Why hast thou deceived me, for thou art Saul?" There is a strong presumption that she would have known him under any circumstances. He was "head and shoulders above all the people"; his face must have been familiar; his camp was less than twelve miles from her cave. It is incredible, in that small country, with Saul ranging over it, and great public processions, that the witch had never seen him. Said he, "Be not afraid." She said, "I see gods ascending out of the earth." "What form is he of?" "An old man covered with a mantle." Then Saul, who never saw anything, but depended upon her description, "perceived that it was Samuel."

What such women did in those times they are doing now in the East. She had retired—her cave, according to the Oriental custom, being divided by a curtain—and had been performing her incantations and muttering. It has often been remarked that when such a giant as Saul appeared and said, "Bring me up *Samuel!*" the witch must have been indeed a foolish woman not to suspect who he was that made such a strange request. Before Samuel is represented as speaking she knew that her interlocutor was Saul. Her motive for pretending not to know him at first was to increase her influence over his mind — a common device of such performers.

Before the witch spoke the words attributed to Samuel, Saul had given her all the facts that she needed to form the answer, in this full description of his situation and confession of helplessness and distress: "I am sore distressed, for the Philistines make war against me, and God is departed from me, and answereth me no more, neither by prophets nor by dreams: therefore I have called thee, that thou mayest make known unto me what I shall do."

The answer plainly consists of things which Samuel had said while living, and of things that could be conjectured from the situation. It is not necessary to assume that the woman was wholly a deceiver. Possibly she believed that her incantations brought up the dead, and she may have fallen into a species of trance in which she imagined the character suggested by her applicant. If so, she would naturally imitate the tone of the supposed responder, and would speak to a great degree in harmony with what the character might be expected to say under the known circumstances. The narrator, as certain ancient Church decrees, according to Reginald Scot, declare, "set foorth Saule's mind and Samuel's estate and certeine things which were said and scene, omitting whether they were true or false."

TRIAL OF CASES

LITTLE aid in the understanding of the trials of witches in New England in 1692 can be derived from courts as now conducted. The Honorable William

Sullivan, in an address before the Bar of Suffolk, Massachusetts, in March, 1824, says that in Massachusetts the governor and assistants were the only depositaries of power, exercising legislative, judicial, and executive authority. They inferred from the charter the rights to exercise whatever power the welfare of the community required; when that was silent the Scriptures were the resort, the clergy and the elders being the expounders in all new emergencies. Hutchinson says that for a number of years "the jury, if not satisfied with the opinion of the court, were allowed to consult any bystander." For several years there were no lawyers, though there were a few attorneys, in the country. According to Mr. Sullivan, the importation in 1647 of two copies each of several law-books, including "Coke on Lyttleton," "Magna Charta," and "Coke's Reports," was probably the first introduction of the common law into the colony. Few or none of the judges were professional lawyers.

On the 8th of December, 1885, the Honorable William D. Northend delivered an address before the Bar of Sussex County, which is to be found in the twenty-second volume of the "Historical Collections of the Sussex Institute." His estimate of the judges is that there was not a regularly educated lawyer on the Superior Court Bench of Massachusetts until 1712, long after the witch trials were over. At that time, and for many years afterward, counsel were not assigned or allowed in capital cases, except on questions of law when the court was in doubt, the theory being that the judges were counsel for the prisoner. On May 14, 1692, Sir William Phipps arrived, bringing the new charter. He was a weak man and a believer in witchcraft. One of the first of his official acts was to appoint seven persons of Oyer and Terminer to try the prisoners who had been committed under suspicion of witchcraft in Essex County.

The kind of evidence admitted appears from the records, which are now accessible. One case may serve to illustrate all. Against Rebecca Nurse there were four indictments. The first sets forth that "she has afflicted Ann Puttnam, Jr., by certain detestable arts called witchcraft, and sorceries, wherewith she has hurt, tortured, afflicted, wasted, and tormented." [1] The other indictments use nearly the same language.

Mrs. Nurse was an aged woman of unspotted reputation, and was more tenderly treated during a portion of the time than any of the rest. The jury at first acquitted her, but the judges sent them out again, and practically forced them to bring in a verdict of guilty, notwithstanding Mrs. Nurse's assertion that she had failed to answer a question (which failure was used against her) because, being deaf, she did not hear it. The judges appeared to be convinced of the guilt of all from the time the afflicted declared them guilty, and badgered prisoners in a manner almost incredible. Most of the examinations were written down by the Rev. Samuel Parris; one of the strongest proofs of the utter blindness of the times being the frank and unequivocal manner in which the record is prepared.

The prejudices of the judges and the spirit in which they dealt with the defendants appear from the account of the examination of Elizabeth Cary, of Charlestown, given by her husband, a shipmaster.

His wife, being conscious of innocence, went to the church. The girls came in, fell in fits, and cried out, "Cary! Cary!" Mrs. Cary had never seen nor heard of one of them in her life.

[1] From the "Records of Salem Witchcraft," copied from the original documents, and privately printed for W. Elliott Woodward. Volume I.

As at every motion of the defendant the afflicted made the same, Mrs. Cary was ordered to stand with her arms stretched out. Mr. Cary says, "I requested that I might hold one of her hands, but it was denied me; then she desired me to wipe the tears from her eyes and the sweat from her face, which I did; then she desired that she might lean herself on me, saying she should faint. Justice Hathorne replied, 'She had strength enough to torment these persons, and she should have strength enough to stand.' I speaking something against their cruel proceedings, they commanded me to be silent or else I should be turned out of the room."

Mrs. Cary was committed, but escaped from jail, went to Rhode Island, and finally to New York, where the governor of the State interested himself in her and protected her. Captain Cary, after describing her sufferings, says: "To speak of their usage of the prisoners, and the inhumanity shown to them at the time of their execution, no sober Christian could bear."

No testimony as to previous good conduct and character availed anything. This may be illustrated by the case of a woman of whom the Rev. William Hubbard, one of the most honored ministers in New England, characterized by Hutchinson as "a man of learning, and a logical and benevolent mind, accompanied with a good degree of catholicism," certifies:

I have known the wife of William Buckley of Salem Village . . . ever since she was brought out of England, which is above fifty years ago. . . . She was bred by Christian parents, . . . was admitted as a member into the Church at Ipswich [of which he was the pastor] above forty years since. I never heard from others, or observed by myself, anything of her which was inconsistent with her profession, or unsuitable to Christianity.

But on evidence similar to that which convicted the others, and mostly from the same witnesses, she was hurried off to prison.

John Proctor went with his wife to support her under the charges; the "afflicted" cried out against him, and though many of the citizens testified to his good character, as well as to hers, he was executed. But the children cried out that they could see "his shape afflicting them."

Against George Burroughs, a graduate of Harvard College and former minister of Salem, the principal evidence was that though a puny man he was remarkably strong physically; that he made nothing of carrying barrels of sugar, flour, etc., from one place to another, and that he could hold a gun straight out at arm's-length by taking hold of the end of the stock; that his wife told some one that he said "he knew all secrets, and made her promise to reveal none of his"; and that he accused his brother-in-law and his wife of talking about him on one occasion.

In his address Judge Northend remarks, "No better illustration can be given of the fallacy of the views of those who look upon legal rules as only a clog and hindrance in the administration of justice. Under the rules of laws now fully established, none of the evidence upon which the convictions were found would be admitted; spectral and kindred evidence could not be allowed, and without it not one of the accused could have been convicted."

EXPLANATION OF CONFESSIONS

MANY persons acknowledged themselves witches, both in Europe and America, and gave detailed accounts of their interviews with the devil. This has led various writers to suppose that witchcraft has an objective reality; and certainly the problem is complicated by the fact that some who confessed were persons of undoubted piety. Yet it is not difficult of explanation.

In Europe tortures the most terrible were inflicted to compel confession. In "Superstition and Force," Mr. Henry C. Lea quotes Rickens, a magistrate during an epidemic of witchcraft at the close of the seventeenth century, as complaining that no reliance could be placed on legal witnesses to procure conviction. Del Rio avers that torture is to be more readily resorted to in witchcraft than in other crimes, in consequence of the *extreme difficulty of its proof.* This, Mr. Lea says, was the common opinion of the time. Constantine issued a decree A. D. 358 that no dignity of birth or station should protect those accused of sorcery or magic from the severest application of torture. Old German records are full of accounts of men and women yielding and confessing, usually in language put into their mouths by the inquisitors.

In New England *none* of those who confessed themselves to be witches were executed, and every effort was made to induce them to do so. If any one confessed to being a witch, and afterward, driven by conscience, retracted, he was certain to be executed. This was the case with Samuel Wardwell, who confessed, retracted his confession, and died upon the gallows protesting his innocence.

But why did some religious and spiritually minded persons confess? Because they were saturated with erroneous views of the power of the devil, and his mode of exercising it. They believed that he was very near them all the time, endeavoring to effect an entrance; and when they were accused, saw "the afflicted," and realized that the magistrates and ministers thought they were guilty, their minds being weakened by the terrible pressure upon them, they came to the conclusion that in some unguarded moment the devil had gained an advantage over them; and that, though "they were unconscious of having done such things, their *spirits* must have committed them," and they therefore confessed.

Many thousands of persons in former centuries concluded in the same manner that they had committed " the unpardonable sin "; while of these very few had any clear idea of what the sin is. The pressure of the doctrinal beliefs of the age upon morbid conscientiousness, with a natural distrust, antagonized all the promises of the Gospel, and they despaired.

Many abandoned persons who believed in witchcraft and sought to obtain the power could easily find coincidences seeming to prove the truth of their claims, and in this way thought themselves to be wizards and witches.

EXPLANATION OF PHENOMENA

In the progress of science principles have been established and illustrative facts accumulated whereby the greater part of the authentic phenomena can be fully explained. There was a large amount of fraud and jugglery. Dr. Hutchinson of England, the second edition of whose work appeared in 1720, has a chapter on " Seven Notorious Impostures Detected."

Seventy-eight years after the Salem witchcrafts, at Littleton, Middlesex County, Massachusetts, a case involving three children whose performances were fully as remarkable and mysterious as those of the Goodwin children attracted great attention. But several years later the oldest girl offered herself as a candidate at the Rev. Mr. Terrell's church in Medford. " Her experience was considered satisfactory, but the minister chancing to preach against *liars* " (though he had not the least idea that she was an impostor), his sermon so powerfully affected her that she went to him and confessed the whole imposture,

20

and showed how her sisters were drawn into it, "by love of mischief, imitation, vanity, and *necessity of going on after they had begun*." In the case of "the afflicted girls" of New England there is positive evidence that some were consciously and intentionally performing a part.

If those who were not intentional deceivers believed that they were afflicted by the accused, their evidence and actions become simple. If the accused moved her head, they would move theirs automatically. Hypnotic performances, now well known, furnish a perfect analogy. Every hypnotizer has to be constantly on his guard lest all with whom he is experimenting should do whatever is done by one. That this is an adequate explanation appears from the fact that in those parts of the world where witchcraft is still believed in, and where a scientific knowledge of epidemic hysteria and of hypnotism does not exist, such attacks are believed to be produced by witchcraft.

The "London Medical Record" has recently published an article quoted from an Italian medical journal, giving an account of an epidemic of hysteria among the peasants of Albania. The priests had tried to exorcise the evil spirits, but without success. Fourteen girls under twenty years of age, one boy of eleven, a woman of fifty, and a robust peasant of nineteen were carefully studied. The muscles of the face and neck became rigid, and afterward those of the limbs. The woman went through the most violent contortions and muscular motions, beating her chest with her hands and then falling motionless. This was sometimes repeated again and again. She said that during the attacks she "saw the figure of the woman who bewitched her." The origin and history of the case are here given in brief:

A band of seventy girls had agreed to work for an old woman in rice-fields. Thinking that they could make a better bargain, they broke their engagement. The old woman was angry, and as she was generally supposed to possess the power of witchcraft, the girls were constantly in dread of being bewitched. As they worked eleven hours a day, standing in water in the hot sun, living chiefly on unsalable beans, bad bacon, and decaying rice, they were reduced "to a state of very unstable mental equilibrium, which was completely upset by seeing the hystero-epileptic fits of the first patient." The medical men sent them off to their own homes, thus isolating them, and they were speedily cured.

The imitative principle in such cases sometimes goes so far that what one thinks he sees hundreds will think they see; what one does scores and hundreds will do. The precise manner of dissemination of the dominant idea is well known.

Testimony to marvels of a different kind is occasionally introduced, such as mysterious noises, the fastening of doors, overthrowing of chairs, tables, crockery, the extinguishing of lights without apparent cause, the entrance of hogs and other animals into a house, the appearance of lights the origin of which is not understood. A case of this kind occurred in New England in 1680, and was before the courts at Ipswich. William Morse and his wife, with whom in the house no one but a grandson lived, were disturbed by such occurrences. A neighbor, Caleb Powell, looked into the matter, and declared that the boy played the tricks; and that he had seen him fling things at his grandfather's head while the old gentleman was at prayer. But the mere attempt to explain the mystery nearly cost Caleb Powell his life, for he was arrested on suspicion of witchcraft, and many witnesses were brought to swear that he said that by astronomy and astrology he could find out, as he "knew the working of spirits, some in one country and some in another." Little investigation could take place in any country where the investigator was liable to be accused of witchcraft and to lose his life for denying its reality.

Scientific investigation, with the meaning which is now given to these words, was never applied to the phenomena. Drake does not exaggerate when he declares that, during the period, "if anything occurred, the origin or reason of which was neither understood nor comprehended, and appeared stranger than usual, the mind instead of investigating fell back upon the ever-ready and easy solution that such was caused by witchcraft." There were a few doubters; but they seldom obtained access to primary sources of information, and when they did were denounced as "Sadducees," "defenders of witches," or "agents of the devil." So strong was this influence that certain clergymen who plainly did not approve the proceedings, were compelled to reaffirm continually their belief in witchcraft, and to protest against being considered defenders of witches. If persons became aggressive in the defense of the accused they were cried out upon by the accusers, and a mortal terror of the consequences led many to avoid being present at the investigation.

Electricity, magnetism, and the action of gases, as well as meteorological phenomena, were imperfectly understood in the times of the epidemic of witchcraft. Many mysteries then inscrutable could now be easily explained. The science of bacteriology, a discovery of the present generation, illustrates many of the facts which, being misunderstood, were supposed to indicate the presence of the devil, and to be the results of witchcraft. Dr. Prudden's "Story of the Bacteria, and their Relations to Health and Disease" gives many instances, and a circumstance easily explained recently occurred which two hundred years ago might have been the means of the death of many. Some time since there was brought to the physiological and pathological laboratory of the Alumni Asso-

ciation of the College of Physicians and Surgeons of
the City of New York, for examination, "a cluster of
sausages which had been destined to grace a board-
ing-house breakfast-table. To the consternation of
the maid who went into the dark cellar for them in
the early morning, there hung in the place of the
sausages a fiery effigy, which seemed to her more like
the quondam spirits of their mysterious ingredients
than the unctuous, homely friend of the homeless
boarder." The microscope revealed at once the bacteria which produced the effect.

REACTION FROM THE FRENZY

A DEEP conviction of the fallibility of spectral evidence arose in the minds of many. The recollection
of the characters and good deeds of several who had
been executed, of their dying protestations of innocence, and their religious bearing at the place of execution, and the recognition of the fact that if they had
confessed they might have saved their lives, were
powerful causes of the reaction.

But there were two others of still greater influence.
The "afflicted" began to accuse persons of such high
standing that the community instinctively felt that
the charge was false. The Rev. Mr. Hale of Beverly
had supported the prosecutions; but when his own
wife was accused, he saw that they were going too
far, and turned against them. Her case was but one
of several: spiritual, devout, and consistent, she was
not better than some of those to whose condemnation
and execution her husband had consented, upon evidence similar in all points to that alleged against her.
But they were without such social relations as could
effectually stem the tide, and were accused before a

suspicion of the trustworthiness of the evidence had been engendered.

The other cause was the *retraction of the confessions.* In all fifty-five confessed. Some of them retracted, though they knew it would be certain death. Such was the case of Samuel Wardwell, who was executed protesting his innocence. Margaret Jacobs, who had testified against her grandfather in her confession, was so overwhelmed with grief and shame when she came to herself that she took it back, and addressed the court, saying:

They told me if I would not confess I should be put down into the dungeon, and would be hanged; but if I would confess I should have my life; the which did so affright me with my own vile, wicked heart, to save my life, made me make the like confession, I did, which confession, may it please the honored Court, is altogether false and untrue. The very first night after I had made confession I was in such horror of conscience that I could not sleep for fear the Devil should carry me away for telling such horrid lies.

The entire confession is one of the most touching compositions in literature. She was afterward tried and condemned to death, but escaped because her case was not disposed of until after the reaction.

Six of the women of Andover who had confessed signed a declaration retracting, and fifty of the inhabitants of that town testified to their good character. They say that their nearest and dearest relations told them that there was no hope of saving their lives but by confessing themselves to be witches; that the confession which they made was suggested by some gentlemen,

they telling us that we were witches and they knew it, and we knew it, which made us think that it was so; and our understanding, our reason, our faculties almost gone, we were not capable of judging of our condition. . . . And most of what we said was but, in fact, consenting to what they said. Some time after when we were better composed, they telling us what we had confessed, we did profess that we were innocent and ignorant of such things; and we learning that Samuel Wardwell had renounced his confession and was quickly after condemned and executed, some of us were told we were going after Wardwell.

Andover was " the first to recover its senses"; juries began to acquit; the governor of the State issued a proclamation opening the prisons, and a general fast was ordered. The jurors who had convicted the accused signed and circulated a document confessing that, "for want of knowledge in themselves and better information from others, they had taken up with evidence which on further consideration and better information they believed was insufficient for touching the lives of any"; and they "humbly asked forgiveness of all and the surviving sufferers in special," and declared that *"according to our present minds we would none of us do such things again on such grounds* for the whole world."

In 1697 the Rev. Mr. Hale wrote a book to show that the proceedings were erroneous. Memorials were sent and the ministers of the County of Essex presented an address to the General Court under date of July 8, 1703, expressing their belief that innocent persons had suffered; and finally the General Court, October 17, 1711, only nineteen years after the executions, and while the majority of the people were still living, reversed "the attainders of George Burroughs and others for witchcraft." This act declares that "some of the principal accusers and witnesses in these dark and severe persecutions have since discovered themselves to be persons of profligate and vicious conversation," and reversed the convictions, judgments, and attainders against all that died. The General Court reimbursed survivors and their heirs for expenses incurred. The petitions of such heirs, duly approved and admitted, are found in Woodward's "Records of Salem Witchcraft," and are valuable as testimony to the characters of the accused, apart from the impossible crime with which they were charged.

Judge Sewall, on the day of the general fast, arose in the old South Church in Boston and sent up to the pulpit a written confession of his error. This scene Whittier describes in the lines beginning, "Touching and sad a tale is told." To the day of his death this conscientious man set apart one day of every year for humiliation and prayer on account of the part he had taken.

The clergy of Salem and vicinity in the beginning fostered the delusion. Mr. Parris and Mr. Noyes, especially the former, must be classed with those representatives of any religion, true or false, who will stop at nothing to destroy those whose orthodoxy they doubt, or whose persons or characters they dislike.

There is evidence that many of the clergy of Massachusetts disapproved the proceedings, but because of the sentiments of the ruling civil authorities of Massachusetts were not able to exert a restraining influence. In a petition drawn up by the opponents of Mr. Parris in Salem Village, they say that the reason they would not hold communion with him is "his declared and published sentiments referring to our molestations from the invisible world: differing from the *opinion of the generality of orthodox ministers of this whole country.*" This was under date of April 21, 1693.

The terrible consequences of the belief forced the issue upon mind and heart; common sense and common humanity reasserted themselves. The horrid fiction was cast off; some denying the reality of witchcraft, others admitting it possible in the *abstract*, but affirming that it was impossible to prove it. As soon as the prosecutions ceased there was no further trouble. The transactions in New England exerted a weighty influence on the other side of the Atlantic against witchcraft, and in 1736 the English statute was repealed.

The investigation justifies the conclusion that where witchcraft is not believed in there are no cases of it; where it is believed there are many, and in proportion to the intensity of the belief. It must be remembered that medical men generally were ignorant and superstitious, and the scientific practice of the healing art unknown. The press did not exist; there was no opportunity for the kind of investigation now made by reporters, for the free utterance of adverse opinion, or for any proper or generally circulated report of trials. If most of the clergy of this country believed in witchcraft, they could find an abundance of the kind of evidence that was admitted in 1692; and were there no press, free, active, and intelligent, it would be possible in a few weeks to originate an epidemic which would parallel any in the past.

The crucifixion of Christ, the cruelties of the Inquisition, the burning of Servetus, the atrocities of the first French Revolution, the hanging of witches and Quakers, are but manifestations of the possible excesses of human nature when governed by false and deeply rooted ideas, when strong passions are excited, and no adequate force, either of authority or of public opinion, restrains.

The solemn words of Longfellow are true of New England's part in the universal tragedy:

> Be not too swift in casting the first stone,
> Nor think New England bears the guilt alone;
> This sudden burst of wickedness and crime
> Was but the common madness of the time,
> When in all lands that lie beneath the sound
> Of Sabbath bells a witch was burned or drowned.

Had not mankind as a whole been stronger than any of its passions, the race would long since have annihilated itself. Superstition and barbarism, though ostensibly expelled by modern civilization, lurk in the shadows stealthily seeking an entrance; and the united forces of reason, science, religion, law, self-interest, freedom of speech and of the press, with "eternal vigilance," are needed to prevent them from regaining a direful ascendancy.

"CHRISTIAN SCIENCE" AND "MIND CURE"

THIRTY years ago the phrases Christian Science and Mind Cure, in the sense now attached to them, were unknown; to-day in the press, in conversation, in literature, and especially in discussions relating to health and disease, and to the more occult phenomena of human nature, they frequently occur. To many they have no definite meaning, and long conversations are carried on concerning them in which the most diverse views are maintained, ending in confusion and contradiction, because those who converse have not a uniform conception of the signification of the terms. Some declare Christian Science and Mind Cure to be the same; others stoutly deny this, and seek to establish a radical distinction. Some represent Christian Science as a great advance upon ordinary Christianity; others denounce it as but refined Pantheism; while many more brand both Christian Science and Mind Cure as delusion, a reaction from the uncompromising materialism of the age.

Mrs. Mary Baker Glover Eddy, President of the Massachusetts Metaphysical College, claims to have been the first to use the phrase "Christian Science."

It was in Massachusetts, in the year 1866, that I discovered the Science of Metaphysical Healing, which I afterwards named Christian Science. The discovery came to pass in this way.

During twenty years prior to my discovery I had been trying to trace all physical effects to a mental cause; and in January of 1866 I gained the scientific certainty that all causation was Mind, and every effect a mental phenomenon.

Mrs. Eddy further states that about the year 1862 her health was failing rapidly, and she "employed a distinguished mesmerist, Mr. P. P. Quimby — a sensible, elderly gentleman, with some advanced views about healing. . . . There were no Metaphysical Healers then. The Science of Mental Healing had not been discovered."

Whether or not Mrs. Eddy is indebted for her ideas to Mr. Quimby has since been the subject of heated discussion; for the short time which has elapsed since the "discovery" has been long enough for the development of several rival schools, which have engendered toward one another as much intensity of feeling as the *odium theologicum* and *odium medicum* combined. Speaking of her rivals, Mrs. Eddy modestly observes: "Some silly publications, whose only correct or salient points are borrowed, without credit, from 'Science and Health,' would set the world right on Metaphysical Healing, like children thrumming a piano and pretending to teach music or criticise Mozart."

The history of the discovery is of sufficient importance to be given. "The cowardly claim that I am not the originator of my own writings, but that one P. P. Quimby is, has been legally met and punished. . . . Mr. Quimby died in 1865, and my first knowledge of Christian Science, or Metaphysical Healing, was gained in 1866. . . . When he doctored me I was ignorant of the nature of mesmerism, but subsequent knowledge has convinced me that he practiced it." Mrs. Eddy says that after having been for many years a sufferer from chronic diseases, she met with an accident which produced, according to physicians, a fatal injury. They gave her up to die, and declared that she would not live till noon. She replied that she would be well at that time. Her pastor called after service and found her busy about the house. One of her assistants says that "while she knew that she was healed by the direct and gracious exercise of the divine power, she was indisposed to make an old-time miracle of it."

After three years' meditation she concluded that her recovery was in accordance with general spiritual laws, capable of being known and clearly stated. She then began to teach and write; though prior to the expiration of the three years, namely, in 1867, she taught a purely metaphysical system of healing to, as she says, "the very first student who was ever so instructed since the days of the Apostles and the primitive Church." Her essays were circulated among her students privately. In 1870 she copyrighted her first pamphlet, but did not publish it till six years afterward.

In 1876 she organized the Christian Scientist Association, and in 1879, at a meeting of that association, she organized a Church, "a Mind Healing Church, without creeds, called the Church of Christ." To the pastorate of this she accepted a call, and was ordained in Boston, 1881. The college flourishes, the church has an assistant pastor, and Mrs. Eddy receives so much patronage as a teacher as to compel the publication of the following:

The authoress takes no patients, and has no time for medical consultation.

Practitioners, who of course are not obliged to waste much time upon such sordid things as anat-

21

omy, physiology, or materia medica, are prepared with unusual rapidity. The primary class in Christian Science Mind Healing includes twelve lessons. In the first week six of these are given. The term continues only about three weeks, and the charge for tuition is $300. The normal class requires six lectures. Graduates from the primary class are advised to practise at least one year before entering this class, and for these six lectures they must pay $200. There is also a class of Metaphysical Obstetrics which requires only six lectures, for which $100 must be paid. In addition to these there is a class in Theology, including six lectures on the Scriptures, for which $200 must be paid. The largest discount to an indigent student is $100 on the first course. Husbands and wives, if they enter together the primary class, may pay $300; but, entering at different times, must pay the regular price, and must do that for all other courses, payment being made strictly in advance. It is obvious therefore, that the benefits of the Mind Cure cannot be applied to commercial transactions; and that 800 material dollars, exclusive of board, are required to master the Science of Metaphysical Healing,—unless one were to say that national bank notes are merely material symbols of an immaterial and impalpable essence.

Considering the short time that has elapsed since the "discovery," the number of practitioners, as advertised in one of their magazines, is very large. Sixty-six are women, and twenty-nine men; and all but five of the men appear to be associated with their wives in the practice of the profession. There are also Christian Science institutes and colleges advertised: two in New York, four in Chicago, one in Milwaukee, one in Brooklyn, and one in Colorado. The other institutions do not charge so large a sum as Mrs. Eddy. Some of them agree to give sufficient instruction for $25 to justify the would-be practitioner in beginning. Others communicate all they know, with the privilege of meeting for conversation once a month for a year, on payment of $100. They give diplomas, valued according to the standing of the respective schools. Impostors have arisen, so that Mrs. Eddy has notified the public that all persons claiming to have been her pupils, who cannot show diplomas legally certifying to that effect, are preferring false claims.

THEORY

By a careful examination of the works of those who have written upon this subject, including Evans, Grimké, Stuart, Arens, Taylor, Baldwin, Hazzard, Nichols, Marston, etc., and by conversation with Mental Healers, Christian Scientists, and their patients, I have ascertained that most of them concur with Mrs. Eddy in the fundamental principles of the system, and that where they diverge it is upon minor points.

Her hypothesis is that " the only realities are the Divine Mind and its ideas. . . . That erring mortal views, misnamed *mind*, produce all the organic and animal action of the mortal body. . . . Rightly understood, instead of possessing sentient matter, we have sensationless bodies. . . . Whence came to me this conviction in antagonism to the testimony of the human senses? From the self-evident fact that matter has no sensation; from the common human experience of the falsity of all material things; from the obvious fact that mortal mind is what suffers, feels, sees; since matter cannot suffer."

The method of Mrs. Eddy's reasoning may be seen in the following extracts:

The ineradicable belief that pain is located in a limb which has been removed, when really the sensation is believed to be in the nerves, is an added proof of the unreliability of physical testimony. . . . Electricity is not a vital fluid, but an element of mortal mind,—the thought-essence that forms the link between what is termed matter and mortal mind. Both are different strata of human belief. The grosser substratum is named *matter*. The more ethereal is called *human mind*, which is the nearer counterfeit of the Immortal Mind, and hence the more accountable and sinful belief. . . . You say, "Toil fatigues me." But what is this *you* or *me*? Is it muscle or mind? Which one is tired and so speaks? Without mind, could the muscles be tired? Do the muscles talk, or do you talk for them? Matter is nonintelligent. Mortal mind does the talking, and that which affirms it to be tired first made it so.

Having adopted a theory, she does not shrink from its logical sequences:

You would not say that a wheel is fatigued; and yet, the body is just as material as the wheel. Setting aside what the human mind says of the body, it would never be weary any more than the inanimate wheel. Understanding this great fact rests you more than hours of repose.

Her most frequently repeated assertions are such as these:

God is supreme; is mind; is principle, not person; includes all and is reflected by all that is real and eternal; is Spirit, and Spirit is infinite; is the only substance; is the only life. Man was and is the idea of God; therefore mind can never be in man. Divine Science shows that matter and mortal body are the illusions of human belief, which seem to appear and disappear to mortal sense alone. When this belief changes, as in dreams, the material body changes with it, going wherever we wish, and becoming whatsoever belief may decree. Human mortality proves that error has been engrafted into both the dreams and conclusions of material and mortal humanity. Besiege sickness and death with these principles, and all will disappear.

As these doctrines are unquestionably in substance such as have been held by certain metaphysicians in past ages, Mrs. Eddy feels called upon to answer those who make that charge:

Those who formerly sneered at it as foolish and eccentric now declare Bishop Berkeley, David Hume, Ralph Waldo Emerson, certain German philosophers, or some unlearned mesmerist, to have been the real originators of Mind Healing. Emerson's ethics are models of their kind; but even that good man and genial philosopher partially lost his mental faculties before his death, showing that he did not understand the Science of Mind Healing, as elaborated in my "Science and Health"; nor did he pretend to do so.

Sickness, then, is a dream of falsity, to be antagonized by the metaphysical healer, mentally, and audibly when it may be necessary.

Mrs. Eddy's theories are her religion, and her Science—so called—is based upon the religious principles which she holds.

One of Mrs. Eddy's former students, named Arens, for whom she entertains a strong spiritual antipathy, has published a volume called "Old Theology in its Application to the Healing of the Sick." In the introduction he writes:

It will be unnecessary to ask the reader for charitable criticism when I say that I make no claims to being a ripe scholar, and that my knowledge of the English language is very imperfect. The truths set forth in this volume have been expressed as clearly as possible, considering the disadvantages under which I have labored, one of which is the poverty of words in the English language to express spiritual thoughts. It has been found necessary to employ close punctuation, and in some instances to disregard some rules of grammar and rhetoric, in order to give the requisite shade of thought.

The mental difficulty in understanding him arises from his incompetency as a writer. His reflection upon the poverty of the English language is another form of confessing his ignorance of it; and his disregard of the rules of grammar and rhetoric does not result from his difficulty in giving shades of thought, but from his lack of knowledge of the language. Mrs. Eddy thus described him in 1883:

When he entered the class of my husband, the late Asa G. Eddy, in 1879, he had no knowledge whatever, and claimed none, as can be shown under his own signature, of Metaphysics or Christian Science. . . . While teaching him my system of Mental Healing, his motives and aims and the general constitution of his mind were found so remote from the requirements of Christian Science, that his teacher despaired of imparting to him a due understanding of the subject. Perhaps it was to meet this great want without remedying it, and cover his lack of learning, that he committed to memory many paragraphs from my works, and is in the habit of repeating them in his attempts to lecture. He, who now proclaims himself a professor in the solemn department that he assumes as a jay in borrowed plumes, was the most ignorant and empty-minded scholar I ever remember of examining.

That his earlier work consists largely of passages taken from Mrs. Eddy's writings, and that it is as a whole in every respect inferior to them, is the simple statement of a fact. He has, however, acquired considerable reputation, and has a constituency. Before advancing the fundamental principles of his system, he attempts to show the inconsistencies of medical science in the following passage:

Materia medica teaches that mercury cures, also that mercury kills; that ipecac causes vomiting, and that an overdose checks it, etc.; these are contradictions in themselves. A rule that can be contradicted is not demonstrable, and therefore not truth. If one and one made two only occasionally, and at other times made three or more, it would be no fact or rule, because not demonstrable, and no dependence could be placed upon it. If from a science (truth) it is found that mercury cures, it would be found that the more of that so-called necessary quality taken into the system, the better it would be for the patient; such would be the result from a perfect rule or from truth.

Here is an example of his style:

Suppose I should be walking past a house, and a pane of glass should fall from an upper window cutting me and causing my death; the glass was made and placed by life, and life broke it and caused it to fall. My life brought me here from Prussia and carried me by the house at the time that happened; therefore life was the cause of my death, and, strange as it may seem, is the cause of all action.

From this profound (?) reasoning he concludes:

If life is the cause of all action it must be the cause of sickness. . . . Thought is the first product of life, and as the thought is so will the action be. Life cannot act contrary to the thoughts which are become beliefs or opinions, that is, which have taken root or are become attached to it, unless it acts unconsciously.

Mrs. Eddy sued this Dr. Arens for infringing her copyright, and obtained judgment against him, so that he was compelled to destroy a large edition of one of his pamphlets.

Dr. Arens established a university in the city of Boston, incorporated five or six years, called the "University of the Science of Spirit." It confers the following degrees: "F. D.," Defender of the Faith, and "S. S. D.," Doctor of the Science of Spirit. The charge for instruction in the general course is one hundred dollars. These courses are somewhat pretentious. The first treats the "Scientific Basis of Theology," "the Difference between God and the Universe," etc., and, proceeding through twenty-one theological points, concludes by setting forth "the First Step in Immortality," and "How to Destroy Sickness." The second course discusses "Theos, Chaos, and Cosmos"; gives a theory of the creation of the universe down to the creation of the "first material human body," which it treats under "its outline and quality; the necessity for respiration; the first consciousness of existence; the separation of male and female; the origin of self-will and its results." And finally, "the beginning of sickness and trouble."

Dr. Marston treats "God, Man, Matter, Disease, Sin, and Death, Healing, Treatment, and Universal Truth." In his book he states that "the mental healer does not care by what medical name the distress is known; it may be nervousness, dyspepsia, asthma, fever,—words all alike to him, since the effects they denote are simply reflections or registers of wrong thinking." In illustrating this he says:

A case may be cited to illustrate the meaning: A middle-aged man who has suffered many years with chronic rheumatism, until it is torture for him to move, has also an excitable temper, a despotic will, and is so intolerant that he cannot abide opposition, but flies into a towering rage if he is crossed. He has had many physicians who ascribe the painful inflammation of his joints to an improper secretion of uric acid; and his nervousness and irritability are easily accounted for by the prolonged suffering he has endured. This case presents the same conditions to the mental healer, but his conclusions are different. To him the bodily trouble is a reflection or effect of lack of mental ease; and the unamiable nature results from a dominant feeling that other people are enemies seeking to oppose the poor man's wishes and thwart his plans. In treating the case, the doctor addresses remedies to the disturbed secretions which are an effect, while the mental healer directs his to the primary cause, which is fear.

His cure is reduced to its simplest form as follows: "The senses say matter can suffer pain; God says matter is insensible. The senses declare a man sick; God says the real man knows nothing of disease." Under the head of Sin and Death he says: "Scientific Christianity does not recognize the definition of theology, but holds that, strictly speaking, there is no sin." He finally describes the cure thus: "A mental cure is the discovery made by a sick person that he is well."

W. F. Evans, a voluminous writer, formerly an evangelical minister, then a Swedenborgian, and lately a mental healer, remarks:

The process is essentially a spiritual work; *it is held that there is a part of us that is never sick, and this part is mentally worked upon so as to control the sick person's consciousness, this destroys the sickness*, for mind cures matter. A disciple of this school is sick—no, he is not sick, for that is something which he will not admit; he has a belief that he is sick; he then says mentally to the rebellious body, "What are you? You have no power over me; you are merely the covering given to me for present purposes; it is an error to suppose that I am sick; I recognize the great truth that I myself, my individuality, my personality, my mind, cannot be sick, for it is immortal, made in the image of God; when I recognize the existence of that truth there is no room left for the existence of error; two things cannot occupy one and the same place; error cannot exist in the same place with truth, therefore error is not in existence; hence I am not sick."

Mrs. Grimké, author of "Personified Unthinkables," says:

Now, rheumatism or pneumonia, etc., are *verbal* expressions for unthinkables, just as $2+2=5$ is a verbal expression for a lie. By means of the picturing faculty, both of the individual and of those about him, the outward manifestation of the unthinkable will express itself upon the body just as surely as the magic-lantern will reflect the picture inserted between the light

and the lenses when the proper conditions are met. . . .
The problem of Health, then, would be how to cultivate and
keep clean and healthy pictures in the mind. Health would
then be an essential part of the ego. Man would be a strict
unity, not a trinity, of Intellect, Body, and Morals, and the absolutely necessary postulates of this *Unity* would be Infinite
Mind, Freedom, and Eternal Life.

There are those who in their own opinion have
reached a greater elevation than either the Christian
Scientists or the Mind Curers, "and profess to heal
by the transfer of psychic energy." The chief practitioner in this sphere informed me that the relative rank of these sciences is, 1. The lower grade—
the mere physical system. 2. What is called animal
magnetism. 3. The mind cure. 4. The spirits (when
they are good spirits). 5. Including all that is good
in the others, he places in the *supernal*. He claimed
that there has been in all ages an order called the
Inspirati, who practised this method, and offered to
make me a Knight of that order.

This will suffice until it fails to attract patients,
when, no doubt, a sixth order, that of the *Empyrean*,
will be devised.

Some of the Christian Scientists have attempted to
construct a technical language, which, when translated, shows that they attach as much importance to
learned terms as does any form of the material science
that they denounce. "Gnosis.—The 'Spiritual Understanding,' the 'Immediate Intuition.' VIR.—
The God in Man. HARMATIA.—Off-the-trackness.
HOMO.—The Creature of God. EGO.—The Homo *as
he is*. NEMO.—The Homo as he sees himself. ENTHE-
ASM.—Direct Communication with God. NIHILOID.—
Like unto nothing, the proper name of disease, disorder, discomfort. YOGA.—Concentration of Thought.
DAMA.—Subjugation of Sense. KARMA.—Law of

Cause and Effect. MAYA.—Illusion, 'Mortal Mind,' False Beliefs.—Chaos, The *Habitat* of Humbug."

Most of these terms appear to have had an oriental origin, and are as valuable in affecting the ordinary mind as chloride of sodium for salt, capsicum for pepper, and H_2O for water. They serve also to make it appear that the Science is difficult, and that large fees for instruction are reasonable.

They make use of certain forms of expression which savor more strongly of cant than any phrases that have ever been used by religious sects. They use the word "belief" in speaking of a disease, or even of a defect of character. A lady, talking with a practitioner of this school of a mutual acquaintance, said she thought her selfish. "Yes," replied the Christian Scientist, "I believe she has a strong belief in selfishness."

To a patient who had every symptom of a torpid liver another healer of the school said, "It is unfortunate that you have such a belief in bile." To which the astonished patient, new to the Science, replied that he thought any one would have the same belief who had the same kind of liver.

PRACTICE

THE manner in which Christian Science antagonizes dreams of falsity is interesting, whether the theories be accepted or not.

First.—Both the patient and the metaphysical healer must be taught that

Anatomy, Physiology, Treatises on Health, sustained by what is termed material law, are the husbandmen of sickness and disease. It is proverbial that as long as you read medical works

you will be sick. . . . Clairvoyants and medical charlatans
are the prolific sources of sickness. . . . They first help to
form the image of illness in mortal minds, by telling patients
that they have a disease; and then they go to work to destroy
that disease. They unweave their own webs. . . . When
there were fewer doctors, and less thought was given to sani-
tary subjects, there were better constitutions and less disease.

Second.—Diet is a matter of no importance.

We are told that the simple food our forefathers ate assisted
to make them healthy; but that is a mistake. Their diet would
not cure dyspepsia at this period. With rules of health in the
head, and the most digestible food in the stomach, there would
still be dyspeptics.

Third.—Exercise is of no importance.

Because the muscles of the blacksmith's arm are strongly developed, it does not follow that exercise did it, or that an arm
less used must be fragile. If matter were the cause of action,
and muscles, without the coöperation of mortal mind, could lift
the hammer and smite the nail, it might be thought true that
hammering enlarges the muscles. But the trip-hammer is not
increased in size by exercise. Why not, since muscles are as
material as wood and iron?

Fourth.—A proper view of Mrs. Eddy's publications is, however, of great importance.

My publications alone heal more sickness than an unconsci-
entious student can begin to reach. If patients seem the worse
for reading my book, this change may either arise from the
frightened mind of the physician, or mark the crisis of the disease. Perseverance in its perusal would heal them completely.

Fifth.

Never tell the sick they have more courage than strength.
Tell them rather that their strength is in proportion to their
courage. . . . Instruct the sick that they are not helpless
victims; but that, if they only know how, they can resist dis-

ease and ward it off, just as positively as they can a temptation to sin.

Sixth.—In preparing to treat patients, the healer must strengthen and steady his own mind.

Be firm in your understanding that Mind governs the body. Have no foolish fears that matter governs, and can ache, swell, and be inflamed from a law of its own; when it is self-evident that matter can have no pain or inflammation. . . . If you believe in inflamed or weak nerves, you are liable to an attack from that source. You will call it neuralgia, but I call it Illusion. . . . When treating the sick, first make your mental plea in behalf of harmony, . . . then realize the absence of disease. . . . Use such powerful eloquence as a Congressman would employ to defeat the passage of an inhuman law.

Seventh.—You are fortunate if your patient knows little or nothing, for "a patient thoroughly booked in medical theories has less sense of the divine power, and is more difficult to heal through Mind, than an aboriginal Indian who never bowed the knee to the Baal of civilization."

Eighth.—See that the "minds which surround your patient do not act against your influence by continually expressing such opinions as may alarm or discourage. . . . You should seek to be alone with the sick while treating them."

Ninth.—Bathing and rubbing are of no use.

Bathing and rubbing to alter the secretions, or remove unhealthy exhalations from the cuticle, receive a useful rebuke from Christian Healing. . . . John Quincy Adams presents an instance of firm health and an adherence to hygienic rules, but there are few others.

Tenth.—What if the patient grow worse?

Suppose the patient should appear to grow worse. This I term *chemicalization*. It is the upheaval produced when Immor-

22

tal Truth is destroying erroneous and mortal belief. Chemicalization brings sin and sickness to the surface, as in a fermenting fluid, allowing impurities to pass away. Patients unfamiliar with the cause of this commotion, and ignorant that it is a favorable omen, may be alarmed. If such is the case, explain to them the law of this action.

Eleventh.— Subtle mental practices are recommended.

I will here state a phenomenon which I have observed. If you call mentally and silently the disease by name, as you argue against it, as a general rule the body will respond more quickly; just as a person replies more readily when his name is spoken; but this is because you are not perfectly attuned to Divine Science, and need the arguments of truth for reminders. To let Spirit bear witness without words is the more scientific way.

This is further modified:

You may call the disease by name when you address it mentally; but by naming it *audibly*, you are liable to impress it upon the mind. The Silence of Science is eloquent and powerful to unclasp the hand of disease and reduce it to nothingness.

Twelfth.— Some of the things that are *not* to be done.

A Christian Scientist never gives medicine, never recommends hygiene, never manipulates. He never tries to "focus mind." He never places patient and practitioner "back to back," never consults "spirits," nor requires the life history of his patient. Above all, he cannot trespass on the rights of Mind through animal magnetism.

The foregoing rules for practice are taken from Mrs. Eddy's different works.

The difference between the views of Mrs. Eddy and those who diverge from her is superficial, though neither she nor they will admit it. Miss Kate Taylor, in "Selfhood Lost in Godhood," referring to Mrs. Eddy's large work, says : "It can be read with profit by any who are seeking truth with sincerity, and with no tendency to become biased." She also says that she was formerly a member of the Christian Science Association, and "learned that limitations are not conducive to growth, and that, as Emerson truly says, 'God always disappoints monopolies,'" and frankly gives her opinion of those denounced by her former preceptor.

The so-called mal-practitioners and mesmerists therein mentioned, on thorough investigation,—not only by myself, but in company with others who seek to be liberal-minded and to give Truth its due wherever it exists,—I find to be simply those who have separated themselves from the Association, that they might pursue their own convictions of right, and step out of the regular ranks of stereotyped terms to let their thoughts find expression in their own words.

The chief point of departure in Miss Taylor's theories from those of Mrs. Eddy is in the value attached to a knowledge of the preceding life of the patient.

Physical disease has many different causes. The physician treating a patient is often narrowed in his efforts to do good, because of some hidden moral or mental cause, some underlying fear, some sorrow, some inherited proclivity, some wrong unforgiven, some trait of character, some past occurrence which has tinged, perhaps almost unconsciously, the whole tenor of a life. It is not necessary that a person's innermost sacred thoughts and life be unveiled, as the physician does not expect, neither does he like, to receive confidences, unless, indeed, they are given voluntarily with a feeling of trust. Some word or hint, though, to the physician would often aid materially. . . . The treatment consists in a vigorous holding of the patient to his right of soul-growth, unobstructed and unretarded by physical defects. . . . In answer to the question, "Is it prayer?" I would first quote Victor Hugo's definition of prayer,—"Every thought is a prayer; there are moments when, whatever be the attitude of the body, the soul is on its knees,"—

and then answer, Yes, it *is* prayer. *Prayer* with the old interpretation begs the Father to change the unchangeable, while *prayer* with the new interpretation lifts the beggar to a comprehension that he himself has omitted to take the gifts already prepared for him from the foundation of the world.

She gives this advice to the sick:

Eradicate all thoughts of physiology, drugs, laws of health, sickness, and pain, and know that God is the only panacea,— divine love the only medicine. . . . Seek the help of a Christian Healer. . . . Judge him not unjustly, . . . neither be in opposition, for his is a good motive. . . . While under his treatment obey any natural impulse, without fear of consequence. Remember! without fear. This does not mean to be foolhardy in the beginning,—unless the cure should be almost instantaneous,—but advance gradually. . . . If you have a time during the treatment when you should feel worse, do not be discouraged. . . . Look forward. . . . One little secret it is well to know. . . . Deny every thought of sickness every time it enters your mind. . . . Never use will-power, mistaking it for divine Truth.

Also Mrs. Stuart teaches the importance of a knowledge of the previous life:

A man came to me from Erie, Penn., with what was called by different M. D's softening of the brain and Bright's disease of the kidneys. After questioning him I found his trouble dated back to the Chicago fire. Now he was not conscious of any fear, was in no personal danger for himself or family. But he was in that atmosphere of mental confusion and terror all through the city. He was cured by treatment on that point and nothing else. A woman came to me who had suffered five years with what the doctors called rheumatism. I happened to know that the death of a child had caused this effect. By silently erasing that picture of death and holding in its place an image of Life, eternal Life, she was entirely cured in twenty minutes.

SPECIMEN TREATMENTS

MENTAL treatment is that which the metaphysical healer is supposed to be giving the patient when she sits silently before him for a period longer or shorter according to her judgment of the necessities of the case. Some of the practitioners have revealed the thoughts which constitute a mental treatment, so that if truth is an element of their system, we can speak confidently upon this part of it.

I said to him mentally: "You have no disease; what you call your disease is a fixed mode of thought arising from the absence of positive belief in absolute good. Be stronger," I said, "you must believe in absolute good; I am looking at you, and I see you a beautiful, strong spirit, perfectly sound. What makes you think yourself diseased? You are not diseased; the shadow of a doubt is reflected on your feet, but it has no real existence. There, look down yourself and see that it is gone. Why, it was a mere negation, and the place where you located it now shows for itself as sound as the rest of your body. Don't you know that imperfection is impossible to that beautiful creature, your real self? Since there is no evil in all the universe, and since man is the highest expression of good amidst ubiquitous Good, how can you be diseased? You are not diseased. There is not an angel in all the spheres sounder or more divine than you." Then I spoke out aloud: "There now," I said, "you won't have that pain again." *As I said it there was a surge of conviction through me that seemed to act on the blood-vessels of my body and made me tingle all over*."—HELEN WIL-MANS.

To this treatment I shall refer in elucidating the causes of the phenomena.

Dr. Evans controverts some of Mrs. Eddy's theories:

To modify a patient's thinking in regard to himself and his disease, we employ the principle of suggestion or positive *affirmation*—not mental argument, as it is sometimes called, for argument creates doubt and reaction. No sick man was ever cured by reasoning with him, mentally or verbally. It is the business of the man who *knows* the truth, not to argue, but to *affirm*. . . . No *intelligent* practitioner of the mind cure will ignore wholly all medical science. . . . The phreno-pathic system is not necessarily antagonistic to other methods of cure, as the various hygienic regulations, and even the use of the harmless specific remedies.

He repudiates Mrs. Eddy's ideas about the personality of God, and says:

It is not necessary to deny the personality of God. . . . Neither is it necessary to deny the personality and persistent individuality of the human spirit.

He also flatly denies Miss Taylor's theories, saying, "The selfhood is not lost in Godhood." "It is not necessary to tell a man dying of consumption that he is not sick, for that is not true." He says that one may or may not use the imposition of hands in healing the sick.

As an example of Christian Science superstition exceeding anything attempted by the most ignorant advocates of patent Faith Healing, read the following, taken *verbatim*, italics, small caps, etc., from a text-book on Mind Cure, issued by the President of the "New York School of Primitive and Practical Christian Science," who states that *his* school will be free from "eccentricity, pretension, and fanaticism"!

PRAYER FOR A DYSPEPTIC.

Holy Reality! We BELIEVE in Thee that Thou art EVERY-WHERE present. We *really* believe it. Blessed Reality we do not pretend to believe, think we believe, believe that we believe. WE BELIEVE. Believing that Thou art every where present, we believe that Thou art in this patient's stomach, in every fibre, in every cell, in every atom, that Thou are the sole, only Reality of that stomach. Heavenly, Holy Reality, we *will* try not to be such hypocrites and infidels, as every day of our lives to affirm our faith in Thee and then immediately begin to tell how sick we are, forgetting that Thou art everything and that Thou art not sick, and therefore that nothing in this universe was ever sick, is now sick, or can be sick. Forgive us our sins in that we have this day talked about our backaches, that we have told our neighbors that our food hurts us, that we mentioned to a visitor that there was a lump in our stomach, that we have wasted our valuable time which should have been spent in Thy service, in worrying for fear that our stomach would grow worse, in that we have disobeyed Thy blessed law in thinking that some kind of medicine would help us. We know, Father and Mother of us all, that there is no such a thing as a really diseased stomach, that the disease is the Carnal Mortal Mind given over to the World, the Flesh, and the Devil; that the mortal mind is a twist, a distortion, a false attitude, the HARMATIA of Thought. Shining and Glorious Verity, we recognize the great and splendid FACT that the moment we really believe the Truth, Disease ceases to trouble us, that the Truth is that there is no Disease in either *real* Body or Mind; that in the Mind what *seems* to be a *disease* is a False Belief, a Parasite, a hateful Excrescence, and that what happens in the Body is the shadow of the LIE in the Soul. Lord, help us to believe that ALL Evil is Utterly Unreal; that it is silly to be sick, absurd to be ailing, wicked to be wailing, atheism and denial of God to say "I am sick." Help us to stoutly affirm with our hand in Your hand, with our eyes fixed on Thee that we have no Dyspepsia, that we never had Dyspepsia, that we will never have Dyspepsia, that there is no such thing, that there never was any such thing, that there never will be any such thing. Amen.—HAZZARD.

It is claimed by all the Christian Science and Mind Cure practitioners that they can operate upon patients *at a distance.*

There is no space nor time to mind. A person in St. Louis may be near to me while I am in New York. A person in the same room may be very distant. Sit down and think about the person you wish to affect. Think long enough and strong enough and you are sure to reach him.—HAZZARD.

The following is a case of heart disease which I cured without having seen the patient: "Please find enclosed a check for five hundred dollars, in reward for your services that can never be repaid. The day you received my husband's letter I became conscious for the first time in forty-eight hours. My servant brought my wrapper, and I arose from bed and sat up. . . . The enlargement of my left side is all gone, and the doctors pronounce me rid of heart disease. I had been afflicted with it from infancy. It became organic enlargement of the heart and dropsy of the chest. I was only waiting and almost longing to die, but you have healed me. How wonderful to think of it, when you and I have never seen each other."—EDDY.

One of them says:

Remember that every thought that you think will be transferred to the persons thought of if you think long enough and strong enough.—HAZZARD.

This surpasses the love-powders that are sold among the colored people and the ignorant, as it is necessary to purchase and administer them, which is sometimes considerable trouble.

The practical directions to attain this power are as follows:

How to "concentrate." 1. Look at an object on the ceiling ten minutes; think of that object alone. 2. Write a proposition on a sheet of paper, as "God is the only reality." Think it for ten minutes with your eyes fixed upon the paper. 3. Begin to think of a subject, and give a dollar to the poor for every time your mind wanders. How to "subjugate." Forget yourself, forget the world, forget you have a body, forget you have any business or friends. Empty your mind of its contents. Be a man of one idea. Get out of yourself.—HAZZARD.

The rules for absent treatment are:

1. Seat yourself alone. Let the room be silent. 2. Subjugate your senses to all else but your thought. 3. Fix your thought upon the patient. 4. Picture him in your mind. 5. Go through the treatment.—HAZZARD.

The patient may be in three different ways. He may be sympathetic ; that will help you greatly. He may be apathetic ; that is not so good, but better than the next. He may be antipathetic, hostile ; then say not a word, but *silently* "give it to him" till he becomes less "cantankerous" and more Christlike.— HAZZARD.

MIND CURERS *versus* FAITH HEALERS, MESMERISTS, ETC.

MRS. EDDY speaks of Mesmerism in this way:

Mortal mind, acting from the basis of sensuous belief in matter, is animal magnetism. . . . In proportion as you understand Christian Science you lose animal magnetism. . . . Its basis being a belief and this belief an error, animal magnetism, or mesmerism, is a mere negation, possessing neither intelligence nor power. . . . An evil mind at work mesmerically is an engine of mischief little understood. . . . Animal magnetism, clairvoyance, mediumship, and mesmerism are antagonistic to this Science, and would prevent the demonstration thereof. . . . The Mesmeriser produces pain by making his subjects believe that he feels it ; here pain is proved to be a belief without any adequate cause. That social curse, the mesmerist, by making his victims believe they cannot move a limb, renders it impossible for them to do so until their belief or understanding masters his.

Of Spiritualism :

Spiritualism with its material accompaniments would destroy the supremacy of Spirit.

And of Clairvoyance specifically :

Clairvoyance investigates and influences mortal thought only. . . . Clairvoyance can do evil, can accuse wrongfully, and err in every direction.

Of Faith Cure :

It is asked, Why are faith cures sometimes more speedy than some of the cures wrought through Christian Scientists? Because faith is belief, and not understanding; and it is easier to believe than to understand Spiritual Truth. It demands less cross-bearing, self-renunciation, and Divine Science, to admit the claims of the personal senses, and appeal for relief to a humanized God, than to deny those claims and learn the divine way, drinking his cup, being baptized with his baptism, gaining the end through persecution and purity. Millions are believing in God, or Good, without sharing the fruits of goodness, not having reached its Science. Belief is mental blindness, if it admits Truth without understanding it. It cannot say with the Apostle, "I know in whom I have believed." There is even danger in the mental state called belief, for if Truth is admitted but not understood, error may enter through this same channel of ignorance. The Faith cure has devout followers, whose Christian practice is far in advance of mere theory.

Marston, speaking of change in the inverted thought of the sick person, says:

Since a change of the inverted thought of the sick person is all that can be produced by extraneous influence, the treatment of a professional Healer is not the only means of securing it. While a majority of cases are affected in that way, there are well-attested instances to show that anything that will enable the sick person to change his thought may put him in a condition to receive spiritual healing. A text from Scripture or some other writings may be brought to his mind with such force as to do this, or some sudden event may startle him out of his chronic delusion. It is in this way alone that we can account for cures that seem to result from prayer, a resort to relics, charms, and other things believed to possess peculiar virtue. This is why good results follow any one of the thousand absurd acts, by the performance of which superstitious and credulous people seek to be restored to health.

Another remarks:

The question is often asked, In what does the Christian Science healing differ from the faith cure? In the faith cure the patient must have faith; in Christian Science that is not necessary; patients have frequently been helped or entirely cured, without knowing they were being treated. . . . No great faith is necessary on the part of the patient; but it will expedite his recovery if he take interest enough in the method by which he is being healed to read suitable books on the subject, and converse profitably with the healer. . . . Prayer to a personal God affects the sick like a drug that has no efficacy of its own, but borrows its power from human faith and belief. The drug does nothing because it has no intelligence.

TESTS OF THE THEORY

First Test. If their principles be true, food should not be necessary. Mrs. Eddy affirms this:

Gustatory pleasure is a sensuous illusion, an illusion that diminishes as we understand our spiritual being and ascend the ladder of Life. This woman learned that food neither strengthens nor weakens the body, — that mind alone does this. . . . Teach them that their bodies are nourished more by Truth than by food.

Then, finding herself unable to silence the testimony of the senses, she endeavors to circumvent it thus:

Admitting the common hypothesis, that food is requisite to sustain human life, there follows the necessity for another admission, in the opposite direction, — namely, that food has power to destroy life, through its deficiency or excess, in quality or quantity. This is a specimen of the ambiguous character of all material health-theories. They are self-contradictory and self-destructive, — "a kingdom divided against itself, that is brought to desolation." If food preserves life, it cannot destroy it. The truth is, food does not affect the life of man; and this becomes self-evident when we learn that God is our only life. Because sin and sickness are not qualities of Soul or Life, we have hope in immortality; but it would be foolish to venture beyond our present understanding, foolish to stop eating, until we gain more goodness and a clearer comprehension of the living God. In that perfect day of understanding, we shall neither eat to live, nor live to eat.

When they dispense with food because "mortal mind" is under the influence of an illusion concerning it, — absurdly supposing "that food supports life," — and continue to live with the accidents of the human body sustained entirely by the divine "substance" of which they speak, they will furnish a demonstration which will utterly destroy every remaining illusion of mortal mind. But so long as they eat, they are either voluntarily perpetuating an illusion, or demonstrating that they are wrong in their notions. If they are in such a low stage as to be compelled to eat when it would not be necessary if they were in a higher plane, they may, for the same reason, be compelled to use drugs.

Second Test. They deny that drugs, *per se,* as taken into the human system, have any power.

Christian Science divests material drugs of their imaginary power. . . . The uselessness of drugs, the emptiness of knowledge, the nothingness of matter and its imaginary laws, are apparent as we rise from the rubbish of belief to the acquisition and demonstration of spiritual understanding. . . . When the sick recover by the use of drugs, it is the law of a general belief, culminating in individual faith that heals, and according to this faith will the effect be. — EDDY.

Surely the mind needs healing that could invent the following absurdity:

The not uncommon notion that drugs possess absolute, inherent curative virtues of their own involves an error. Arnica, quinine, opium, could not produce the effects ascribed to them except by imputed virtue. Men think they will act thus on the physical system, consequently they do. The property of alcohol is to intoxicate; but if the common thought had endowed it simply with a nourishing quality like milk, it would produce a similar effect. A curious question arises about the origin of healing virtues, if it be admitted that all drugs were originally destitute of them. We can conceive of a time in the mental history of the race when no therapeutic value was assigned to certain drugs, when, in fact, it was not known that they possessed any. How did it come to pass that common thought, or any thought, endowed them with healing virtue, in the first place? Simply in this way: Man finding himself unprotected, and liable to be hurt by the elements in the midst of which he lived, forgot the true source of healing, and began to seek earnestly for material remedies for disease and wounds. The desire for something led to experiments; and with each trial there was associated the hope that the means applied would prove efficacious. Then what was at first an earnest hope came at length to be a belief; and thus, by gradual steps, a belief in the contents of the entire pharmacopœia was established.— MARSTON.

It is true that in many cases the effect of a medicine is to be attributed entirely to the imagination, or to the belief that it will have such and such effects; but the statement of such extreme positions as these shows the irrationality of the theories upon which they are based. According to the above, if it were generally believed that alcohol were unintoxicating, nourishing, and bland as milk, it would be an excellent article with which to nourish infants; and, on the other hand, if it were generally believed that milk were intoxicating, all the influences of alcohol would be produced upon those who drank it. If the public could only be educated to believe alcohol to be nourishing, the entire mammalian genus might be nursing their offspring upon alcohol with equally good results. No insane asylum can furnish a more transparent delusion.

That drugs produce effects upon animals has been demonstrated beyond the possibility of contradiction, and that, when the animals did not know that they were taking drugs; and small doses have produced not the slightest effect, while large doses—the animals in each case not knowing that they were tak-

23

ing medicines—have produced great effect, and do so with uniformity. Also the effect of medicines upon idiots and unconscious infants is capable of exact demonstration.

Allied to the effect of drugs is that of *poisons*, almost every drug having the effect of a poison if taken in excess. Some poisons, however, are of such nature that the smallest possible dose may be attended with fatal results. In the case of animals, poisons introduced into the system without the knowledge of the animals do their work effectually. Strychnine carefully introduced into a piece of meat so small that a cat will swallow it whole, will in a very short time show its effects. The instinct of the animal will cause its rejection if there be the slightest possibility of perceiving it; but if sufficient means be taken to keep the animal from knowing that it is taking anything except meat, it will swallow the meat, and the poison will do its work.

These facts are admitted by the advocates of Christian Science and Mind Cure, and the absolute lunacy of their theories is seen in the manner in which they attempt to account for the effects.

If a dose of poison is swallowed through mistake, the patient dies, while physician and patient are expecting favorable results. Did belief cause this death? Even so, and as directly as if the poison had been intentionally taken. . . . The few who think a drug harmless, where a mistake has been made in the prescription, are unequal to the many who have named it poison, and so the majority opinion governs the result.—EDDY.

It is said that arsenic kills; but it would be very difficult for any one to prove how it kills; since persons have had all the symptoms of arsenic poisoning without having taken any arsenic; and again, persons have taken arsenic and did not die. . . . Suppose you take a child that knows nothing about arsenic, and administer the usual dose, the child will probably die, but I will show you that the arsenic was not the cause of the death. . . . Here you may say, "What had the life of the child to do with the action, the child not knowing anything about arsenic?" We will admit that the child was ignorant of the nature of the poison, but all who are educated in physiology and materia medica know that it kills, therefore the thought, although unconscious to the child, was hereditary in its life. It is, indeed, a universal thought admitted as a fact in every life or soul. A thought is a product of life and is action, and this thought, produced and accepted by life, acts upon the life of the child and produces unconsciously a confusion therein. This confusion produces a fear; this fear in the child's life heats the blood and causes the first conscious action.—ARENS.

The effects of various experiments, with chemicals and medicine, upon cats and dogs, are studied most minutely by distinguished scientific men, and the results witnessed published to the world with a presumption of wisdom and profundity of learning that carry the conviction to most minds that the properties of such drugs, and their effects upon the *human system*, have been forever established. And Materia Medica falls back upon these so-called demonstrations of Science as absolutely indisputable proofs of its Theories. Now it never seems to have occurred to them that all the effects witnessed of such experimenting might be accounted for on the basis of *Thought*, and with the view of investigating the subject to establish a totally opposite explanation; and to show that Mind acting on Matter could account for all their facts, the following experiments have been recently made: The object of the experiments was a dog, a noble thoroughbred, of great sagacity and intelligence. The first experiment consisted in conveying commands to him entirely through *mind*. Not a word was *spoken*, but his mistress would say to him *mentally*,—"Carlo, come here," or "Carlo, lie down," and although the *thought* might have to be repeated mentally a number of times, yet it would reach him, and sometimes he would respond almost immediately. Second experiment: One day his master discovered an appearance to which he gave the name *Mange*. All the dogs around were having it. It was catching,—Dr. So-and-So had pronounced it mange, and prescribed a mixture of Sulphur and Castor Oil, etc., which was to be applied *externally* in such a way that Carlo, in attempting to remove the preparation with his tongue, would get a dose into his system. But here the mistress interposed, and insisted that Carlo should be subjected wholly to mental treatment. The result was entirely satisfactory. The appearance vanished as it came. Again the experiment of placing Carlo entirely under the intelligence of his master's mind and thoughts for a certain period was tried, and compared with the effects of leaving him wholly under his mistress's mind. In the former case he soon exhibited every symptom of dyspepsia and indigestion in every form to which the master was subject, and in a very marked degree. But under the thought of the mistress, every symptom and appearance vanished at once. He soon attained a perfection of physical condition which constantly attracted the notice of every one. Experiments of this kind were carried much further, and can be by any one who wishes to test the matter for themselves. In all the instances just mentioned, the physical condition of the dog responded to the mind under whose influence it chanced to be. Love and Fear (*especially fear*) are the most marked characteristics of the animal mind. The instances are innumerable where the instinct of the animal surpasses the reason of man in detecting the kindly thought, or the thought of *harm*, toward itself. When a scientific experimenter gives a drug to a dog, it is done with a perfect certainty in his mind that disorder, derangement of the system, suffering, etc., in some form or another, are sure to follow. A *fear* corresponding to the thought of the man instantly seizes upon the dog, and various results *do* follow. The experimenter notes them down and then proceeds to try his drug on dog number 2, all the while holding in his mind an image of the results of experiment number 1, expecting to see similar results. In all probability he sees them.—STUART.[1]

Third Test. Extraordinary accidents to the body. Whatever may be said of the power of thought in the production of ordinary disease, the effects of accidents to persons who are entirely unconscious when

[1] Mrs. Stuart in the foregoing passage is only a little more absurd than Mrs. Eddy. "The preference of mortal mind for any method creates a demand for it, and the body seems to require it. You can even educate a healthy horse so far in physiology that he will take cold without his blanket; whereas the wild animal, left to his instincts, sniffs the wind with delight." The connection of this quotation with what goes before shows that the horse does not take cold, in the opinion of Mrs. Eddy, because, having been accustomed to the blanket, his system is so weakened that he will take cold without it; but because the training of the said horse has been such that he is led to believe that if the blanket is not on he will take cold!

they occur, as the sleeping victims of railroad disasters, are facts which, if they do not terminate human life at once, require the aid of surgery.

Mrs. Eddy says:

> The fear of dissevered bodily members, or a belief in such a possibility, is reflected on the body, in the shape of headache, fractured bones, dislocated joints, and so on, as directly as shame is seen in the blush rising to the cheek. This human error about physical wounds and colics is part and parcel of the delusion that matter can feel and see, having sensation and substance.

It is confessed, however, that very little progress has been made in this department:

> Christian Science is always the most skilful surgeon, but surgery is the branch of its healing that will be last demonstrated. However, it is but just to say that I have already in my possession well-authenticated records of the cure, by mental surgery alone, of dislocated hip-joints and spinal vertebræ.

But records, to be well authenticated, require more than an assertion. And the records may be authentic, and what they contain may never have been thoroughly tested. As they affirm that "bones have only the substance of thought, they are only an appearance to mortal mind"; if their theories be true at all, they should be able to rectify every result of accident to the body as readily and speedily as diseases originating within the system.

Fourth Test. Insanity. It is a well-established fact that blows upon the head produce insanity. It is equally well established that surgery in many cases is able to remove the difficulty by an obviously physical readjustment, where the surgeon himself cannot be positive what the effect will be until after the experiment, and the victim has no knowledge whatever upon the subject. During the late war, a negro was wounded in the head by the explosion of a shell. He wandered about for several years, to all appearance a driveling idiot, when certain surgeons took an interest in his case, and concluded that the removal of a piece of the skull which had been driven in and pressed upon the brain, might restore his reason. Knowing that no damage could be done to his mind by the operation, they performed it, and were almost appalled when, after the lapse of so many years, as they lifted the piece of skull and removed the pressure upon the brain, the light of intelligence returned to the eye of the man, who said, "We were at Manassas yesterday ; where are we to-day?" A similar case, where there had been delirium alternating with coma for a week, occurred in March last.

The transient effect of stimulants upon persons who have been in a state of dementia apparently for a long time, is also well known.

Mrs. Eddy upon this subject directs practitioners to tell the moderately sick man,

that he suffers only as the insane suffer, from a mere belief. The only difference is that insanity implies belief in a diseased brain, while physical ailments (so called) arise from belief that some other portions of the body are deranged. . . . The entire mortal body is evolved from mortal mind. A bunion would produce insanity as perceptible as that produced by congestion of the brain, were it not that mortal mind calls the bunion an unconscious portion of the body. Reverse this belief, and the results would be different.

It may be readily admitted that if a man believed his mind was in his foot, and believed it was out of order, he might be crazy. But in selecting the bunion for an illustration, Mrs. Eddy was not so wide of the mark as she might have been. More than twenty years ago, while listening to the lectures of Dr. C. E.

Brown-Séquard, before the physicians of Brooklyn, I heard him give the following case: A youth (fourteen years old) went to bed perfectly sane, nor had he ever had a symptom of insanity. The next morning when he arose and stepped upon the floor he became a maniac. With great difficulty he was replaced upon the bed, and the moment he touched it he was sane. During the morning he made several attempts to rise, always with the same result. A physician was called, who in his account of the case says: "When sitting up in his bed he drew on his stockings; but on *putting his feet on the floor and standing up, his countenance instantly changed, the jaw became violently convulsed,* etc. He was pushed back on the bed, was at once calm, looked surprised, and asked what was the matter. Inquiry showed that he had been fishing the preceding day, but had met with no accident. His legs were examined minutely, but nothing unusual was seen; but, says the physician, *"On holding up the right great toe with my finger and thumb to examine the sole of that foot, the leg was drawn up and the muscles of the jaws were suddenly convulsed, and on releasing the toe these effects instantly ceased."* After further experiment, an irritated point, so small as to be scarcely visible, was taken away by the cutting of a piece of skin, and "the strange sensation was gone and never returned."[1]

---

[1] This case can be found (No. 44) in "Lectures on the Physiology and Pathology of the Central Nervous System," by Brown-Séquard; published, 1860, in Philadelphia. Also in Holmes's "Annals of Surgery," vol. 3, p. 330.

A similar account can be found of insanity produced four years after a boy trod on a piece of glass, which was entirely relieved by removing from a point near the ball of the big toe a trifling piece of glass. What is called the nervous temperament or condition is of importance.

Post-mortem examinations which exhibit the degeneration of the brain structure are of no importance in the eyes of these professors of dreams.

Fifth Test. The perpetuation of youth and the abolition of death should also be within the range of these magicians.

Baldwin, of Chicago, says:

Man should grow younger as he grows older; the principle is simple. "As we think so are we" is stereotyped. Thoughts and ideas are ever striving for external expression. By keeping the mind young we have a perfect guarantee for continued youthfulness of body. Thought will externalize itself; thus growing thought will ever keep us young. Reliance on drugs makes the mind, consequently the body, prematurely old. This new system will make us younger at seventy than at seventeen, for then we will have more of genuine philosophy.

Mrs. Eddy meets this matter in the style of Jules Verne:

The error of thinking that we are growing old, and the benefits of destroying that illusion, are illustrated in a sketch from the history of an English lady, published in the London "Lancet." Disappointed in love in early years she became insane. She lost all calculation of time. Believing that she still lived in the same hour that parted her from her lover, she took no note of years, but daily stood before the window, watching for his coming. In this mental state she remained young. Having no appearance of age, she literally grew no older. Some American travelers saw her when she was seventy-four, and supposed her a young lady. Not a wrinkle or gray hair appeared, but youth sat gently on cheek and brow. Asked to judge her age, and being unacquainted with her history, each visitor conjectured that she must be under twenty.

That the above should be adduced as proof of anything would be wonderful if the person adducing it had not previously adopted a theory which supersedes the necessity of demonstration. It is important to notice that if the belief had anything to do with it, this amazing result grew from a belief in a falsehood. She did *not* live in the same hour that parted her from her lover; she believed that she did, and, according to Mrs. Eddy, this belief of a falsehood counteracted all the ordinary consequences of the flight of time.

But the delusion among the insane that they are young, that they are independent of time and of this world, is very common; and the most painfully paradoxical sights that I have ever witnessed have been men and women, toothless, denuded of hair, and with all the signs of age, — sans teeth, sans eyes, sans taste, sans everything, — some of them declaring that they were young girls and engaged to be married to presidents and kings, and even to divine beings. These delusions in some instances have been fixed for many years. Having had an official connection with an insane asylum for five years, I have had more opportunities than were desired for conversing with persons of this class.

Granting the case adduced by Mrs. Eddy to be true, and admitting that the state of the mind may have had some effect, it is of no scientific importance; for the number who show no signs of age until fifty, sixty, or even seventy years have passed, is by no means small in the aggregate; we meet them everywhere. One of the most astute observers of human nature, himself a physician, solemnly warned a gentleman that if he continued to take only four hours' sleep in twenty-four, he would die before he was fifty years of age. "What do you suppose my age to be now?" said the gentleman. "Thirty," said the physician. "I am sixty-nine," was the reply, which proved to be the fact.

Mrs. Eddy, not content with this case, continues: "I have seen age regain two of the elements it had lost, sight and teeth.   A lady of eighty-five whom I knew had a return of sight.   Another lady at ninety had new teeth, — incisors, cuspids, bicuspids, and one molar."   Such instances as these are not uncommon, but are generally a great surprise to the persons themselves, and unconnected with any delusion as to flight of time.   They are simply freaks of nature.

There is a flattening of the eye which comes on with advancing years, and necessitates the use of glasses. Many persons who have few signs of age, retain the color of the cheek, have lost no teeth, and whose natural force is not abated, find their eyes dim.   According to these metaphysical healers this is not necessary, but I have observed that a number of them say nothing about being themselves compelled to use glasses.

Much is made of one case of a metaphysical healer, who, after using glasses fifteen years, threw them away, and can now read even in the railroad cars without them.   Such cases of second sight have occurred at intervals always, and under all systems, and sometimes when the progress of old age had been so great that the persons had suffered many infirmities, and had but a few months left in which to "see as well as ever they did in their lives."

Some famous actors and actresses, without the use of pigments, dyes, or paints, notwithstanding the irregular hours and other accidents of their professional life, have maintained an astonishing youthfulness of appearance down to nearly threescore years and ten.

John Wesley at seventy-five, according to testimony indubitable and from a variety of sources, not only presented the appearance of a man not yet past the prime of life, but, what is more remarkable, had the undiminished energy, vivacity, melody and strength of voice which accompany youth. Nor at eighty-five had he exhibited much change. In the city of Chicago there died recently a professional man nearly seventy-five years of age, whose teeth, complexion, color, hair, voice, and mind showed no signs of his being over forty-five years of age. Henry Ward Beecher, the January before his death, could write to his oldest brother that he had no rheumatism, neuralgia, sleeplessness, or deafness, was not bald, and did not need spectacles.

Meanwhile it is impossible not to suppose that the case as described by Mrs. Eddy has been greatly exaggerated. That some Americans who saw her at the age of seventy-four supposed her to be under twenty, is to be taken "*cum grano salis.*"

As for death, if the theories of these romantic philosophers be true, it should give way; if not in every case, at least in some. It is said that there are hundreds of persons in Boston who believe that Mrs. Eddy will never die. Joanna Southcott, who arose in England in 1792, made many disciples, by some estimated at one hundred thousand, who believed that she would never die; but unfortunately for their credulity she succumbed to the inevitable decree.

Sixth Test. If these theories are true, clothing, so far as sustaining warmth and life is concerned, is superfluous, and fire unnecessary. This conclusion reduces the whole scheme to an absurdity.

EXPLANATION OF THEIR ALLEGED SUCCESS

IN endeavoring to ascertain the causes of recoveries which undoubtedly occur when the patient is under the supervision of Christian Scientists and Mind Curers, it would be a blunder to omit the testimony of Mrs. Eddy as to her experiments with homeopathy. She says that she has attenuated common table salt until there was not a single saline property left; and yet with one drop of that in a goblet of water, and a teaspoonful administered every three hours, she has cured a patient sinking in the last stage of typhoid fever. Describing a case of dropsy given up by the faculty, she says that after giving some medicines of high attenuation, she gave the patient unmedicated pellets for a while, and found that she continued to improve. Finally she induced the patient to give up her medicine for one day, and risk the effects. After trying this, she informed Mrs. Eddy that she could get along two days without the globules; but on the third day had to take them. She went on in this way, taking unmedicated pellets, with occasional visits from Mrs. Eddy, and employing no other means was cured. Thus Mrs. Eddy says she discovered that mind was potent over matter and that drugs have no power.

It is not to be inferred from the above that homeopathic remedies, which have been modified by the discoveries made and the experience attained since the time of Hahnemann, are generally powerless. That question is not essential to this inquiry. But the confession of Mrs. Eddy that her experiments were the means of teaching her that mind and not matter effects the cure, will be regarded by all who do not accept her theories as containing the principal key to the problem. She made the common error of generalizing from a few particulars, and ever since has endeavored to test facts by theory instead of making facts the test. Because she found a supposed mental cause adequate to a cure in a few cases, she leaped to the wild conclusion that all causes are mental. Notwithstanding these numerous absurdities and the radical error, it would be unwise to lose sight of the specific elements in the practice of Christian Science and the various forms of Mind Cure as a profession.

The patients who are treated by these practitioners have, to begin with, the *vis medicatrix naturæ*, which is the final element in every cure, recognized to be such by the leaders of the medical profession for a long period of time. Sir John Forbes, M. D., one of the most eminent regular physicians of England, remarks of the practice of his own School in his famous article on homeopathy:

First, that in a large proportion of the cases treated by allopathic physicians, the disease is cured by nature, and not by them. Second, that in a lesser but still not a small proportion, the disease is cured by nature in spite of them; in other words, their interference retarding instead of assisting the cure. Third, that in, consequently, a considerable proportion of diseases it would fare as well or better with patients if all remedies—at least all active remedies, especially drugs—were abandoned.

Sydenham long ago said, "I often think more could be left to Nature than we are in the habit of leaving to her; to imagine that she always wants the help of art is an error, and an unlearned error too."

Sir John Marshall, F. R. S., in opening the session of the London University Medical School in 1865, said,

The *vis medicatrix naturæ* is the agent to employ in the healing of an ulcer, or the union of a broken bone; and it is equally true that the physician or surgeon never cured a disease; he only assists the natural processes of cure performed by the intrinsic conservative energy of the frame, and this is but the extension of the force imparted at the origination of the individual being.

Under the Mind Cure this force of nature is still at work, and in the great number of self-limited diseases which tend to recovery, it is left free from all error of practitioners. If it loses any advantages

24

which the introduction of the proper drugs might give, it is saved from the consequences of the administration of the wrong ones.

The number of instances in which the prescriptions interfere with nature is so great that Dr. Paris wrote, many years ago, "The file of every apothecary would furnish a volume of instances where the ingredients of the prescription were fighting together in the dark. This is especially true of diseases of children. The late Dr. Marshall Hall said, "Of the whole number of fatal cases of diseases in infancy, a great proportion occur from the inappropriate or undue application of exhausting remedies."

Further, those who are treated by the Mind Curers in many cases derive benefit from the freedom of diet, air, and exercise allowed. They are told to pay no attention to symptoms, think nothing whatever about their diseases, and not talk about them; to eat, sleep, drink, and act as nearly as possible as if they were well; and in a large majority of chronic diseases, this is all that is needed to produce a return to health.

They have also the benefits of faith and fancy; as they are taught to imagine healthy, vigorous organs, and their whole bodies in the condition of health, and with such mental pictures to drive away all consciousness of symptoms, they summon to their aid that most potent of all influences, a calm and fearless mind. The presence of the practitioner and her methods greatly contribute to this calming influence.

She enters with a cheerful air and, without taking your hand or approaching your bed, seats herself and asks you to tell her all your symptoms. [She may, however, belong to the class which will not allow any description of symptoms.] She receives your budget of ailments calmly, without one expression of sympathy, for she has none, considering all your maladies as an illusion or dream from which it is her divine mission to awaken you. You are made to feel, immediately, that there is little of consequence in all that you have been telling her. She then relapses into a silence of ten or fifteen minutes, in which her kind face wears a resolute expression, making it almost stern. . . . After this silent treatment she speaks to you in the most encouraging manner, endeavoring to call you away from yourself to the contemplation of spiritual truth.

A point of difference between Faith Healers and Mind Curers is worthy of observation. Faith Healers require the patient to have faith; Mind Curers make a boast of the fact that faith is not necessary. A close analysis, however, shows that this boast is vain. Before they are sent for there is usually some faith, and often much, combined with a distrust of other systems. This was, as some of their authorities affirm, the case when they began. Sufficient time has elapsed to develop a constituency who employ no other methods. If there is no faith, there must be a distrust of other forms of practice, or there would be no reason for turning to the new. Where there is no faith on the part of the patient, usually his friends believe, and have induced him to make the experiment. Thus he is surrounded by an atmosphere of faith which is so important that all the writers attach great weight to it.

Friends and attendants who are believers in Mental cure, and know what sort of a mental atmosphere is favorable to restoring health, may do much to help the metaphysician in his work. But, unfortunately, this is seldom the case ; and the friends are usually ignorant on the subject, and innocently burdening the invalid with just that kind of hurtful sympathy which keeps him under a cloud of depression. When such is the case, their absence is more helpful than their presence, and it is desirable to be alone with the patient while treating him.— MARSTON.

Some even go so far as to say that they should be, if possible, removed from the society of those who do not believe.

But a favorable atmosphere exists to some extent among those who have induced an unbelieving invalid to send for a mental healer. Assuming that the healer has arrived, it is easy to see how faith is engendered. She takes her seat, and after a few unimportant questions becomes silent. The thoughts that wander through the mind of the invalid, as told me by a patient of thorough intelligence, an alumnus of one of the first universities of this country, were such as these: "Can there be anything in this? I don't believe there is, and yet a great many people are believing in it, and some most wonderful cures have taken place. There is Mrs. ——. I *know* that she was given up to die by our best physicians, and I *know* that she is well." Then the eye will turn to the face of the metaphysician, who seems looking at far-off things and wrestling with some problem not yet solved, but of the certainty of the solution of which she has no doubt. Sometimes the practitioners cover their eyes, and this would add to the effect in many temperaments. The fifteen minutes pass and leave the unbeliever passive; as a quotation elsewhere describes it, "less cantankerous."

The encouraging words of the healer on departing are not without effect, differing as they do from the uncertain or preternaturally solemn forthgivings, or ill-concealed misgivings, of many ordinary physicians. There are no medicines to take, no symptoms to watch, and only the certainty of recovery to be dwelt upon. Whatever the appetite calls for is to be eaten without anxiety as to the consequences, and if there be no appetite there is to be no eating and no anxiety as to the result of abstinence.

The effect of the treatment having been pleasant, the patient rather longs than otherwise for the next day to come, and for the next. If the disease be one that under ordinary circumstances would require an operation, the dreadful image of the surgeon's knife no longer appals the patient's mind. The invalid discovers that he does not die, that he sleeps a little better; certainly he is not aroused to take medicine, and there is no fear that he will take cold; he feels decidedly better at the next visit, and now faith is not only born but turned into sight. His friends assure him that he is better, and he tells them that he is so.

Perhaps the most potent cause in awakening faith is the sublime audacity displayed by the practitioner who dares to dispense with drugs, manipulation, hygiene, prayer, and religious ceremony. That spectacle would infallibly produce either such opposition and contempt as would result in the termination of the experiment, or faith. It is impossible to be in a negative position in its presence, where the responsibilities of life and death are assumed.

As for "absent treatments," these are based on the theory that to think of another entirely and abstractedly occasions a spiritual presence of that other. "Distance is annihilated, and his living image and inner personality seem to stand before us, and what we say to it we say to him."

These persons catch up and incorporate with their theories the yet immature investigations of the Society for Psychical Research, in which it is claimed that a sensitive subject can form in the mind a distinct mental picture or idea of words and letters which had been in the mind of an agent. Healers endeavor to extend those phenomena so as to make them annihilate space; and, according to them, "it is as easy to affect a person in the interior of Africa by a mental influence, as in the same room." Here they affiliate with the whole mass of superstitions which accumulated in the early history of the human race, and reappear in certain temperaments in each generation. Whether such a thing as thought-transference exists, there is not space here to inquire; nor is it necessary, for the effects of the "absent treatment," so called, can all be accounted for without any such assumption.

Patients thus treated *know* or they do *not* know that they are being treated. When they know, there is nothing to explain, for it is the same as if patient and practitioner were in each other's presence. All the mental operations, as well as the original force of nature, proceed under the conviction that they are being treated by a mental healer. If they do not know the entire field of coincidence and the *vis medicatrix naturæ* remain inviolate; and to determine that there is any connection between the alleged treatment and the change in the condition of the patient would require a vast number of cases and detailed coincidence of time and symptom, for which these practitioners do not display ability, and for which, on their own testimony, they have had no opportunity. Indeed, their theories are such as to make all investigation superfluous and tedious.

The case upon which Mrs. Eddy appears to rely is described thus: "The day you received my husband's letter I became conscious for the first time in forty-eight hours." What can this prove? What evidence is there that she would not have become conscious if the letter had never been written? If she were ever to come out of an unconscious state and recover, it must be at some time. The coincidence of Mrs. Eddy's receiving a letter from the husband does not show any connection between the two facts, for such letters have been sent and the patients have died. To my personal knowledge her treatments have failed, and her predictions have not been fulfilled, the patient dying in excruciating agony. Instances which have occurred, and can be reproduced at any time, of the attempted absent treatment of persons *who never existed*, are numerous; for there is not one of this class of healers that cannot be so imposed upon. This is sufficient to raise a powerful presumption that the spiritual presence which they evoke, and to which they speak, is " such stuff as dreams are made of."

It is not to be denied that they make more cures than any bungler or extremist of a school using drugs would expect. But their failures are numerous, and, like faith healers, they never publish *these*. Compelled, however, to admit this, the chancellor of the University of the Science of Spirit says :

Our inability to heal instantaneously as they (Jesus and the Apostles) are recorded to have done, is attributable to our deficiency in the realization of the doctrine. While we claim that our theory of healing is applicable to all diseases, we do not claim to possess sufficient understanding in it at the present time to heal all diseases instantaneously, neither would we now guarantee to cure certain diseases, such as cancer or consumption in the last stages. Of one thing, however, we are confident, *i. e.*, that we can do more good in all cases of illness than can be done with any other theory, or with materia medica.—ARENS.

They are rather more successful than faith healers for this reason : with the faith healers it is generally either an instantaneous cure, or none at all. And an instantaneous cure cannot be made to apply to a great many cases, and what is supposed to be such is very frequently a delusion followed by a complete relapse. The Christian Scientists, however, and their congeners make many visits and give nature a much better opportunity without the destruction of the patient's faith in them by a failure at a critical juncture; thus it happens that the proportion of recoveries is more numerous.

The principal practical element has been more or less recognized and employed by the greatest physicians of every school through the whole history of medical practice, as well as by quacks and superstitious pagan priests. "The History of Medical Economy during the Middle Ages," by George F. Fort, contains numerous illustrations of this subject, though adduced for another purpose, and, unlike many other treatises, giving the authorities with most painstaking accuracy.

Dr. Rush, of whom Dr. Tuke affirms that few physicians have had more practical experience of disease, says:

I have frequently prescribed remedies of doubtful efficacy in the critical stage of acute diseases, but never till I had worked up my patients into a confidence bordering upon certainty of their probable good effects. The success of this measure has much oftener answered than disappointed my expectations.

The "British and Foreign Medical Review" for January, 1846, whose editor then was Sir John Forbes, contained an article written by himself which encourages "the administration of simple, feeble, and altogether powerless, non-perturbing medicines, in all cases in which drugs are prescribed *pro forma*, for the satisfaction of the patient's mind, and not with the view of producing any direct remedial effect."

"Physic and Physicians," published in 1839, speaking of the celebrated and extraordinarily successful Dr. Radcliffe, who was the founder of the Radcliffe Library at Oxford University, and died in 1714, says that he paid particular attention to the mind of the patient under his care, and had been heard to say that he attributed much of his success and eminence to this circumstance. There is a very good anecdote illustrating his views upon this subject:

A lady of rank consulted Radcliffe in great distress about her daughter, and the doctor began the investigation of the case by asking, "Why, what ails her?" "Alas! doctor," replied the mother, "I cannot tell; but she has lost her humor, her looks, her stomach; her strength consumes every day, and we are apprehensive that she cannot live." "Why do you not marry her?" said Radcliffe. "Alas! doctor, that we would fain do, and have offered her as good a match as ever she could expect." "Is there no other that you think she would be content to marry?" "Ah, doctor, that is what troubles us; for there is a young gentleman we doubt she loves, that her father and I can never consent to." "Why, look you, madam," replied Radcliffe gravely, "then the case is this: your daughter would marry one man, and you would have her marry another. In all my books I find no remedy for such a disease as this."

This principle has also been employed by certain priests and clergymen of every sect. A young woman, a teacher, was, as she believed and as her friends supposed, at the point of death. Her physician was not quite certain that she was as ill as she seemed, and requested the pastor to assist him in breaking up her delusion that she must die. He attempted it, but she refused to hear him, and intrusted him with messages for her friends, especially for her class in the Sunday School. When about to bid her farewell, he informed her that he would return in the afternoon; she replied that she would like him to pray with her, but that it was useless to ask for her recovery. Having in view her hearing what he had to say, he prayed in such a way as to break the spell and cause her to believe that she would recover; as he did this, the morbid symptoms of approaching death gave way, and she is still living.

Another case was still more remarkable. A woman, ill and bedridden, conceived a high regard for the piety and intelligence of her pastor. He entered her room and in a loud and solemn voice said, "I command you to arise!" Involuntarily she arose and resumed the duties of housekeeping, which after the lapse of ten years she still performs.

A Roman Catholic priest, of high position in his church, told the writer that he thought he had saved scores of lives by refusing to administer the Sacrament of Extreme Unction, which led the patients to say "Father —— does not think I am going to die."

In 1832, when the cholera raged in Norfolk, Virginia, Dr. Buzzell, a physician of great local celebrity, lived there. He was driving night and day, and on one occasion was summoned to see a stalwart negro who was apparently in the state of collapse. Instead of beginning at once to treat him, he accused him of shamming, denounced and derided him in every possible way for calling him when he was at work night and day, driven almost to death. Then, assuming the appearance of intense excitement, he procured a switch and began to thrash the negro very severely. The more he groaned, and the more he said he was dying, the more Dr. Buzzell thrashed him, and with his threatenings and beatings brought on such a tremendous reaction that the man recovered.

In a visit to a branch of the Oneida Community at Wallingford, in 1856, I asked Mrs. Miller, the sister of John H. Noyes, the founder of the community, what they did if any of the inmates became ill, as they repudiated medicines. She said they had very little sickness. "But, have I not heard of an epidemic of diphtheria among you?" She said there had been, but by their treatment they saved every case. "What was that treatment?" "It was treatment by criticism." "How was it applied?" "So soon as a person was taken ill, a committee was appointed who went into the room and sat down, paying no attention to the patient; they began at once to speak about him or her, criticizing the patient's peculiarities, bringing every defect to the surface, and unsparingly condemning it." Mrs. Miller added that no one could endure this more than an hour. The mental and moral irritation was so great that they began to perspire and invariably recovered. The universal efficacy of this method may well be doubted, for many persons live in such an atmosphere that if that treatment would save them, they would never die; while others are so callous to all criticism that the remedy would be without effect.

In a certain lunatic asylum was a patient, a very attractive young lady, whose delusion took the form that she was specially called of God to do some great work which had not yet been indicated to her. With this were connected several pernicious practices, such as fasting, excessive prayer, and others of similar character. The asylum physicians were very much interested in her, but the months passed away and she did not improve.

At last one of the assistant physicians, especially interested in the influence of the mind upon the body, determined upon a plan to effect her cure by a powerful mental operation. Accordingly, he introduced a tube into her room, without her knowledge, and also prepared a calcium light so that, at a certain time, he could flood the room with rays of intense brilliancy.

The young woman had not walked a step for many months. At the appointed hour, with all the physicians standing in the hall, and the wife of the physician in chief—a thoroughly Christian woman, intensely sympathetic with the patient—also with them, the physician spoke through the tube in the name of the Lord, informing the girl that He had heard her prayers, that she should soon be sent upon her mission, and that she should go forth from the place to her own home to testify to His glory. At the same instant that the voice was heard, the room was flooded with a light much brighter than the sun at noonday.

Her face, with the utmost simplicity of faith, was lighted up with a joy that seemed too great for mortal; and those who were situated where they could see it, declared that hardly ever in their lives had they seen such an expression of seraphic bliss.

Of course, great interest centered in the conduct of the young woman the next morning. She said not a word to a human being upon her vision, but in the morning rose and walked the entire length of the hall, and continued to improve in physical and mental health till discharged from the asylum as practically cured.

Our informant, an official of the institution, of entire credibility, has not heard from her for some time; but, up to a recent period, she remained in good health.

This is an instance of cure effected by the operation of the mind upon the body, as extraordinary as any instance of cure which can be adduced by Faith Healers or Christian Scientists.

The nervous "temperament" or condition of the healer appears to be of no special importance; that is, it is of importance only in the same sense that it is to salesmen, public speakers, school-teachers, lawyers, sea-captains, detectives, military leaders, physicians, and all who impress themselves upon others. I have seen successful healers thin and tall; others short and fat; some pale, others florid; some intelligent, others unintelligent; some intellectual, more only intelligent; some in good health, others diseased; one of the best was so feeble as to seem on the verge of death.[1]

The specimen mental treatment given on page 257 shows how the practitioner worked herself up to the point; and it is easy to fancy how forcibly she spoke when a surge of conviction that seemed to act on all the blood-vessels of her body and made her tingle all over, went through her; and it is equally easy to imagine the effect upon the patient.

The relation of the Mind Cure movement to ordinary medical practice is important. It emphasizes what the most philosophical physicians of all schools have always deemed of the first importance, though many have neglected it. It teaches that medicine is but occasionally necessary. It hastens the time when patients of discrimination will rather pay more for advice how to live, and for frank declarations that they do not need medicine, than for drugs. It promotes general reliance upon those processes which go on equally in health and disease.

But these ethereal practitioners have no new force to offer; there is no causal connection between their cures and their theories.

What they believe has practically nothing to do with their success. If a new school were to arise

[1] In practice it seems to be more difficult to successfully treat one's self than to treat another person. The reason for this is that, when personally under the influence of supposed disease, the appeal of the senses is more forcible than when the deception shows itself in another. But that one can conquer the results of his own inverted thinking, there is not the slightest occasion to doubt. . . . We must not, however, make the mistake of supposing that he who would attempt to bring healing to others must first be sound himself. . . . The effect of a treatment depends not on its length, but on the condition of the healer who exercises it, and the dynamic power of the thought exerted. — MARSTON.

25

claiming to heal diseases without drugs or hygiene, or prayer, by the hypothetical odylic force invented by Baron Reichenbach, the effects would be the same, if the practice were the same.

Recoveries as remarkable have been occurring through all the ages, as the results of mental states and nature's own powers.

They will not be able to displace either the skilled surgeon or the educated physician; for their arrogant and exclusive pretensions are of the nature of a "craze." Most sensible persons will prefer a physician who understands both the mind and the body; who can be a "father confessor" to the sick man, relieving him of the responsibility of treating himself, quieting his mind, strengthening him by hope, and stimulating him by his personal presence; one who, understanding the mineral, plant, and animal substances included in the materia medica, can assist nature, interfering only when absolutely necessary and certainly safe; too learned and honest, when not knowing what to do, ever to do he knows not what.

They will also prefer a physician who can relieve their pains when incurable, smooth their pathway to the inevitable end, or, when he has the happiness to see them convalescent, will be able to give them such hygienic hints as may prevent a recurrence of the malady, or save them from something worse.

The verdict of mankind, excepting minds prone to vagaries on the borderland of insanity, will be that pronounced by Ecclesiasticus more than two thousand years ago:

"THE LORD HATH CREATED MEDICINES OUT OF THE EARTH; AND HE THAT IS WISE WILL NOT ABHOR THEM. MY SON, IN THY SICKNESS BE NOT NEGLIGENT; BUT PRAY UNTO THE LORD, AND HE WILL MAKE THEE WHOLE. LEAVE OFF FROM SIN, AND ORDER THY HANDS

ARIGHT, AND CLEANSE THY HEART FROM ALL WICKED-
NESS. THEN GIVE PLACE TO THE PHYSICIAN, FOR THE
LORD HATH CREATED HIM: LET HIM NOT GO FROM
THEE, FOR THOU HAST NEED OF HIM. THERE IS A
TIME WHEN IN THEIR HANDS THERE IS GOOD SUCCESS.
FOR THEY SHALL ALSO PRAY UNTO THE LORD, THAT
HE WOULD PROSPER THAT WHICH THEY GIVE FOR EASE
AND TO PROLONG LIFE."

INDEX